EXPLORING
THE PSYCHOLOGY
OF INTEREST

Psychology of Human Motivation

Edited by C. R. Snyder

Exploring the Psychology of Interest
Paul J. Silvia

EXPLORING THE PSYCHOLOGY OF INTEREST

Paul J. Silvia

UNIVERSITY PRESS

2006

OXFORD

UNIVERSITY PRESS

Oxford University Press, Inc., publishes works that further
Oxford University's objective of excellence
in research, scholarship, and education.

Oxford   New York
Auckland   Cape Town   Dar es Salaam   Hong Kong   Karachi
Kuala Lumpur   Madrid   Melbourne   Mexico City   Nairobi
New Delhi   Shanghai   Taipei   Toronto

With offices in
Argentina   Austria   Brazil   Chile   Czech Republic   France   Greece
Guatemala   Hungary   Italy   Japan   Poland   Portugal   Singapore
South Korea   Switzerland   Thailand   Turkey   Ukraine   Vietnam

Published by Oxford University Press, Inc.
198 Madison Avenue, New York, New York 10016

www.oup.com

Oxford is a registered trademark of Oxford University Press

Library of Congress Cataloging-in-Publication Data
Silvia, Paul J., 1976–
Exploring the psychology of interest / by Paul J. Silvia.
    p. cm.—(Psychology of human motivation)
Includes bibliographical references and indexes.
ISBN-13 978-0-19-515855-7
ISBN 0-19-515855-5
1. Interest (Psychology)   I. Title.   II. Series.
BF321.S48 2006
153.1'533—dc22   2005018240

9 8 7 6 5 4 3 2

Printed in the United States of America
on acid-free paper

Dieses Buch ist natürlich für Beate

Preface and Acknowledgments

Psychology has always been interested in interest. Theories of interest, curiosity, and intrinsic motivation appear in historical classics and in far-flung areas of modern research. The study of interest currently has a home in the psychology of emotion, education, development, personality, motivation, vocations, aesthetics, gerontology, and text processing, to name a few. But despite this—or perhaps because of it—the psychology of interest is a scattered field. Many areas within the psychology of interest have proposed the same ideas and struggled with the same problems. Sometimes one area has solved another area's problem, but researchers in neither area knew it. The central goals of this book are to review research on interest from diverse areas of psychology, to reveal similarities between seemingly different areas, and to stimulate new research by critically evaluating current theories and proposing untested hypotheses. It's hard for me to tell how well the roles of impartial reviewer and motivated critic were balanced—fortunately, two wrongs make a right if they're multiplied rather than added.

The best part of writing a book is thanking the people who helped. This book occupied me through several years, eight apartments and houses, and two countries. I would like to thank Andrea Abele and Guido Gendolla at the Social Psychology Program at the University of Erlangen,

Germany, where I wrote much of an early draft. The Universität der Bundeswehr in Hamburg, Germany, graciously provided library access— my thanks to Gisela Dahme and Jan Eichstaedt. I thank my many friends in the Department of Psychology at the University of North Carolina at Greensboro for being critical sounding boards and for creating a fun and lively place to think. Finally, I thank the members of the Psychology Department's infamous weekly Agraphia Group—Wesley Allan, Mike Kane, Tom Kwapil, Cheryl Logan, Stuart Marcovitch, and Matt Paradise—for showing me that large carrots can be brandished like sticks.

Writing a book that spans many fields of psychology showed me how little I know. I'm grateful to Jack Brehm, John Dunlosky, the late Shelley Duval, David Feldman, Guido Gendolla, Suzanne Hidi, Todd Kashdan, Jordan Litman, Adam Powell, Rick Snyder, and Ed Wisniewski for their comments on various parts of this book and for suggesting articles and ideas. The writers of anonymous reviews of early drafts deserve special thanks for their incisive criticisms and encouragement. I also thank everyone who sent me copies of unpublished and in-press papers; extra thanks go to the authors who allowed me to discuss their unpublished work. Any errors and oversights are due to my own considerable recalcitrance and ignorance.

A platitude among social scientists is that some people study their antitheses—the teetotaler studies alcoholism, the straight-arrow studies pathology, the provincial studies the peculiar. If this is true, what cruel torpor awaits people who study interest? This book is dedicated to Beate—thanks for dragging me from Curiosity Central, for tolerating my capricious hobbies, and for being my best friend.

Contents

EXPLORING THE PSYCHOLOGY OF INTEREST

Introduction

We live in interesting places in an interesting time. Yet that may not be saying much. *Interest* has many meanings in everyday usage (Benedict, 2001; Savickas, 1999; Spacks, 1995), many of them too vague. Everyday speech gives us *interesting*, a convenient phrase when we want to be evasive or spare a friend's feelings. People also use *interest* casually to express general motivational states like wanting and caring—as in "I'm not interested in eating Indian food twice today"—or to characterize people's stake in a situation, often called their "best interests." These meanings reflect the roots of interest in *inter esse*, meaning "to be between," "to take part in." Other meanings of interest—such as the interest charged by mortgage lenders—are, thankfully, outside of psychology altogether.

Psychology's interest in interest has a long and complex history. Early psychologists, particularly educational and vocational psychologists, had a lot to say about interest. A few books, such as Felix Arnold's (1910) *Attention and Interest* and John Dewey's (1913) *Interest and Effort in Education*, made strong cases for the role of interest in learning, cognition, and motivation. The advent of behaviorism dampened research on interest—much as it dampened most of the interesting concepts in psychology—until the 1960s and 1970s, when psychologists from an eclectic group of areas turned their attention to interest. Experimental psychologists examined curiosity and exploratory behavior (Berlyne, 1960; Fowler, 1965); vocational psychologists explored the psychological structure of interest in occupations (Holland, 1973); psychologists studying aesthetics explored interest in response to art (Berlyne, 1971a); and the nascent field of emotion psychology began exploring interest as an emotional state (Tomkins, 1962).

Theories of interest split into two fields: (1) interest as a part of emotional experience, curiosity, and momentary motivation; and (2) interest as a part of personality, individual differences, and people's idiosyncratic hobbies, goals, and avocations. For convenience we'll refer to these constructs with the simple terms *interest* and *interests*. This is analogous to the classic distinction between states and traits, and it's roughly similar to a long-standing distinction (Hidi, 1990; Krapp, Hidi, & Renninger, 1992) between *situational interest* (for state interest) and *individual interest* (for stable interests; see chapter 8). Distinguishing between interest and interests is helpful because it organizes the vast and eclectic body of work on interest. By doing so, it highlights bridges between seemingly different areas.

As an example of these bridges, momentary feelings of interest have been studied in the context of when people find paintings and music interesting (Berlyne, 1972, 1974d), when texts are interesting to read (Schraw & Lehman, 2001), the cognitive processes that cause interest (Silvia, 2005c), facial and vocal expressions associated with feelings of interest and boredom (Banse & Scherer, 1996; Reeve, 1993), motivational effects of interest (Sansone & Smith, 2000b), and the effects of feeling interested on learning and performance (Ainley, Hidi, & Berndorff, 2002; Fisher & Noble, 2004). Recognizing that these areas have something fundamental in common—they all examine the causes and consequences of feeling interested—is the first step toward developing models and concepts that can bring these diverse areas together.

The same is true for interests. Stable and enduring aspects of interest have been studied in the context of individual differences in interest-related traits such as trait curiosity, openness to experience, sensation seeking, boredom proneness, and breadth of interest (Kashdan, 2004; see chapter 4); theories of how unique interests and hobbies develop (Super, 1940; see chapters 5 and 6); attempts to bolster students' interests related to math, science, and literature (Hoffman & Häussler, 1998); and theories of interests related to vocations and occupations (Savickas & Spokane, 1999). As before, recognizing that researchers in these diverse fields are talking about the same thing sets the stage for a broader theoretical integration.

Interest and Emotion

Exploring the state of interest takes us into the realm of emotion psychology. The psychology of emotions is a dynamic and flourishing field. It's hard to imagine, even with the generosity of hindsight, that psychologists once avoided studying emotions. For many decades, psychology viewed emotions as simple states of activation and arousal (Duffy, 1934), as disruptive influences on rational behavior (Leeper, 1948), or as specious concepts undeserving of a place in scientific psychology (Meyer, 1933). Pioneering books by Magda Arnold (1960), Robert Plutchik (1962), and Silvan Tomkins (1962, 1963) reintroduced emotions to psychology and inspired decades of future research on appraisal, facial expressions, and psychobiology.

The modern psychology of emotions has formed a partnership with cognitive psychology, another once-peripheral field of psychological science. This alliance is natural and powerful because cognitions and emotions have a lot to do with each other. Cognitive processes give rise to emotions (Ellsworth & Scherer, 2003), and emotions affect perception, attention, memory, judgment, and reasoning (Silvia & Warburton, 2006). Throughout this book, cognition-emotion interactions will recur as central mechanisms in the psychology of interest. For example, chapter 2 develops a model of what makes things interesting using cognitive-appraisal theories of emotions (Lazarus, 2001; Scherer, 2001a), and chapter 6 develops a model of the development of interests using research on emotional knowledge.

Looking at interest from the perspective of emotion psychology provides a set of predictions about what interest is, what features it should have, and what it should do. Modern theories of emotions assert that emotions consist of a set of organized components (Ekman, 1992; Ellsworth & Scherer, 2003; Frijda, 1986; Roseman, 2001), such as facial and vocal expressions, physiological changes, subjective experience, readiness to act, and psychosocial functions. As we'll see later in this book, other points of view on interest would not make these predictions or expect interest to have these features. Viewing interest as a simple motivational state (e.g., Hidi, 1990; Krapp, 1999; Schraw & Lehman, 2001), for example, does not imply the presence of facial or vocal expressions associated with interest. Furthermore, emotion psychology provides broad, overarching theories that can bring coherence to otherwise scattered findings. Studies of text-based interest, for instance, have examined how interest affects attention during reading (Hidi, 1995). An emotion approach would point out that similar studies have been done on interest and attention to faces during infancy (Langsdorf, Izard, Rayias, & Hembree, 1983), on interest and attention to visual art (Evans & Day, 1971; Silvia, 2005c), and on interest and psychophysiological markers of attention (Libby, Lacey, & Lacey, 1973), and that all of these areas can be informed by research on attention and emotion.

Interests and Personality

Exploring enduring interests takes us into the realm of personality psychology. The struggle between the general and the unique has preoccupied personality psychology for many decades (Allport, 1962). Much of personality psychology has concerned itself with abstract traits. This approach, labeled *generic structuralism*, asserts that " 'the' human personality is structured in terms of a finite number of underlying qualities (or attributes, characteristics, predispositions, traits) in some amount of which every individual is endowed by nature and/or nurture" (Lamiell, 1987, p. 8). There's no question that the study of individual differences has been popular, fertile, and controversial (Eysenck & Eysenck, 1985). It has had many distinguished antagonists who advocated the study of what is unique and idiosyncratic about people. Lamiell (1987) called individual differences research "impersonality psychology" because it focuses on distributions of people rather than people themselves. Gordon Allport (1961), perhaps the most famous critic of generic structuralism, once asked, "Is it reasonable to assume that all people do in fact possess the same basic constitution of personality? Must the units of organization in all lives be the same?" (p. 329).

Fortunately, personality psychologists have reframed this trenchant conflict. Modern theories of personality recognize that personality can be productively studied at several levels (McAdams, 1992, 1996). In addition to traits and dispositions, personality psychologists study idiosyncratic goals and motives (Emmons, 1999; Klinger, 1971), personally constructed narratives of one's life (McAdams, 1993), and the enactment of abstract traits in the daily lives of individuals (Fleeson, 2001). An integration of the levels of personality seems possible, and some studies examine several levels of personality at once. For instance, research has explored how general traits and specific goals change over time (Paloutzian, Richardson, & Rambo, 1999) and how traits and goals influence each other during adulthood (Abele, 2003).

The scope of modern personality psychology is seen in the psychology of interest. On the side of traits, a large body of work has examined traits related to interest, curiosity, and intrinsic motivation. Some of these traits, such as openness to experience and sensation seeking, have been widely studied (McCrae, 1996; Zuckerman, 1994); others are newcomers to the study of interest (Kashdan, Rose, & Fincham, 2004; Litman & Jimerson, 2004; Litman & Spielberger, 2003). On the side of unique aspects of personality, a growing literature is concerned with interests, hobbies, and avocations. Vocational psychologists have examined avocational interests related to hobbies and leisure pursuits (Hansen & Scullard, 2002; Roe & Siegelman, 1964; Super, 1940), personality psychologists have considered the role of interests in motivation (White, 1972), and educational psychologists have studied how interests affect learning (Alexander & Jetton, 1996; Renninger, 2000). We'll explore both the general and the unique aspects of interests.

An Overview of This Book

By now, the study of interest is an eclectic and sprawling area of research. Psychologists interested in emotions, aesthetics, education, metacognition, vocations, personality, life-span development, exercise science, organizational behavior, neuroscience, and text processing have intriguing ideas about what interest is and how it works. It isn't surprising that so many areas of psychology study interest. It is surprising, though, that these areas of psychology have little to do with each other. Those researching theories of vocational interests, for instance, are unaware of research on interest as an emotion; those in emotion psychology, in turn, are unaware of what aesthetics research has shown about interest; and those involved in the study of interest and education are generally unaware of all of these areas. The central goal of this book is to introduce the reader to these isolated pockets of research.

We hope, though, to do more than review the vast body of work on interest. Whenever people in many fields struggle with similar problems, one naturally wonders if a single solution can be found. There are parallels between different areas of the psychology of interest. As one example, emotion psychology has shown that appraising something as easy to understand increases interest (Silvia, 2005c), education psychology has found that finding a text easy to read makes it more interesting (Schraw, Bruning, & Svoboda, 1995), and vocational psychology has found that occupational activities are more interesting when people feel efficacious about doing them well (Betz, 1999). Remarkably, no one has yet explored these striking similarities and considered possible general models that explain all of these relationships.

Part I of this book explores interest as an emotion. Chapter 1 reviews what is known about emotional qualities of interest. Most theories of emotions assume that emotions consist of a set of components (Ekman, 1992; Ellsworth & Scherer, 2003), such as facial expressions, physiological changes, patterns of cognitive appraisals, subjective affective experience, and action tendencies. Chapter 1 describes research that examined whether interest has any of these features, and it explores differences between interest and the related emotion of happiness. These two emotions are often lumped together under the umbrella of "positive affect," and interest is sometimes defined as feelings of enjoyment (e.g., Chen, 2001). We'll see that interest and enjoyment differ in critical ways, thus supporting the notion of interest as a distinct emotion.

People are not constantly interested in everything all the time—something makes them experience interest. Chapter 2 tackles the tricky problem of what makes something interesting. That chapter reviews the long history of thought, beginning with Daniel Berlyne's (1960, 1971a) seminal and sophisticated theories of curiosity and ending with recent models (Chen, 2001; Loewenstein, 1994). The chapter concludes by re-locating the question of "what makes things interesting" within modern appraisal theories of emotion. According to appraisal theories, evaluations of events, not events themselves, cause emotional experience (Ellsworth & Scherer, 2003; Lazarus, 1991; Roseman, 2001). The chapter then reviews a program of experiments that examines interest's *appraisal structure*: the pattern of cognitions that leads to feelings of interest (Silvia, 2005c).

In light of the historical and theoretical aspects of interest covered in chapters 1 and 2, chapter 3 reviews research on interest and reading. Educational psychologists have generated a large and insightful literature on how interest affects learning. Consistent with the fragmentation of the psychology of interest, however, theories of what makes text interesting are disconnected from theories of what makes everything else interest-ing. After reviewing this work, we'll reframe models of text-based interest in terms of the appraisal model developed in chapter 2. Viewing the causes of text-based interest as an instance of a broader appraisal model enables new predictions and new bridges to other areas of research. We'll also examine research on how interest promotes learning from text. This research may be the best evidence for the view that interest's function is to enable the acquisition of knowledge and skills (Fredrickson, 1998; Izard, 1977; Tomkins, 1962).

Part II of this book considers interests as stable aspects of personality. Chapter 4 examines individual differences related to interest. One class of models assumes individual differences in curiosity (Kashdan, 2004; Spielberger & Starr, 1994), proneness to boredom (Farmer & Sundberg, 1986), and the tendency to seek strong sensations and new experiences (McCrae, 1996; Zuckerman, 1994). Others have posited differences in the breadth, depth, or complexity of one's interests (Ainley, 1998; Boyle, 1989; Langevin, 1971). In reviewing these traits, we consider how well the underlying dynamics of the trait are understood. Individual differences research is most powerful when it illuminates psychological processes instead of simply documenting differences (Cronbach, 1957; Underwood, 1975). We'll see how individual differences research has informed basic problems in other areas of the psychology of interest.

The following two chapters examine the development of interests. Where interests come from is a thorny problem—many theories have had something to say about it. Chapter 5 takes a look at the history of thought on *motivational development*—the study of how idiosyncratic motives develop and change. Theorists as diverse as Sigmund Freud, Clark Hull, William McDougall, Gordon Allport, Anne Roe, Silvan Tomkins, and Edward Thorndike have weighed in on how interests develop. Despite their apparent differences, most theories of interest development have taken the same basic approach: (1) identifying a general source of motivation, and (2) positing a mechanism that directs or connects motivation to specific activities.

Appreciating abstract similarities among past theories provides a foundation for developing a new theory of how interests develop. In chapter 6, we return to the interface of cognition and emotion to consider how momentary states influence the development of enduring aspects of personality. People don't simply experience emotions—they think about their emotions, form ideas about what emotions are like, and develop theories about the causes and consequences of emotions (Gilbert & Wilson, 2000; Seager, 2002). By thinking about their feelings—especially the causes of their feelings—people cultivate knowledge about the activities, objects, and events that should create feelings of interest and enjoyment. Thus, this model emphasizes attributions for emotions as a cognitive mechanism that bridges transient experience and enduring aspects of personality. Some contrasts between the emotion–attribution theory and other theories are considered (Prenzel, 1992; Tomkins, 1979).

The study of vocational interests is the biggest—and probably the most isolated—area of research in the psychology of interest. Vocational psychology has studied interests related to the world of work for nearly a century (Savickas, 1999). The study of vocational interests has a lot to offer other areas, but, for whatever reason, it hasn't received the attention it deserves (Tinsley, 2001; Walsh, 2001). Vocational psychologists have developed sophisticated tools for assessing interests, proposed intriguing theories of how interests develop, and conducted longitudinal and experimental studies that test these theories. In chapter 7, we examine theories of interest structure, models of how vocational interests develop, and new directions for vocational interest research.

Part III of this book considers some implications for models of interest and for future research. Chapter 8 reviews some theoretical problems that are best appreciated in light of the rest of the psychology of interest. This book looks at interest and interests primarily in terms of emotion and personality. This isn't the only way to view interest and interests; in fact, several well-known models preceded the view advocated in this book. In chapter 8, we analyze alternative models of interest. One well-known model distinguishes among *situational interest, individual interest,* and *actualized interest* (Hidi, 2001; Krapp, 1999; Renninger, 2000). Another distinguishes between *emotional interest* and *cognitive interest* (Harp & Mayer, 1997; Kintsch, 1980). Still another argues for a distinction between *interest* and *curiosity* (e.g., Hidi & Berndorff, 1998; Reeve, 1996). Comparing and contrasting these models highlights the strengths of our model founded on theories of emotion and personality.

Chapter 9 wraps up our exploration of the psychology of interest. It looks back at the terrain that was covered and looks ahead to unknown lands awaiting interested researchers.

PART I

INTEREST
AND
EMOTION

1

Interest as an Emotion

The study of emotions has exploded in recent years, emerging as an integrative and interdisciplinary part of psychological science. For modern psychologists, situated within a flurry of research and writing on emotions, it seems odd that emotions were once considered irrelevant, fictional, or unscientific. During behaviorism's heyday, subjective experience was considered anachronistic to the true concerns of psychology. If subjective experience existed, it was too ephemeral to be captured by the cold, objective eye of scientific scrutiny. In hindsight, the behaviorists' exclusion of emotions is ironic—observable facial and vocal expressions are among the most popular topics in the study of emotions (Keltner & Ekman, 2000; Johnstone & Scherer, 2000).

This chapter reviews what research says about interest as an emotion. Interest has had a checkered history in the study of emotions. Some researchers place it among the most important of the emotions (Fredrickson, 1998; Izard, 1977; Tomkins, 1962). Others doubt its status as an emotion, arguing that interest is a nonemotional state of motivation or attention (Lazarus, 1991; Ortony & Turner, 1990; see chapter 8). There isn't much scientific evidence either way. The champions of interest as an emotion never did much research on interest—other emotions took center stage. Likewise, the skeptics dismissed interest without conducting the research that would support their alternative position. The best approach is to see what research has found, discuss limitations and gaps in the evidence, and outline the key directions for future work.

The Psychology of Emotions

The decline of behavior theory in the early 1960s corresponded with the rise of the first modern theories of emotions (Arnold, 1960; Plutchik, 1962; Tomkins, 1962, 1963). Many contemporary theories assume that emotions are discrete (Ellsworth & Scherer, 2003; Izard & Ackerman, 2000; Johnson-Laird & Oatley, 1992; Lazarus, 2001). Emotions can be described in dimensional terms—such as valence, activity level, or arousal (Feldman-Barrett & Russell, 1999; Watson & Tellegen, 1985)—but emotions themselves are not quantitative variations on abstract dimensions. Instead, there are a limited number of distinct emotions. Emotion theories differ in how many emotions they posit, although most theories agree on a core group of emotions. Nearly all theories include happiness, fear, anger, sadness, and disgust; some include interest, surprise, contempt, guilt, embarrassment, regret, and jealousy.

What makes an emotion an emotion? Contemporary theories typically define emotions as coherent clusters of components. Ekman (1992, pp. 174–189), for instance, proposed nine features, such as distinctive universal expressive signals, distinctive physiology, rapid onset and brief duration, coherence among the emotion's components, appearance in related species, distinctive universals in the emotion's antecedents, and unbidden occurrence. Other researchers include distinctive subjective conscious experiences (Izard & Ackerman, 2000), appearance in early life (Izard, 1978), and adaptive functions across the life span as defining features of basic emotions (Keltner & Gross, 1999; Oatley & Jenkins, 1992). Appraisal theories emphasize distinctive cognitive patterns that give rise to the emotions (Roseman & Smith, 2001). If interest is an emotion, then it should have these features. In the following sections, we'll review the evidence regarding interest's emotional qualities.[1]

1. Readers familiar with emotion psychology may notice that we're obscuring a distinction between *basic emotions* theories (Ekman, 1992; Izard, 1977) and *appraisal theories* (Roseman & Smith, 2001). By emphasizing pan-cultural, psychobiological programs, models of basic emotions posit a small group of emotions. Appraisal theories, in contrast, view emotions as caused and constituted by evaluations of events—there are as many emotions as there are coherent patterns of appraisal (see Ellsworth & Scherer, 2003). The differences between these theories are unimportant for now because both theories define emotions as sets of components. Later in this book we'll see some advantages of an appraisal perspective for understanding the causes of interest (chapters 2 and 3).

Expressions of Interest

Facial Expressions

Emotions have distinctive facial expressions (Darwin, 1872/1998; Ekman, 1993; Izard, 1971). Emotional expressions are holistic—they are perceived as coherent patterns of expressions, not as collections of isolated muscle movements (Etcoff & Magee, 1992). Consistent with the presumed biological basis of emotions and their expressions, there are brain regions dedicated to producing spontaneous facial expressions as well as biological dysfunctions related to producing facial expressions (Rinn, 1984). Some emotional expressions—happiness, anger, fear, sadness, and disgust—are considered to be universal (Ekman, 1992). Research regarding the universality of other emotions—such as contempt, shame, confusion, and embarrassment—is still in progress (Keltner & Busswell, 1996; Keltner & Ekman, 2000; Matsumoto, 1992; Rozin & Cohen, 2003).

Within the enormous literature on facial expressions (Keltner & Ekman, 2000), only a few studies have explored interest expressions. Tomkins (1962) and Izard (1971) speculated that interest involves either slightly lowered or raised eyebrows, raised lower eyelids (to sharpen visual focus), and parted lips and a dropped jaw, although they had few studies at the time. Tomkins (1962) cited an early study of "attentive listening," in which people listened to an audio-recording three consecutive times (Wallerstein, 1954). One group listened to a detective story; another group listened to a philosophy essay. Electromyographic (EMG) measures were taken of movements of the frontalis muscle, which controls forehead and brow movements. Repeating the story was expected to reduce interest. In fact, several participants fell asleep toward the end of the experiment, and most participants reported greater boredom during the later repetitions. Measures of frontalis movement showed that facial activity decreased as the detective story was repeated, presumably reflecting less interest. Facial activity during the philosophy essay showed a similar trend. Although intriguing, this experiment is limited by its inclusion of only one measure of muscle activity.

A more comprehensive experiment explored facial expressions of interest during infancy (Langsdorf, Izard, Rayias, & Hembree, 1983). Infants ages 2, 4, 6, or 8 months viewed a live human face, a realistically dressed mannequin, and an inanimate object. The primary measures were heart rate, visual attention to the object, and facial expressions of interest. Based on coding systems developed by Izard, the researchers coded the following facial movements as signs of interest: raised or lowered brows, widened and rounded eyes, squinted eyes, raised cheeks, opened and relaxed mouth, moved tongue, and pursed lips. The duration and intensity of the facial movements were two indexes of interest. A third, more complex index of interest expressions was formed by taking each time period that an infant spent looking at the object and then computing the percentage of the time period spent expressing interest. This index avoids confounding the facial movements that might be expressed only during visual attention with the separate measure of visual attention.

Infants expressed significantly more interest in the live face than in the mannequin; both of these stimuli elicited more interest expression than did the inanimate object. This finding appeared for all three measures of interest expression. The measure of visual attention found that infants also spent the most time looking at the face, less time looking at the mannequin, and the least time looking at the inanimate object. Heart rate deceleration showed a similar pattern. Mediation analyses found that the effects of the stimuli on visual attention were significantly mediated by interest facial expressions. The faces and objects induced interest; in turn, interest determined the time spent looking at the faces and objects. This analysis was significant for each of the three stimuli.

A recent study explored 11-month-old infants' facial and nonfacial expressions in response to an impossible event (Camras et al., 2002). Infants first saw an expected event—a toy was placed under a cloth, and removing the cloth revealed the toy. After several trials, the toy was secretly switched: removing the cloth revealed a new toy. Facial expressions and bodily expressions for the normal event and the expectancy-violating event were videotaped and shown to adult observers. The observers tried to guess, based on the infants' expressions, which trial had a normal event and which had an impossible event. They also rated the infants for surprise, interest, and negative affect. Observers correctly identified the impossible event above chance levels. Surprise and interest were both higher during the impossible event relative to the normal event. The observers' ratings of interest seemed to be driven by postural changes more than by facial changes. Observers rated interest in the impossible events as higher when infants showed more body stilling, more sober facial expressions, and a ceasing of distress and fussing.

Reeve (1993) conducted a broad, exploratory study of interest expressions in adults. In his first study, undergraduates watched a series of three film clips. Facial expressions were measured by videotaping participants and applying the Facial Action Coding System (Ekman & Friesen, 1978). Physiological measures of heart rate and skin conductance were also taken. The first clip was a moderately interesting film used to familiarize the participant with the context and to allow the physiological responses to stabilize. The subsequent clips were highly interesting (diving into the ocean) and uninteresting (an outdated business talk show). Pretesting found that the films evoked different levels of interest but equal levels of enjoyment. Self-reports of interest and enjoyment were taken after each film.

The findings are summarized in table 1.1. Some of the movements differed significantly between the interesting and uninteresting films. During the interesting film, people widened their eyelids more, blinked and glanced away less often, spent less time with their eyes closed or away from the film, moved their head away less often, and kept their head more still. A few of these expressions didn't replicate when correlated with self-reported feelings of interest, but overall the internal analyses showed the same effects. No effects were found for the physiological measures. The overall pattern of expressions—increased stillness of the head and eye movements associated with visual attention—fits with what one would expect from an interest expression.

Reeve's (1993) second study replicated the findings with a different procedure. Undergraduates watched films while being monitored for facial expressions, heart rate, and skin conductance. This time the interestingness of the film was manipulated between subjects, enabling a cleaner test of condition differences, and a second manipulation was added. The interesting film group watched the highly interesting film three consecutive times, while the uninteresting film group watched three consecutive uninteresting films. This design thus provides between- and within-person comparisons of interest expressions. The findings were similar to the first study, as table 1.1 shows. Not every expression was replicated, but some were robust across both studies and across experimental and internal analyses. An additional measure—the amount of exposed eyeball surface—was also significant, with the interested group showing a greater percentage of the eye's area.

TABLE 1.1 Facial Movements Associated With Interest

	Study 1		Study 2		
	Condition	Interest	Condition	Time	Interest
Eye blinks	S	S	S		
Eyes closed	S	S			S
Glances away (no.)	S	S		S	S
Glances away (time)	S			S	S
Eyelid widening	S		S	S	
Eyeball surface area	nm	nm	S	S	
Lips parting				S	S
Jaw drop					
Yawns				S	S
Smiles		S			
Lip wipes					
Head turning	S	S	S		S
Head tilt					S
Shoulder tilt					
Head stillness	S	S		S	
Skin conductance				S	
Heart rate					

Notes: nm = expression not measured; S = significant. *Condition* refers to interesting vs. uninteresting film comparisons; *Interest* refers to correlations between the expression and self-reported interest; *Time* refers to differences between the first and last viewing of the same film.

Source: Adapted from Reeve 1993, Experiments 1 & 2.

A later study validated some of these expressions in the context of free-choice activity (Reeve & Nix, 1997). Undergraduates were asked to work on an engaging puzzle task. While they worked on the puzzle, four facial expressions were videotaped: eye contact with the puzzle, eyeball exposure, eye closing, and lip parting. Eye contact with the puzzle was significantly correlated with self-reported feelings of interest and with feelings of perceived self-determination. Feelings of competence correlated negatively with the amount of time spent with closed eyes; lip parting was correlated with the speed with which the hands manipulated the puzzles. Given the large number of measures included in this study, these findings seem a bit scattered. Nevertheless, this is the first attempt to connect interest expressions to motivated activity, and the findings should encourage more research.

Vocal Expressions

Studies of vocal expressions of emotion explore many of the same issues as studies of facial expressions: the universality of vocal expressions, differences between spontaneous and deliberate expressions, the accuracy of judgments of emotions based on vocalizations, and the underlying dimensions of vocal expressions that vary for different emotions (Frick, 1985). Assessments of the dimensions of vocal expressions sort into three rough categories (Johnstone & Scherer, 2000). Measures of *time* focus on the durations of sounds and pauses in speech and the overall speech rate. Measures of *intensity* focus on the energy in the speech signal that affects the perceived loudness of speech. Measures of *frequency* focus on the pitch of the voice, quantified as the rate at which the vocal folds open and close. Frequency measures can describe the base level of the pitch, the range of the pitch, and the variability of the pitch during the utterance.

Vocal expressions for different emotions show different arrangements of the three dimensions. Fear, for example, is characterized by a higher rate of articulation, higher intensity of speech, and increases in the range and average pitch of the voice (Scherer, 1986). Vocal expressions of interest and boredom have not been widely studied, but research finds expressive patterns corresponding to these emotions. Johnstone and Scherer (2000) describe bored speech as "generally slow and monotonous" (p. 227): the base level of pitch declines, speech rate declines, and the voice's pitch becomes less variable and shows a smaller range of frequency. Interested speech, in contrast, shows a quicker rate of speech and a wider range of frequency.

Recognition of emotions from vocal features tends to be high, but not all emotions are recognized equally well. In one study (Banse & Scherer, 1996), professional actors portrayed 14 emotions by communicating sentences of meaningless utterances. People then listened to the sentences and judged the emotion expressed by the speaker. The three emotions recognized most accurately were hot anger (78%), boredom (76%), and interest (75%); the emotions recognized least accurately were disgust (15%) and shame (22%). Analysis of the errors found that confusions of emotions were systematic rather than random. Vocal expressions of interest were most often confused with happiness; expressions of boredom were most often confused with sadness.

Subjective Experience

Emotions have distinctive feelings—subjective qualities that remain the same across the life span (Izard, 1984). Collecting quantitative data on the conscious experience of emotions can be difficult. As William Mc-Dougall (1908/1960) observed, "a person who had not experienced [an emotion] could no more be made to understand its quality than a totally colour-blind person can be made to understand the experience of colour-sensation" (p. 61). Nonetheless, Izard (1977) provides a description of the conscious experience of interest:

> At the experiential level interest . . . is the feeling of being engaged, caught-up, fascinated, curious. There is a feeling of wanting to investigate, become involved, or extend or expand the self by incorporating new information and having new experiences with the person or object that has stimulated the interest. In intense interest or excitement the person feels animated and enlivened. It is this enlivenment that guarantees the association between interest and cognitive or motor activity. Even when relatively immobile the interested or excited person has the feeling that he is "alive and active." (p. 216)

Studies of the subjective experience of interest suggest that interest has a positive and active experiential quality. Izard (1977, pp. 216–222) asked people to describe their past experiences of interest, using self-report rating scales for emotional and subjective experiences. Past experiences of interest were characterized by elevated feelings of pleasantness, self-assurance, impulsiveness, and tension. Interest was most closely related to the emotions of enjoyment and surprise. Appraisal research finds that situations that arouse interest are rated as pleasant (Smith & Ellsworth, 1985), and that interest most often blends with positive emotions (Ellsworth & Smith, 1988). Research on the structure of self-reported affect reveals similar findings. Interest is located on the high *Positive Affect* pole in Watson's Positive Affect × Negative Affect model (Watson, 2000; Watson, Wiese, Vaidya, & Tellegen, 1999). The Pleasure × Arousal model locates interest within the *Pleasure–High Arousal* quadrant (Feldman-Barrett & Russell, 1999). In a study of momentary experience, high school students read essays about television and prehistoric people (Schiefele, 1996). Scales for affective experience were inserted into the text to obtain online ratings of subjective responses to the essays. Feelings of interest were reflected in a joint increase in positive feelings and activation.

Emotion theories contend that emotions involve coherence among their components—the subjective, expressive, behavioral, and physiological aspects of an emotion should correlate (Reisenzein, 2000; Rosenberg & Ekman, 1994). As a result, the subjective experience of interest should coincide with other emotional features. Some evidence for coherence comes from research on interest expressions. Reeve (1993) found that self-reported feelings of interest correlated with several facial actions (see table 1.1). In Reeve and Nix's (1997) experiment, self-reported feelings of interest correlated with several behavioral measures (how long people spent working on a puzzle as well as how comprehensively and deeply people explored the puzzle). In infants, the amount of time spent viewing human and inanimate faces correlated with facial expressions of interest (Langsdorf et al., 1983). Taken together, these findings suggest coherence among subjective, expressive, and behavioral components of interest.

Functions of Interest

Most theories of emotions assume that emotions have adaptive functions (Keltner & Gross, 1999). As evolved mechanisms, emotions should be roughly functional in helping people deal with "fundamental life-tasks" (Ekman, 1992, p. 171). The strongest form of the functionalist view asserts that each emotion serves useful functions for modern humans. Weaker forms acknowledge that some emotions might be less useful now than they were in the ancestral past, or that functionalism applies to the species rather than to the individual. Either way, the issues involved in functionalist analysis are clearly complex (Oatley & Jenkins, 1992; Parrott, 2001). To avoid detouring, we'll take a weak form of functionalism. Emotions in general are useful, but whether a specific emotional experience is adaptive depends on many factors beyond the emotion itself (Parrott, 2001).

What is interest good for? Izard and Ackerman (2000) suggest a motivational function—"interest motivates exploration and learning, and guarantees the person's engagement in the environment. Survival and adaptation require such engagement" (p. 257). Diverse areas of research demonstrate beneficial motivational effects of interest. Studies of successful adolescents indicate that "undivided interest" promotes the growth of expertise (Rathunde, 1996, 1998, 2001). An experience-sampling study of high school students assessed subjective experience during school-related activities (Rathunde & Csikszentmihalyi, 1993). Three years later, achievement and talent were measured. Feelings of undivided interest during the first year of high school strongly predicted academic success, engagement with school, and teachers' ratings of achievement three years later. Reading research, reviewed in chapter 3, shows that people process texts more deeply and remember the material more accurately when the texts are interesting (Hidi, 2000; Schiefele, 1999). Furthermore, students are more successful in courses that they find personally interesting (Schiefele, Krapp, & Winteler, 1992). Finally, the experience of interest during an activity predicts the duration of engagement, volunteering to repeat the activity, and the development of skill (Deci & Ryan, 1985; Fisher & Noble, 2004; Prenzel, 1992; Reeve, Cole, & Olson, 1986).

The motivational function of interest extends to activities that are not inherently interesting or appealing. Interest can bolster motivation to complete tasks that are boring and tedious. Much of what people have to do, such as washing dishes or compiling references, is boring. To boost their motivation to complete such tasks, people implement interest-enhancing strategies (Sansone & Harackiewicz, 1996; Sansone & Smith, 2000a, 2000b; Sansone, Wiebe, & Morgan, 1999; Sansone, Weir, Harpster, & Morgan, 1992). For example, when people have to copy letters from a template, they make the task more interesting by competing against time or against their past performance levels, varying the artfulness of the lettering, or cognitively restructuring the task in ways that foster interest. The use of interest-enhancing strategies predicts feelings of interest, which in turn increase persistence at the task (Sansone & Smith, 2000b).

Some researchers suggest a second function—interest is adaptive because it motivates people to develop diverse experiences that can be helpful when unforeseen events occur (Fredrickson, 1998). Berlyne (1971a), for example, writes: "Since every scrap of retained information might help one day and thus adds its quota of security against future perplexity, frustration, and helplessness, it is easy to see that moments of freedom from more urgent claims (including those of sleep and rest) can hardly be better occupied than with activities that add to the nervous system's holdings in this commodity" (p. 295).

The broaden-and-build model of positive emotions (Fredrickson, 1998, 2001) proposes that interest, like other positive emotions, lacks short-term functions associated with survival. Instead, interest serves long-term developmental goals: curiosity about the new and the possible broadens experiences and attracts people to new possibilities. The broaden-and-build model suggests that interest cultivates diverse experience by orienting people to new and unusual events and facilitates the growth of competence by motivating sustained activity in a specific area.

The notion that diverse experience is an adaptive function of interest has an intuitive appeal. Indirect evidence comes from research on sensory deprivation. People typically find sensory deprivation intensely boring and unpleasant (Schultz, 1965). When confined to extended sensory restriction, people often experience hallucinations, show deficits in cognitive and perceptual performance, and exhibit disturbances of normal motivation (Fiske, 1961; Scott, Bexton, Heron, Doane, 1959; Zubeck, Pushkar, Sansom, & Gowing, 1961). Other indirect support comes from longitudinal research on stimulation seeking, a trait relevant to interest (see chapter 4). Stimulation seeking at age 3 strongly predicted intelligence at age 11, suggesting a possible role of diverse experience in cognitive development (Raine, Reynolds, Venables, & Mednick, 2002).

Of the two functions of interest that have been proposed—interest as a motivational resource and interest as a facilitator of diverse experience—only the first function is well supported by research. Many studies, including experiments that manipulate interest, show how interest improves motivation and learning (see Hidi, 2000; Sansone & Smith, 2000b; Schiefele, 1999). The second function seems intuitively plausible, but it has not yet received the empirical attention that it deserves. The indirect evidence is intriguing, however, and future research should explore it further.

Antecedents of Interest

Emotions occur quickly, as indicated by physiological and facial responses within milliseconds of encountering an emotion-eliciting stimulus (Ekman, 1992; LeDoux, 1996). The rapid onset of emotions reflects their adaptive value. As sources of motivation for dealing with fundamental life-tasks (Johnson-Laird & Oatley, 1992), emotions need to be rapid and flexible. An emotion such as fear, for instance, would be ineffective if people required minutes or seconds to become afraid. Emotions must also be brief. People's flexibility would be hindered if emotions persisted for hours because the demands of the situation may have changed since the emotion arose. The intensity of an emotion is thus flexible in the face of new, emotionally relevant events (Brehm, 1999; Silvia & Brehm, 2001).

The antecedents of emotions, like emotions themselves, should be distinctive and universal (Ekman, 1992; Scherer, 2001a). The things that make people happy should differ from the things that make people afraid; both sets of antecedents should appear pan-culturally (Roseman & Smith, 2001). There is solid evidence for distinctive, universal antecedents for many emotions (Boucher, 1983; Boucher & Brandt, 1981; Scherer, 1997). The universal antecedents tend to be abstract rather than specific (e.g., "core relational themes"; Lazarus, 1991), such as expecting or experiencing harm, achieving a goal, or losing a significant other. Exceptions are cases of biologically prepared classes of antecedents (Öhman, 2002), such as snakes as a cause of fear (Öhman, Flykt, & Esteves, 2001).

When do people experience interest? A set of abstract qualities of information, labeled *collative variables* by Berlyne (1960), play a major role. *Novelty, complexity, uncertainty,* and *conflict* have been found to arouse feelings of interest in young infants, children, adults, older adults, and members of other species (Berlyne, 1960, 1971b, 1974a, 1978; Daffner, Scinto, Weintraub, Guinessey, & Mesulam, 1992; McCall & Kennedy, 1980; McCall & McGhee, 1977; Walker, 1980, 1981). Cross-cultural research finds these relationships in several cultures and languages (Berlyne, 1976; Berlyne, Robbins, & Thompson, 1974; Child, 1981). The effects of the collative variables on interest are seen in self-reported feelings, expressions of preference, eye movements, behavioral measures of choice, the amount of time spent watching and listening, and the ability of stimuli to reward other actions.

But the cause of interest is more complex than merely perceiving something novel or ambiguous. Strictly speaking, it is misleading to say that complex and novel things are interesting. Emotions result from the person's subjective appraisals of events, not from the events themselves (Ellsworth & Scherer, 2003; Lazarus, 1991). The antecedents of interest, particularly the cognitive appraisal processes that give rise to feelings of interest, are complex and controversial. The next chapter is devoted to the causes of interest, so we'll defer our discussion until then.

Distinguishing Interest From Happiness

Emotions should be distinct in their antecedents, expressions, functions, and consequences. If interest is an emotion, then it should be different from similar emotions. The closest candidate is the positive emotion of *happiness*, also known as *enjoyment* (Izard, 1977). In structural studies, interest and its synonyms load on a "positive-affect" factor alongside happiness and its synonyms (Mayer & Gaschke, 1988; Watson, 2000). In everyday speech, people often use *interest* to refer to enjoyment or preference. It is thus important to see if interest can be distinguished from happiness. Fortunately, many experiments address the relationship between interest and happiness (see Berlyne, 1971a, pp. 213–220; Cupchik & Gebotys, 1990). Four types of evidence demonstrate differences in the antecedents and consequences of interest and happiness.

Antecedents of Interest and Enjoyment

Interest and enjoyment have different antecedents. This isn't surprising because different emotions should have different causes (Roseman & Smith, 2001). Variables like complexity and novelty have distinct, and sometime opposite, effects on interest and enjoyment. People tend to find complex things interesting and simple things enjoyable (see chapter 2). In some experiments (Aitken, 1974; Eisenman, 1966), people ranked randomly generated polygons according to how interesting and how enjoyable they found each polygon. The complex polygons were the most interesting; the simplest polygons were the most enjoyable. In a similar study (Day, 1967), people viewed polygons and rated them for interest and enjoyment. Fairly simple polygons were more enjoyable, and complex polygons were more interesting (see Russell, 1994; Russell & Gray, 1991). The diverging effect of complexity on interest and enjoyment appears for studies of anagrams (Boykin, 1977), randomly generated melodies (Crozier, 1974), and videos (Normore, 1974). Like complexity, novelty has diverging effects on interest and enjoyment. Familiar things tend to be enjoyable, whereas new things tend to be interesting. Research on mere exposure has demonstrated this many times. Repeatedly showing an object increases how much people like it (Zajonc, 2001); it takes a lot of repetitions before the object wanes in appeal and becomes disliked (Van den Bergh & Vrana, 1998). Yet while increasing liking, repetition reduces interest—things become less interesting with more repetitions (Berlyne, 1974c).

Reeve (1989) studied the antecedents of interest and enjoyment within the context of intrinsically motivated activity. After working on anagram tasks, people reported their feelings of interest and enjoyment. In one condition, the task involved variations in color, lettering, arrangement of words, and so forth, to increase the task's novelty and complexity. People found the task interesting when it was varied and diverse, but they found it enjoyable when they thought that their performance was competent and successful. Reeve proposed that novelty and complexity promote interest, whereas satisfying needs associated with competence and autonomy promotes happiness (Deci & Ryan, 2000). Experiments on short stories show a similar pattern (Iran-Nejad, 1987). People were interested in stories with high uncertainty (e.g., a surprise ending) that was eventually reduced; it didn't matter whether the story had a happy or sad ending. In contrast, people enjoyed stories that had happy endings, regardless of the story's uncertainty.

Effects of Interest and Enjoyment Viewing Sets

Some experiments have manipulated instructional sets associated with interest and happiness. In one experiment, people were asked to view randomly generated polygons (Brown & Farha, 1966). People could control how long they viewed each image. Some people were told to view the polygons according to how enjoyable the polygons were; others were told to view the polygons according to how interesting they were. When viewing was based on interest, people spent more time viewing the more complex polygons. This conceptually replicates the experiments described earlier: interest was associated with greater complexity. An experiment by Day (1968) replicated this finding. People viewed randomly generated polygons according to different instructional sets. People who used an interest set spent more time looking at complex images; people who used an enjoyment set spent less time looking at complex images. The finding appears for forced-choice measures as well (Silvia, 2005c; see chapter 2). People viewed polygons that ranged from simple (4 sides) to complex (160 sides). One group picked the polygon they found to be the most interesting; another group picked the polygon they found to be the most enjoyable. People with the interest set chose polygons that were significantly more complex, relative to people with the enjoyment set.

Behavioral Measures Related to Interest and Happiness

Another group of experiments examined behavioral measures, particularly what people chose to view and how long they chose to view it. Many studies, reviewed by Berlyne (1971a, pp. 216–219), indicate that the interestingness of an image predicts viewing time better than the pleasingness of an image. For example, people briefly viewed two images that had been rated for interest and enjoyment and then chose one of the pictures to view for a longer period (Berlyne, 1963). People typically chose to view the relatively interesting image instead of the relatively enjoyable image. In another forced-choice experiment, people generally chose to view interesting, complex patterns over enjoyable, simple patterns (Berlyne & Crozier, 1971).

Ratings of interest usually predict the amount of time spent viewing an image, whereas ratings of enjoyment do not consistently predict viewing time (Berlyne, 1971a). When both interest and enjoyment predict viewing time, interest tends to have a stronger effect. In a study by Berlyne (1974e), ratings related to interest predicted the amount of time spent viewing images (average $r = .66$) more strongly than did ratings related to enjoyment (average $r = .38$). In an experiment on complexity and music, people listened to music selections as long as they wished and rated the music on dimensions related to interest and enjoyment (Crozier, 1974, Study 4). Their ratings of interest accounted for 78% of the variance in listening time; ratings of enjoyment, in contrast, accounted for only 10% of the variance.

Dimensions Underlying Aesthetic Judgments

A final body of research demonstrates that interest and enjoyment emerge as underlying dimensions for judgments of aesthetic objects (see Berlyne, 1974a, for a review). Some experiments have asked for ratings on a large set of items and then extracted general factors underlying the judgments. Crozier (1974) asked participants to rate musical selections on semantic-differential scales. The melodies were randomly constructed to vary in uncertainty, according to information theory principles (Berlyne, 1957; see chapter 2). A factor analysis of the rating scales found two independent factors: one reflected the music's pleasingness and the other reflected interestingness. Furthermore, the effect of complexity on the factor scores replicated studies that directly asked for interest and enjoyment judgments.

In a similar study (Evans & Day, 1971), people viewed polygons varying in complexity. A wide range of responses was measured, including self-report ratings, behavioral measures (time spent viewing the images), and physiological measures of arousal. A factor analysis uncovered two factors that represented the responses. The first factor resembled interest—ratings of activity, complexity, uncertainty, viewing time, and skin conductance loaded on this factor. The second factor resembled enjoyment—ratings of liking, beauty, pleasingness, goodness, and enjoyment loaded on this factor. In a cross-cultural replication, underlying interest and enjoyment factors emerged from ratings of visual images made by Canadian and Ugandan participants (Berlyne et al., 1974).

Participants in a psychophysiology experiment viewed a series of photographs that had been rated on many dimensions by a different group of people (Libby, Lacey, & Lacey, 1973). Pupillary and cardiac activity were measured while people viewed the photographs. As in past studies, separate interest and enjoyment factors emerged in factor analyses of the ratings. Physiological responses varied according to interesting and enjoyable qualities of the pictures. For pictures rated high in interest, pupil diameter increased and heart rate decreased. (As a tangent, the heart-rate finding replicates the study of visual attention in infants [Langsdorf et al., 1983].) For pictures rated high in enjoyment, however, pupil diameter did not change and heart rate increased.

In a study of responses to real art, as opposed to randomly generated stimuli, participants viewed 15 paintings and ranked them on a large set of rating scales (Russell & George, 1990). Some of the scales reflected the participants' judgments of the paintings' pleasing, enjoyable, and likable qualities; other scales reflected the participants' judgments of the paintings' interestingness; and yet other scales reflected perceptions of complexity and familiarity. Congruent with past research, ratings of interest were uncorrelated with ratings of enjoyment. Cupchik and Gebotys (1990) asked expert and novice artists to rate 12 paintings on many dimensions. An underlying dimension of interest reflected perceptions of complexity, novelty, and meaningfulness; an underlying dimension of enjoyment reflected perceptions of simplicity and emotional warmth.

Functions of Interest and Happiness

Tomkins (1962) argued that interest and enjoyment can be distinguished by their functions (see Consedine, Magai, & King, 2004). Interest motivates people to engage with new and complex aspects of the world. Over time, this cultivates knowledge and competence. Happiness, in contrast, serves a rewarding function—it builds attachments to familiar things and rewards the attainment of goals. Tomkins pointed out that these functions can conflict, particularly when people must choose between unfamiliar things and liked things. Interest motivates trying a new dish at a favorite restaurant; happiness motivates ordering what one has liked in the past. This is an intriguing idea—the empirical differences between interest and enjoyment are consistent with different underlying functions, but no research thus far addresses the point directly.

Summary

Interest and happiness diverge in their antecedents and in their consequences. These effects appear across different types of tasks (viewing randomly generated images, listening to music, looking at art, completing anagrams), types of measures (self-report ratings, duration of visual attention), and types of designs (experimental and correlational). The evidence converges to show that interest and enjoyment are distinct positive emotions.

Chapter Summary and Conclusions

Like all vigorous scientific fields, the psychology of emotions has many ongoing controversies. One controversy involves interest's status as an emotion. Some theories of emotion contend that interest—the emotion involved in creativity, learning, curiosity, and competence—is one of the most significant emotions (Fredrickson, 1998; Izard, 1977; Tomkins, 1962). Others contend that interest is better viewed as a motivational process, a cognitive state, or a component of attention (Ortony & Turner, 1990; Wilson, 1971; see chapter 8). In this chapter we avoided this debate—the evidence is what matters, and neither side of the debate has conducted much research on interest. Negative emotions have received more attention than positive emotions; among theories of positive emotions, happiness usually gets the most attention (Fredrickson, 1998).

We began by considering some defining components of emotions, such as expressions and antecedents, coherence among responses, and subjective experience. Research on facial and vocal expressions of interest in infancy (Camras et al., 2002; Langsdorf et al., 1983) and in adulthood (Banse & Scherer, 1996; Reeve, 1993) show expressive aspects of interest. Other studies find coherence among subjective, expressive, and behavioral components of interest. Strong evidence for distinctive antecedents, particularly with regard to differences between interest and happiness, has been obtained (Berlyne, 1971a; see chapter 2). Measures of subjective experience consistently point to a positive-and-active quality to feelings of interest (Izard, 1977, p. 216), and interest clearly facilitates motivation and learning (Rathunde, 1998; Sansone & Smith, 2000b; see chapter 3). Taken as a whole, the evidence supports viewing interest as an emotion.

2

What Is Interesting?

What makes people emotional? This question, not surprisingly, occupies a central place in the psychology of emotions. The issue's obvious theoretical significance aside, the psychology of emotions would be an impractical science if it couldn't explain why people experience certain emotions at certain times. Treating emotional disorders, controlling one's feelings, and tilting the balance of positive and negative emotions require knowing the antecedents of emotions (Thayer, 2001). People who must create feelings of interest—entertainers, teachers, writers, artists, magicians, and beleaguered babysitters, to name a few—need to know how to manipulate the emotions of other people. This requires understanding the dynamics of emotional experience.

While reviewing the emotional qualities of interest (chapter 1), we deferred discussing when people experience interest. The antecedents of interest—and the huge literature that examines them—require a chapter of their own. In this chapter, we consider the two questions that are fundamental to understanding the sources of interest. First, what is interesting? Researchers in many areas—aesthetics, child development, motivation and emotion, education, text processing, and vocational interests—have studied the antecedents of interest. The findings are consistent, but the explanations are diverse. Does interest come from shifts in arousal relative to an optimal level (Berlyne, 1960)? From a boredom drive (Fowler, 1965)? From perceiving gaps in knowledge (Loewenstein, 1994)? From cognitive appraisals (Roseman & Smith, 2001)? We will re-

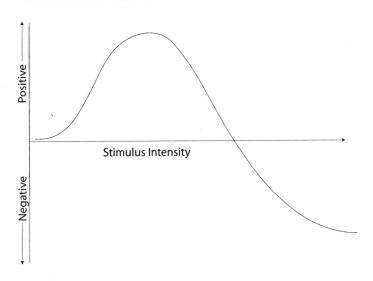

FIGURE 2.1 The Wundt curve

view theories of what makes something interesting, weigh the empirical evidence, and then draw some conclusions.

Second, do the things that induce interest reduce interest when they reach high levels? Some theories have proposed that the antecedents of interest have a quadratic effect on emotional feelings of interest—this is the problem of the *inverted-U* (Walker, 1981). The inverted-U preference function dates back to Wundt, who suggested that the relationship between stimulus intensity and affect had the form shown in figure 2.1. In this function—often called the Wundt curve—positive feelings increase as the stimulus increases in intensity, until the increasing stimulation becomes less pleasant and ultimately aversive (Berlyne, 1971a). Explaining (and demonstrating) the inverted-U has proved to be difficult. After evaluating past theories, we will develop a different perspective grounded in appraisal theories of emotion (Ellsworth & Scherer, 2003) and present new experiments that support it (Silvia, 2005a, 2005c).

Theories of Interest

Berlyne's Theories of Curiosity

The modern study of interest begins with Daniel Berlyne (Day, 1981; Furedy & Furedy, 1981). His work remains influential decades after his death, particularly in the study of aesthetics (Konečni, 1996; Silvia, 2005b). Berlyne was among the first to take interest seriously as a problem for learning theory and for psychology more generally (Berlyne, 1949). Berlyne proposed several related theories of curiosity. Sensitive to developments in neuroscience, he revised his theory of curiosity as physiological research suggested new relationships among perception, arousal, and reward. We will ignore his early curiosity drive theory (Berlyne, 1954a, 1954b) and focus on his two arousal theories advanced in 1960 and 1971. By considering Berlyne's work in detail, we hope to compensate for slighting other important "optimal level" theories (Fiske & Maddi, 1961a; Hebb, 1949, 1955; Hunt, 1965, 1971; Leuba, 1955). Berlyne had more to say about the antecedents of interest than did proponents of these other theories, and his work best demonstrates the conceptual problems that beset optimal level theories.

Berlyne (1960) argued that a family of variables determines whether or not something is potentially interesting. He named these *collative variables* because they involve comparing incoming information with existing knowledge, or comparing several regions of a differentiated stimulus field. Four collative variables—complexity, novelty, uncertainty, and conflict—received the most attention.

COMPLEXITY

Complex patterns have more elements than do simple patterns, more dissimilarity between the elements, and less integration of several elements into a single unit. All told, "one might say roughly that it refers to the amount of variety or diversity in a stimulus pattern" (Berlyne, 1960, p. 38). A common manipulation of complexity involves showing people randomly constructed polygons with different numbers of sides. Some examples are shown in figure 2.2. Complex patterns tend to suggest several different categorizations, and they contain parts that conflict

FIGURE 2.2 Some randomly generated polygons differing in complexity

with other parts. In simple patterns—like the alternation of 1, 0, 1, 0, . . . —the whole is easily predicted from a part. In complex patterns, parts rarely represent, and thus poorly predict, the whole.

NOVELTY

Novelty seems intuitively tied to interest, but Berlyne (1960) noted that novelty is a slippery concept. Novelty is a negative feature—a novel stimulus lacks the quality of previous occurrence. So how does the absence of something cause the presence of interest? Berlyne thought that novelty works because novel stimuli usually fall between the person's existing categorizations. Virtually nothing is truly novel; people can at least categorize an object as tangible and perceptible. Conceptual equidistance creates conflict between competing categorizations and interpretations. Novel events can also conflict with expectations, enabling the absence of an event to be an event in itself. Berlyne distinguished between short-term, long-term, and complete novelty. *Short-term novelty* refers to contrasts with recent experience; *long-term novelty* refers to novelty within a longer period. *Complete novelty* is when people encounter a totally new object.

UNCERTAINTY

Uncertainty has a technical meaning based on information theory (Shannon & Weaver, 1949). Information theory isn't a theory with a specific content or subject matter (Frick, 1959; Garner, 1962). It's probably better described as a perspective, a way of thinking about the nature and structure of information. As noted by Berlyne (1965): "A certain degree of uncertainty is said to exist when (1) any number of alternative events can occur, (2) there is no knowing in advance which will occur at a particular time, and (3) each alternative occurs with a specifiable relative frequency or probability" (p. 31). Information theory specifies uncertainty as $U = \sum_{i=1}^{n} p_i \log_2 1/p_i$, in which p is the probability that event i will occur (Attneave, 1959). According to this formula, uncertainty has some interesting properties. First, uncertainty increases as the number of alternatives increases, all else equal, because uncertainty is a sum across alternatives. For example, an election with five candidates is more uncertain than an election with two candidates. Second, uncertainty increases as the alternative events become equally probable. An election is more uncertain when all five candidates have an equal chance of winning and less uncertain when one candidate is the clear favorite. Combining these two properties, we see that uncertainty approaches a psychological maximum when a large number of alternatives are equally likely.

Sports matches offer a good example of uncertainty. In a tennis tournament, the first-round match between the defending champion and an unranked qualifier is fairly certain. From our equation, we have two events, i_1 (defending champ wins) and i_2 (unseeded player wins). If the defending champ has a 90% chance of winning, then uncertainty about the match's outcome is: $U = (.90 \times (\log_2 1/.90)) + (.10 \times (\log_2 1/.10)) = .47$. In the tournament's final match, however, the two players tend to have equal levels of ability; the probabilities thus become more similar and uncertainty goes up. If the defending champ has a 50% chance of winning, then uncertainty is: $U = (.50 \times (\log_2 1/.50)) + (.50 \times (\log_2 1/.50)) = 1$. This illustrates how uncertainty can change when the number of alternatives is held constant.

CONFLICT

Berlyne (1960) used conflict very generally—"when two or more incompatible responses are aroused simultaneously in an organism, we shall say that the organism is in *conflict*" (p. 10). This definition extends conflict beyond narrower usages referring to motivational and decisional conflicts (Atkinson, 1964). Indeed, Berlyne (1960) noted that "the concept of 'conflict,' as we are using the term, is rather broad. Conflict, in our sense, must accompany virtually every moment of normal waking life in the higher mammals" (p. 31). Conflict is the most clearly collative of the four variables. A common form of conflict is receiving information that differs from existing information, such as expectancy violation, or perceiving incongruent parts within a whole object. Stimuli can also arouse conflict by implying different and incompatible categorizations. People notice conflict quickly and spontaneously (Locher & Nagy, 1996), and the tendency to orient attention toward conflict appears early in infancy (McCall, Kennedy, & Applebaum, 1977).

CORRELATION OF THE FOUR COLLATIVE VARIABLES

Berlyne viewed the four collative variables as members of a family of variables. In his early writings Berlyne usually referred to the collative variables in terms of conflict; in his later writings he subsumed them under uncertainty. With some mathematical maneuvering, all four variables can be expressed with a modified information theory formula (Berlyne, 1957; 1960, pp. 34–36). Furthermore, multivariate studies commonly found that the collative variables formed a unitary factor (e.g., Evans & Day, 1971). But Berlyne never took the final step of proposing a single, unitary collative variable. He was reluctant to reduce them all to conflict or to uncertainty. As he noted in *Aesthetics and Psychobiology*, "the collative stimulus properties can be usefully discussed in the language of information theory, although it seems doubtful at the present time that the concepts introduced by information theory are sufficient to cover all noteworthy aspects of them" (Berlyne, 1971a, p. 69). Most of the things that people find interesting involve all or several of these dimensions. Drawing fine lines around these concepts is difficult and not particularly fruitful. Berlyne was more concerned with their functional relations— how the collative variables affect interest and motivation. We thus turn to the dynamics of the collative variables.

AROUSAL 1: AROUSAL POTENTIAL AND OPTIMAL
AROUSAL LEVELS

Berlyne described his first arousal model in his book *Conflict, Arousal, and Curiosity*. This theory explores how variables like complexity and novelty affect curiosity and exploration. Berlyne didn't link the collative variables to interest directly—a novel stimulus does not itself create curiosity. Instead, he connected the four collative variables to curiosity through the concepts of *arousal potential* and *optimal arousal*, the most important and elusive aspects of his model. Berlyne assumed that the four collative variables have arousal potential, which is the capacity to influence the level of arousal in the reticular activating system (RAS). As a stimulus's complexity increases, the stimulus's arousingness increases—a complex stimulus has more arousal potential than a simple stimulus.

Like his contemporaries, Berlyne viewed motivation and reward in terms of drive and drive reduction. He suggested that the RAS was the neurological source of drive (Hebb, 1955). If so, then increases in RAS activity should be aversive, and decreases in RAS activity should be rewarding. But why do people seek stimuli with high arousal potential? Why do people seek novelty, complexity, uncertainty, and conflict? If people want to reduce drive by reducing arousal, they should avoid stimuli with high arousal potential. This, of course, is drive theory's biggest challenge. Berlyne's solution to this quandary was creative and controversial: he posited a U-shaped relationship between arousal potential and arousal level. Like others, Berlyne argued that high levels of arousal potential create high arousal. But unlike others, he argued that *low* levels of arousal potential also create *high* arousal.

This idea seems odd—why should a lack of stimulation lead to high arousal? Some critics have dismissed it on intuitive grounds (Loewenstein, 1994). But Berlyne's seemingly desperate hypothesis had some support. Participants in sensory-deprivation experiments, for example, try to increase the amount of stimulation by humming, following complex trains of thought, or moving around. Some studies find that people eagerly listen to ordinarily tedious information, such as old stock reports (Schultz, 1965). Bored people are restless and agitated, suggesting a link between low arousal potential and high arousal. Other studies find increases in arousal as the length of sensory deprivation increases (Schultz, 1965). Neurological studies at the time suggested that repetitive stimu-

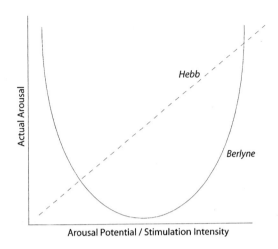

FIGURE 2.3 Relationships among stimulation, arousal potential, and arousal

lation diminished cortical inhibition of the RAS, allowing the RAS to increase arousal (Berlyne, 1960).

Berlyne's theory is often confused with Hebb's (1955) theory. Hebb argued that people prefer a moderate, optimal level of arousal. Berlyne, following Hull (1952) and Spence (1956), argued that people prefer a low level. The relation between arousal potential and arousal is shown in figure 2.3; Hebb's prediction is added for contrast. When arousal potential is low, actual arousal is high: people reduce arousal by increasing the arousal potential of incoming stimulation. When arousal potential is high, actual arousal is high: people reduce arousal by reducing the arousal potential of incoming stimulation. Hebb, in contrast, didn't distinguish between arousal potential and actual arousal. His model assumes that arousal increases as the intensity of stimulation increases.

When arousal potential is low and arousal is thus high, people will seek stimuli and activities with higher arousal potential. This leads to *diversive* exploration—the aimless searching for whatever happens to increase arousal potential. Yet when arousal is suddenly increased by a stimulus with high arousal potential, the person becomes curious and engages in *specific* exploration—the examination of a particular thing (Hutt, 1970). People try to reduce arousal by reducing the object's arousal potential. Through exploration, the person renders the object less novel, uncertain, conflicted, and complex. Arousal then decreases toward the preferred low level. Berlyne could thus explain arousal seeking by assuming that arousal reduction is rewarding—an interesting theory, indeed.

The *arousal jag* is an ancillary idea developed from Berlyne's first arousal model. He argued that people sometimes seek increases in arousal because reducing it is enjoyable. Horror movies, roller coasters, and obstreperous activity in general were problems for drive theories (Hull, 1952). Berlyne assumed that two conditions moderated this effect. First, the level of drive needed to be moderate. People presumably won't seek intense arousal—such as seeking panic by wandering the dockyards at 3 A.M.—just so they can reduce the arousal through escape. Second, people must be certain that relief will follow arousal. In retrospect, the arousal jag notion has a "hit yourself on the head because it feels good when you stop" flavor reminiscent of drive theory.

Advances in neuroscience tempered enthusiasm about the RAS. Drive theorists saw the RAS as a potential neurological basis for drive (Hebb, 1955), but the RAS's halcyon days were few. Research soon showed that there was no unitary arousal system in the body or brain (Lacey, 1967; Pribram & McGuiness, 1975; Routtenberg, 1968). In modern psychology, the concept of general physiological arousal has lost its usefulness (Neiss, 1988). In 1967, Berlyne recognized that a new neurological model was needed to explain curiosity.

As neuroscience cast doubt on the concept of drive, research on learning challenged the drive-reduction model of reinforcement. By the time of Berlyne's (1967) review, many studies had found that animals will seek increases in stimulation without subsequent declines. Brain-stimulation studies (Olds, 1973) and drive-induction studies (Sheffield, Roby, & Campbell, 1954) cast serious doubt on the prevailing view of reward as drive reduction. Worse yet for drive theorists, research found that drive *increases* could reward learning. The forecast for drive theory was grim (Atkinson, 1964; Bolles, 1967). Berlyne (1967) realized that a key assumption of his first arousal model—that the optimal arousal level is low—was untenable:

> There still seem to be ample grounds for holding that high levels of arousal are aversive and that drops from them to more moderate levels are rewarding. . . . Furthermore, I would still contend that the discomfort from boredom is more likely to come from inordinately high arousal than from inordinately low arousal. . . . But I would modify the notion of the arousal jag. Data from

many different sources now compel us to entertain the hypothesis that reinforcement, and in particular reward, can result in some circumstances from an increase in arousal regardless of whether it is soon followed by a decrease. (p. 30)

AROUSAL 2: ANTAGONISTIC REWARD AND AVERSION SYSTEMS

Berlyne's (1971a, 1974b, 1978) second arousal theory overhauled the neuropsychological aspects of his first arousal theory. With ideas from Olds (1962) as his cornerstone, he assumed that three neural systems yield the Wundt curve. The first system—the primary reward system—generates positive affect whenever arousal potential increases. Unlike the first arousal theory, then, arousal increase is rewarding in the second arousal theory. This system's activation increases as arousal potential increases, eventually stabilizing at a high level. The second system—the primary aversion system—generates negative affect whenever arousal potential increases. This system's activation also increases as arousal potential increases, but it has a higher absolute activation threshold than the primary reward system. Figure 2.4 shows the joint operation of these two systems. The two curves form the Wundt curve when summed.

As in his first arousal theory, Berlyne assumed that decreases in arousal were rewarding. This was enabled through the operation of a third system—the secondary reward system—which inhibited the pri-

FIGURE 2.4 Reward and aversion systems in Berlyne's (1971a) second arousal model

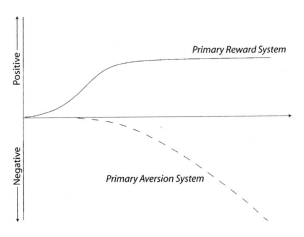

mary aversion system. When arousal potential declines, this system inhibits the primary aversion system. This is experienced as pleasure because the primary reward system is no longer antagonized by a coinciding aversion system. The arousal jag's rewarding effects were thus recast in terms of the secondary reward system's operations.

Although the physiological dynamics differ, the core concepts—collative variables and arousal potential—remain the same. But the second arousal model rejected the U-shaped relationship between arousal potential and arousal level. The first model needed this assumption to explain both approach and avoidance using a single variable. Berlyne's second model was more purely hedonic: people sought arousing stimuli for their own sake, not because they decreased arousal. Increases in arousal potential are rewarding because increases are inherently rewarding, not because they reduce the high arousal resulting from low arousal potential. Reductions are rewarding because they involve inhibiting the aversion system, not because arousal is approaching an optimal level. In the new arousal model Berlyne didn't assume that both low and high degrees of arousal potential are arousing.

The revised arousal theory avoided the problems associated with optimal-level theories, but it encountered new problems. For the primary reward and aversion systems to yield a Wundt curve, two things must be assumed. First, the aversion system's activation must be delayed. If both systems were activated simultaneously, affect would sum to the level of indifference. Second, the aversion system must be stronger than the reward system. When both systems are at the maximum intensities, the aversion system must be more powerful. Otherwise, high arousal potential would create indifference, not discomfort. Berlyne (1971a) admitted that there was no direct evidence for either assumption.

Third, Berlyne's second model assumes that antagonistic emotional experiences can co-exist at high intensities. When arousal potential is high, both the primary reward and the primary aversion systems are operating near their maximum intensities. Modern emotion theories disagree on whether opposing emotions can co-exist (Larsen, McGraw, & Cacioppo, 2001; Panksepp, 1998), and this issue is difficult to resolve empirically. Many theories argue that emotions control perception and cognition monopolistically (Brehm & Brummett, 1998), so several simultaneous emotions would create stasis and conflict. Regardless, both sides of the debate agree that emotions can occur *independently*, particularly that negative affective states can exist without preceding or concurrent positive states. In Berlyne's model, the road to aversion leads through happiness. That is, when people experience unpleasant affect, the pleasure system's activation preceded the aversion system's activation, however briefly. This is questionable. It doesn't seem like fearful stimulation first activates a "pleasure system" and then activates a "fear system" (LeDoux, 1996).

SUMMARY OF BERLYNE'S THEORIES

Berlyne answers our first question—What is interesting?—with the four collative variables: novelty, uncertainty, conflict, and complexity. The collative variables don't induce interest themselves; they affect interest indirectly by moderating the level of arousal (Arousal 1) or the activation of the reward and aversion systems (Arousal 2). Berlyne offered two explanations for the inverted-U. In Arousal 1, the person's arousal level varies depending on momentary stimulation. If the arousal potential of incoming information is too low, people reduce arousal by seeking information with greater arousal potential. If the level of arousal potential is too high, people reduce arousal by exploring the stimulus, avoiding, or both. People at the desired low level of arousal sometimes seek quick increases in arousal to enjoy its subsequent reduction. In his second arousal theory, increases in arousal potential first activated a pleasure system and then activated an antagonistic aversion system. The affective qualities of these systems summed to form the Wundt curve.

After Berlyne's death in 1976, the journal *Motivation and Emotion* published a group of papers discussing his work. The authors agreed that evaluating his contributions would have to wait for future developments in motivational psychology. Three decades later, it's easier to appraise Berlyne's work and to assess his influence. Berlyne's theorizing was flexible in some ways and recalcitrant in others. Berlyne probably did the most to quash conventional drive theory, but he used drive theory concepts longer than nearly anyone. The concepts of arousal and drive, so useful in the early 1960s, plagued his work in the 1970s. In the published portions of his unfinished book *Curiosity and Learning*, Berlyne (1978) struggled with the problems created by equating arousal with drive and by regarding curiosity as a form of drive. These problems vanish when the drive concept is abandoned.

Berlyne also shared the learning theorist's skepticism of emotions. In 1971 he wrote "The word 'emotion' is actually not much used by contemporary psychologists . . . as with many other terms taken over from ordinary language, the boundary lines of what it denotes are not distinct enough or properly located for the purposes of science" (Berlyne, 1971a, p. 62). He then suggested that emotions were simply states of high activation, and hence reduced them to arousal. The major emotion psychologists of his time aren't cited in any of Berlyne's major works (1960, 1967, 1971a, 1974d, 1978), except for a mention of Plutchik's (1962) circumplex model in Berlyne's book on aesthetics (1971a, p. 72). Reviews of Berlyne's legacy and influence have pointed to this as a major limitation of his work (Cupchik, 1988; Konečni, 1996).

Berlyne's predictions about arousal have not fared well. Berlyne contended that the collative variables affected curiosity indirectly by affecting arousal potential: physiological arousal mediated their effects on interest. In some of his later writings, Berlyne (1971b, 1978) speculated about whether the arousal concept was necessary. In response to controversy over "whether there is sufficient evidence for the claim that the collative stimulus properties produce their motivational effects through changes in arousal," Berlyne noted: "I have used the term 'arousal potential' to refer conveniently to a sizable collection of stimulus properties that seem to have a number of effects in common. But the term is defined strictly in terms of these stimulus properties, which means that statements about effects of the variables that make up arousal potential can stand or fall independently of any hypothesis about the role of arousal" (1971b, p. 192).

After reviewing research that suggested a role for arousal, Berlyne conceded that "one must certainly admit that the question is still open and that arousal is not by any means implicated by a watertight chain of argument" (p. 193). The decline of drive theories since Berlyne's time has made his ideas about arousal anachronistic (Neiss, 1988). Most of the post-Berlyne theories connect interest directly to the collative variables (Chen, 2001; Loewenstein, 1994; Nunnally, 1981; Walker, 1980). The concepts of arousal potential and arousal have not proved to be necessary.

Berlyne's most enduring contribution has been his model of the collative variables (Wohlwill, 1987). Berlyne's analysis of the four collative variables remains the most detailed and insightful in the field. Researchers interested in the psychology of emotions, aesthetics, environmental design, music, architecture, and visual perception have relied on Berlyne's discussions to understand how novelty, complexity, uncertainty, and conflict affect interest and enjoyment. The arousal theories that sur-rounded the collative variables, however, have been discarded. Research-ers agree that collative properties have profound effects on curiosity and motivation, but they don't attribute their effects to arousal.

Interest and Affect Gradients

Silvan Tomkins (1962) was the first to view interest as an emotion; he called interest the "affect which has been most seriously neglected" (p. 337). He saw interest as a positive emotion associated with novelty, one that motivated the person to explore new things. The most unusual aspect of Tomkins's theory of emotion is his *innate activator theory* of how emotions are aroused. Tomkins (1991) sharply criticized cognitive ap-praisal theories of emotion, contending that an appraisal explanation was too obvious. He felt that the centuries-old universal agreement on the appraisal basis of emotion should make psychologists suspicious:

> Cognitive theory is in close accord with common sense in its explanation of how affect is triggered—too close, in my view. For some few thousand years everyman has been a "cognitive" theorist in explaining why we feel as we do. Everyone knows that we are happy when (and presumably because) things are go-ing well and that we are unhappy when things do not go well . . . if one asks a child or a random sample of men and women on any street, *all* will agree that one fears harm and whatever is danger-ous, that one becomes angry at insult, and so on. (pp. 55–56)

Furthermore, Tomkins argued that appraisal theories fail to explain emo-tions in reaction to music, emotions during daydreaming and nocturnal dreaming, and emotions in infancy: "It would imply a fetus in its passage down the birth canal collecting its thoughts and, upon being born, emit-ting a birth cry after having appraised the extrauterine world as a vale of tears" (p. 56).

As an alternative, Tomkins (1962, 1991) proposed that each emotion is aroused by a certain density of neural firing, which is determined by the intensity and rate of information input. Figure 2.5 shows how Tom-kins thought each basic emotion was aroused. The total rate and density of information input from all perceptual channels determines which emo-tion will occur. The *gradient* of informational input determines emotional

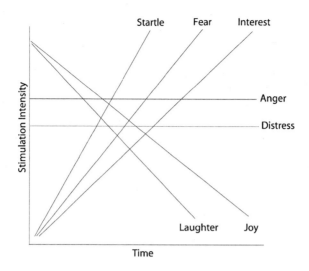

FIGURE 2.5 Tomkins's (1962) innate activator model of emotions

experience. Increases in the rate of information can evoke interest, fear, or startle. Interest occurs when the rate of information increases quickly, but not quickly enough to activate fear or startle. Decreases in the rate of information evoke happiness. Continued changes in the absolute levels of information evoke sadness and anger. Tomkins didn't specify moderators that determined whether a given positive gradient would be too steep or too flat.

Unlike his enduring contributions to the science of emotions—such as his theories of facial expressions—Tomkins's innate activator model of emotion activation has had little influence. This noncognitive model tries to recast all variables that affect emotions in terms of information intensity. Parkinson (1995) argues that it is "difficult to apply this analysis to emotional responses to complex event sequences, where the variable of intensity cannot meaningfully be specified independently of the emotional significance of the situation" (p. 57). Furthermore, emotions have more neural specificity than Tomkins's model assumes (LeDoux, 1996; Panksepp, 1998). Finally, modern research shows that cognitive processes are important for the activation of emotions (Ellsworth & Scherer, 2003; Roseman & Smith, 2001). Emotion psychologists do not have to choose between "cognitive" and "noncognitive" theories (e.g., Izard & Ackerman, 2000; Smith & Kirby, 2001).

In sum, Tomkins answered the first of our questions—What makes something interesting?—by asserting that an increase in information increases interest, provided that the rate isn't high enough to induce fear or startle. Tomkins lacked a good solution for the inverted-U. He posited a stimulation threshold between interest and fear: increases in the rate of informational input arouse interest, until the rate exceeds the interest–fear threshold. This is an unsatisfying answer if we don't know what determines the threshold between interest and fear. Nevertheless, Tomkins's ideas are noteworthy because he was the first to view interest as an emotion.

Interest as a Boredom Drive

Fowler (1965) presented a model of interest that managed to be unique despite its self-imposed orthodoxy. He argued that Hull's (1952) drive theory could easily explain curiosity and exploratory behavior. One need only posit a *boredom drive*, which "may be defined in terms of the animal's length of exposure to or 'familiarity' with a relatively unchanging stimulus condition, or conversely, in terms of the animal's length of deprivation of a change in stimulation" (p. 42). Curiosity had an idiosyncratic meaning for Fowler: "the proposed formulation treats curiosity as a *learned*, anticipatory reaction to the changes in stimulation contingent upon some instrumental act. Accordingly, curiosity is not present when an animal initially encounters a novel or unfamiliar surround, but only on subsequent occasions or trials, and only as a result of the animal learning to anticipate the unfamiliar stimuli" (p. 58).

When a bored animal encounters novelty for the first time, it can't be curious. Only after experiencing a reduction in boredom, which rewards the novelty seeking, can the animal *potentially* be curious. Curiosity requires the development of *fractional anticipatory responses*—learning theory's tortuous term for expectations. For example, the internal feelings of the actions reducing hunger (chewing, salivating) and the feeling of drive reduction are both classically conditioned with the final goal response (actually eating). When an animal responds in a way related to prior drive reduction (starts walking toward the food box), the response produces a fractional version of eating (slight salivating, small mouth movements), which then acts as another stimulus. The animal thus "expects" that walking will lead to food because it can feel itself responding as if it were eating. The full version of this process is known as the "r_g–s_g incentive mechanism" (Hull, 1952; Spence, 1956).

For an example of Fowler's model, imagine a bored rat that stumbles on a colorful maze compartment. Exploring this room (the final goal response) reduces the boredom drive, forming a habit; all responses leading up to the drive reduction (walking toward the room and entering it) are classically conditioned with the feeling of drive reduction. The next time the animal is bored, it begins walking toward the compartment, guided by the formed habit. Walking toward the compartment (response) evokes the fractional version of exploring (slightly twitching whiskers, perhaps). This response evokes its own internal stimulus (the feeling of twitching whiskers), which amplifies the drive and strengthens the tendency to continue the chain of responses leading to the colorful maze compartment. This, in Fowler's terms, is curiosity—the animal now "expects" that walking into the compartment will reduce the drive because feelings of drive reduction were conditioned onto actions that reduced the drive.

There is something elegant and subversive about using drive theory concepts to explain curiosity, classic drive theory's biggest stumbling block. Nevertheless, drive theory is classic for good reasons. Modern motivation psychology finds no evidence for general drive, for reinforcement based solely on drive reduction, for complex and enduring associative chains based on classical conditioning, and for proprioceptive conditioning of fractional responses (Atkinson, 1964; Bolles, 1967). Furthermore, the assertion that actions have miniature-but-incomplete "fractional versions" requires strenuous assumptions about the nature of responses, and it illustrates how preoccupied learning theorists were with simple actions made by hungry rats (Harlow, 1953). Berlyne (1978) criticized Fowler's theory by pointing out that people can be stimulated and still seek more stimulation (e.g., Berlyne, Salapatek, Gelman, & Zener, 1964). Finally, the functional basis of curiosity in Fowler's model seems odd in relation to modern theories. A boredom drive model implies that curiosity has no motivational or epistemic function. Fowler sees curiosity as a concomitant of motivation but not motivational in itself; curiosity is a conditioned r_g response like any other.

What does this model say about our two questions? Fowler says little about what makes something more or less interesting. In his model, people don't seek interestingness, they avoid boredom. When feeling bored, any change will do so long as the change doesn't increase drive. Fowler didn't consider the inverted-U, our second question. In hindsight, Fowler's model seems like learning theory's last desperate attempt to resurrect Hull's drive theory of motivation. Yet there was to be no return of the revenant; Fowler's book was published as traditional motivation concepts were eroding under the steady trickle of cognitivism, expectancy–value theories of motivation, and disinterest. As Fowler was lighting a candle instead of cursing the darkness, everyone else was heading for brighter rooms.

Interest and Information Conflict

Nunnally (1971, 1972, 1981) offered an unusual perspective on interestingness. His theory was the first to disavow intervening motivational and physiological concepts and to assert that cognitive variables could directly affect feelings of interest. He argued that the primary determinant of visual exploration is *information conflict*: "Information conflict is largely synonymous with the term incongruity; however, it is intended to be somewhat more precise and circumscribed. Information conflict refers to the competing information relative to identifying, labeling, remembering, categorizing, and otherwise encoding the stimulus" (Nunnally & Lemond, 1973, p. 67).

Familiar objects in unfamiliar places, novel objects, and objects with contradictory qualities all contain information conflict. The concept most resembles Berlyne's use of *conflict*. Examples include a picture of an airplane with feathered bird wings, ambiguous sentences such as "Man baits dog," and paradoxical epigrams such as "The only difference between a caprice and a life-long passion is that the caprice lasts a little longer" (Wilde, 1998, p. 19).

A unique aspect of Nunnally's model is its view of affect and attention. Like Berlyne, Nunnally argues that affective responses to information conflict follow the Wundt preference curve: "The organism's emotional response to information conflict will vary with the degree of conflict: mild levels of information conflict are experienced as pleasant; moderate levels of information conflict produce giddiness and slight feelings of unreality; and extreme levels of information conflict result in anxiety and confusion" (Nunnally & Lemond, 1973, p. 69). Visual exploration, in contrast to emotion, is a simple linear function of information conflict. Affect might become negative, but the person will keep looking. According to this model, no level of conflict will lead to visual avoidance. This prediction distinguishes Nunnally's model from nearly all other models of interest. Nunnally felt that these effects had nothing to do with arousal, drives, or physiology. The effect of information conflict on affect and attention is seen as foundational, as "a human tropism" (Nunnally, 1972). Regarding the inverted-U, Nunnally notes its existence but doesn't suggest why it occurs.

Nunnally and Lemond's (1973) review of studies on adult visual exploration supported their model: most studies found that visual exploration was a linear function of information conflict. Nevertheless, if perception is the first stage in approach and avoidance, we would expect some point at which people avoided information conflict. There are two reasons visual exploration experiments would fail to find inverted-U effects of information conflict on viewing time. First, the absolute level of information conflict isn't very high in visual exploration experiments (Maddi, 1971). Common stimulus materials—complex checkerboard patterns, random polygons, winged dogs wearing business suits—aren't very complex in an absolute sense. Experiments with complex music found that adults showed a quadratic preference for music of different complexity levels (Bragg & Crozier, 1974). People rated moderately complex music as being more interesting than mildly and highly complex music. And when allowed to choose between pairs of melodies, people selected the moderately complex melodies over the simple and highly complex melodies (Hargreaves, 1986; Kinney & Kagan, 1976; North & Hargreaves, 1995).

A second reason experiments may find linear rather than inverted-U patterns is statistical. Walker (1980, 1981) cautions that aggregated information conceals important information about individual profiles (Nezlek, 2001). Within any data set on conflict and exploration, some people will show linear trends and other people will show inverted-U trends (Aitken, 1974). Averaging across these trends can create a flattened linear trend, or even a U-shaped trend, depending on the proportion of inverted-U trends and on individual differences in baseline viewing times. In some circumstances, only a few linear trends in a large data set can render an overall linear trend, even though most people had inverted-U trends (Walker, 1980). The psychological question, of course, is how to understand why people show different responses to information conflict.

Interest and Information Gaps

Loewenstein (1994) offers an intriguing theory of curiosity based on information theory. He proposes an *information gap theory*, which he says "views curiosity as arising when attention becomes focused on a gap in one's knowledge. Such information gaps produce the feeling of deprivation labeled *curiosity*. The curious individual is motivated to obtain the missing information to reduce or eliminate the feeling of deprivation" (p. 87). Loewenstein defines information gaps using information theory's uncertainty formula, $U = \sum_{i=1}^{n} p_i \log_2 1/p_i$. The absolute size of an information gap is the person's "informational goal" (usually total certainty) minus the person's current level of information.

A knowledge gap, then, is $U > 0$; it's the existence of uncertainty. One wonders how this differs from Berlyne's claim that uncertainty—specified by the same formula—affects curiosity. In fact, the similarities between the information gap theory and Berlyne's theories are striking. Berlyne was the first to suggest that information theory concepts can describe the sources of curiosity, and he developed this idea in several places. Berlyne discussed information theory in every major work, including an article on uncertainty (Berlyne, 1957), his theory of curiosity (Berlyne, 1960, chap. 2), his theory of thinking (Berlyne, 1965, chap. 2), the applications of curiosity to aesthetics (Berlyne, 1971a, 1974b), and his unfinished book on curiosity and learning (Berlyne, 1978).

The theory of motivation presumed by the information gap theory resembles Berlyne's (1960) first theory in other ways. Lowenstein assumes that curiosity is an aversive state. If this is true, then we have what Loewenstein called "the problem of voluntary exposure to curiosity": When do people seek out an aversive state? Loewenstein proposes that curiosity is aversive but that reducing curiosity is enjoyable. This is Berlyne's "arousal jag," discussed earlier: people seek stimuli with high arousal potential because reducing it is pleasant. Regardless, this "voluntary exposure problem" is a problem the theory manufactures by assuming that curiosity is aversive. Research on the subjective experience of interest, described in chapter 1, finds that people rate curiosity as a positive and active affective state. Loewenstein's contradictory prediction requires empirical support.

Its similarity to Berlyne's theory aside, the information gap theory has several gaps of its own. First, the theory cannot explain the inverted-

U pattern. Loewenstein assumes a linear relation between uncertainty and curiosity: there is no level of uncertainty that would lead to avoidance, anxiety, boredom, or flabbergasted surprise. A lot of research, most of it conducted before Loewenstein's review, has found an inverted-U pattern (Walker, 1980, 1981), so a theory of interest should explain why this happens. Second, the information gap theory may be too narrow. The theory attributes curiosity to uncertainty evoked by a disparity between an actual and an ideal informational condition. This analysis works well for some instances of interest. When one of four fictional characters must be the murderer, or one of the 50 states must be the easternmost state, it is easy to represent curiosity in terms of information gaps. But can all inducers of curiosity be reduced to uncertainty and knowledge gaps? Internally inconsistent objects, such as airplanes with feathered wings (Nunnally, 1971), are interesting. What are the actual and ideal knowledge states here? Why do randomly generated polygons evoke interest? A broader view of the causes of curiosity is necessary to account for these cases.

The information gap theory seems like old wine in new, smaller bottles. Like Berlyne, Loewenstein specifies curiosity in terms of information theory principles. Unlike Berlyne, he doesn't address the problems that confront this approach. First, can all inducers of curiosity (such as novelty and complexity) be subsumed under information theory's definition of uncertainty? There are good reasons for viewing the antecedents of interest as a family of related variables instead of reducing all the variables to uncertainty (see Berlyne, 1971a, p. 69). Second, when and why do people avoid high levels of uncertainty? The inverted-U is something that a theory of interest should explain. Finally, is curiosity a negative state motivating its own reduction? Apart from contradicting research on the subjective experience of interest (see chapter 1), the drive reduction model of motivation is almost too quaint to criticize.

Multidimensional Sources of Interest

A recent theory of interestingness suggests that momentary feelings of interest stem from several sources (Chen, 2001). Interest is said to derive from five different sources: novelty, challenge, attention demand, exploration intention, and instant enjoyment. Each source contributes linearly to the experience of interest. A 24-item self-report scale measures these sources (Chen, Darst, & Pangrazi, 1999). The scale has five subscales, one for each source of interest, as well as a *total interest* subscale that assesses general feelings of interest. Research with this scale suggests that each source contributes to the experience of total interest, but that some sources mediate the effects of other sources (Chen, Darst, & Pangrazi, 2001). Specifically, the first four sources (novelty, challenge, attention demand, and exploration intention) affect interest by affecting feelings of *instant enjoyment*—the degree to which an activity quickly evokes happiness. Instant enjoyment, in turn, evokes feelings of interest. In short, interest has five sources, but some of the sources work through other sources. Apart from this new prediction, Chen's work is noteworthy because it explores interest in physical activities rather than interest in pictures and texts (Chen & Darst, 2001, 2002).

Chen's (2001) theory is the first model to suggest a hierarchical view of what makes something interesting. Yet like the information gap theory, Chen's theory doesn't allow for nonlinear relations between the sources of interest and the feelings of interest. As a result, it can't predict or explain inverted-U functions. This is a big liability of the model because past research shows that interest won't increase linearly with increases in these five sources. High levels of novelty, for example, sometimes evoke irritation rather than interest (Berlyne, 1970). Levels of challenge beyond one's abilities can reduce interest and promote disengagement (Silvia, 2003; Wright & Kirby, 2001).

Furthermore, Chen's (2001) theory proposes that *instant enjoyment* is the precursor to general feelings of interest. Factors such as novelty increase instant enjoyment, which then increases interest. Including enjoyment as a source of interest is questionable in light of empirical differences between interest and enjoyment (see chapter 1), particularly research on how novelty and complexity have opposite effects on interest and enjoyment. Why, then, did instant enjoyment mediate the effects of the other four sources on interest? A look at Chen's scale reveals high overlap between the measures of interest and those of enjoyment. Half of the items measuring "total interest" refer to feelings of enjoyment; none of the other subscales has items that overlap with the total interest scale. Item overlap guarantees relatively higher correlations between the instant-enjoyment and the total-interest subscales and thus biases how the parts relate to the whole.

Evaluating Past Theories of Interest

This chapter has reviewed many theories of the sources of interest, from drive reduction and arousal modification to knowledge gaps and information conflicts. Many of these theories are obviously anachronistic, but they illustrate the diversity of approaches to this problem. How have these theories explained the sources of interest? For the first question—What is interesting?—the theories generally converge. Most theories proposed Berlyne's family of collative variables—conflict, uncertainty, novelty, and complexity—or something like them, such as information conflict (Nunnally, 1981) or information gaps (Loewenstein, 1994). This convergence reflects the strong empirical support for the effects of collative variables on interest. Their effects generalize across types of measurement (self-reports; behavioral measures of exploration, choice, and attention; physiological measures), types of samples (human infants, children, and adults; nonhuman animals), types of stimuli (paintings, text, movie sequences, music, physical activities, randomly generated images), types of research designs (correlational ratings, manipulation of the collative variables), and different cultures.

But the theories diverge in their answers to the question of the inverted-U. Two factors are needed for an inverted-U pattern. One factor is apparently the intensity of the collative variables; the second factor is a moderator that creates the hinge between interest and disinterest. The theories disagree about the second factor. Some theorists thought it was a threshold between interest and fear (Tomkins, 1962), a threshold between reward and aversion systems (Berlyne, 1971a), or a threshold defining an optimal level of stimulation (Berlyne, 1960; Hebb, 1955). Other theorists took the inverted-U as an empirical fact but didn't offer explanations for it (Nunnally, 1981; Walker, 1981); a few didn't discuss the inverted-U (Chen, 2001; Loewenstein, 1994). Explaining the inverted-U by positing thresholds is a dead end. Research has not been kind to any of the proposed thresholds, particularly those founded on optimal levels of stimulation. And proposing a threshold raises new questions about why a threshold exists, why it varies over time, and why people have different thresholds. These new questions increase a theory's burden and reduce its simplicity.

One limitation applies to all of the theories described thus far, a problem that may be the reason for their failure. Each theory implicitly takes a behavioristic stance toward cognition and emotion: they trace interest to events rather than to interpretations and appraisals of events. The difference is subtle but critical. Do people *perceive* that something is complex and feel interest because of the object's complexity, or do people *appraise* something as complex and feel interest because of their appraisal? As a parallel, consider two ways of explaining the experience of fear: is fear caused by *perceiving* that something is harmful or by *appraising* something as harmful? The first approach attributes interest to events; the second attributes interest to cognitive processing of events. Attributing the causes of emotions to objective qualities of stimuli and events reflects the behaviorist climate in which most theories of interest developed. Much of the responsibility for this can be attributed to Berlyne's behavioristic roots and his distrust of cognitive psychology (Berlyne, 1965, 1975; Cupchik, 1988).

Why is this a problem? What's wrong with attributing emotions to objective features of events instead of to subjective interpretations of events? By attributing interest to events rather than to the person's subjective interpretations of the events, proponents of the theories have problems explaining variability in emotional experience (Roseman & Smith, 2001). For example, experts, relative to novices, find complex art more interesting (Crozier, 1974; Hekkert & van Wieringen, 1996; Walker, 1980). The objective complexity of the artwork alone cannot explain such differences, and positing different thresholds for experts is a hollow explanation (Berlyne, 1971a). Explaining why an event has different effects on different people, and why an event has different effects on the same person over time, requires considering subjective appraisals of the event (Lazarus, 1991; Roseman & Smith, 2001).

Modern appraisal theories of emotions, by shifting the focus from events to cognitive appraisals of events, have been enormously successful in advancing the science of emotions (see Scherer, Schorr, & Johnstone, 2001). According to Scherer (2001b), "As far as one can see, there is, at present, no viable alternative to an appraisal (in the broad sense of the word) explanation for the general prediction of the elicitation and differentiation of emotions" (pp. 389–390). A model of the causes of interest should capitalize on the many advances in the study of how cognitive processes cause emotional experiences.

Appraisals and Interest

Theories of *appraisal*—the cognitive processes involved in the generation of emotions—were developed to resolve problems that encumbered past theories of emotion (Roseman & Smith, 2001). The idea that thoughts cause emotions has a long history, although systematic research on appraisal is relatively recent (Schorr, 2001a). Researchers are still sorting out the disagreements between different theories of appraisal. But these disagreements shouldn't obscure the substantial agreement among appraisal theorists, particularly on fundamental questions of how cognition and emotion intertwine (Lazarus, 1991; Roseman, 2001; Scherer, 2001a).

A core assumption shared by all appraisal theorists is that cognitive appraisals of events cause and constitute emotional experience (Roseman & Evdokas, 2004). Theories of appraisal are sometimes criticized for proposing mechanisms that are too slow to explain the causes of emotions (Ellsworth & Scherer, 2003). For many people, the phrase *cognitive appraisal* conjures images of slow, deliberate processing of the meaning and implications of events. But no theory of appraisal assumes that appraisal processes must be conscious, deliberate, reflective, effortful, or intentional. To the contrary, modern theories assert that appraisals can occur automatically and outside of awareness (Smith & Kirby, 2001). Many appraisals—such as whether an event is new, good or bad, or relevant to a goal—appear to unfold very rapidly (Scherer, 2001a).

The study of appraisal splits into the study of *appraisal structure* and *appraisal processes*. Research on appraisal structure identifies the pattern of cognitions involved in an emotion. Most theories describe an emotion's appraisal structure through a set of elemental appraisal components. Common appraisal components, for example, include appraising events as relevant to a goal, evaluating resources for coping with an event, making attributions of causality and responsibility, judging an event's congruence with a motive or goal, and assessing whether an action falls short of personal and moral standards (Lazarus, 1991; Roseman, 2001; Scherer, 2001a; Weiner, 1985). Each emotion has a unique appraisal structure.[1] Happiness, for instance, involves (1) appraising an event as rele-

---

1. Not all theories agree on each emotion's appraisal structure, although the theories overlap substantially (Ellsworth & Scherer, 2003). This chapter cannot delve into the intricate differences between theories of appraisal (see Scherer et al., 2001). For our purposes, the important point is that cognitive appraisals are fundamental to emotional experience.

vant to a goal; (2) appraising the event as congruent with the goal; and (3) expecting the beneficial event to continue (Lazarus, 1991, p. 268). Anger, in contrast, involves (1) appraising an event as relevant to a goal; (2) appraising the event as incongruent with the goal; (3) judging a threat to one's social- or self-esteem; and (4) blaming someone for the threat.

Some theories synthesize the set of appraisal components into a holistic, abstract theme, known as a *core relational theme* (Lazarus, 1991). The core relational theme for happiness, for instance, is expressed as "making reasonable progress toward the realization of a goal" (Lazarus, 2001, p. 64). Anger's core relational theme is expressed as "a demeaning offense against me and mine" (Lazarus, 2001, p. 64). Thematic and structural descriptions of appraisals complement each other. Expressing appraisals as abstract themes highlights the coherent, subjective meaning generated by the appraisal process; expressing appraisals as a set of judgments highlights an emotion's subtle cognitive architecture.

In contrast to the structure of appraisal, the process of appraisal has not received much attention (Smith & Kirby, 2001). A key process issue is the temporal nature of appraisals. Some theories contend that the appraisal process is sequential (Scherer, 2001a): early appraisals serve as inputs into later appraisals. For example, appraisals of an event's novelty and congruence with goals should occur before appraisals of coping potential, or how well one can deal with the event. Presumably, people must notice an event and appraise it as pressing before appraising their ability to deal with the pressing event. Other theories, in contrast, contend that multiple appraisals unfold parallel to one another or that events are appraised in terms of abstract themes (Lazarus, 1991). Few studies have tackled the temporal aspect of appraisal (Scherer, 1999). Another issue involves how people arrive at answers to appraisal questions. For example, when judging an event as congruent or incongruent with a goal, what information do people use? How do people estimate their ability to deal with a stressful event?

The process of appraisal over the course of an emotional episode explains why emotions arise, change, and end. The process of appraisal is recursive: after appraising an event, people respond to changes in the emotional event though *reappraisal* (Lazarus, 2001). Consider a person who experiences fear upon appraising an event as dangerous. If the person's attempts to avoid harm work, then reappraisals of the situation would indicate an absence of threat and an increased ability to deal with the threat. Reappraising the threat as eliminated should reduce the experience of fear. The process of appraisal and reappraisal shows the fluid, dynamic nature of emotion. A parent who is angry with a child may learn that the negative event was the parent's fault. Reappraising the dimension of blame should lead to a change in emotion, from anger with the child to anger or shame directed at the self.

What Is the Appraisal Structure of Interest?

Theories of appraisal differ in the number of emotions that they describe. Thus far, appraisal theories have had little to say about the appraisal structure of interest (see Ellsworth & Smith, 1988). Needless to say, this complicates an analysis of interest in terms of cognitive appraisals. Using dimensions of appraisal that affect other emotions, we can develop a model of the appraisal structure of interest. This preliminary appraisal structure can be evaluated against findings from past research, tested in new experiments, and modified as needed by future research.

One of the first judgments in the appraisal sequence, according to Scherer (2001a), is a *novelty check*—whether or not an event is new, sudden, or unfamiliar. For interest, this novelty check includes whether people judge something as new, ambiguous, complex, obscure, uncertain, mysterious, contradictory, unexpected, or otherwise not understood. People probably experience the output of this appraisal as a disruption in processing and a subjective feeling of surprise and uncertainty. The first appraisal dimension is clearly rooted in Berlyne's (1960) analysis of the collative variables. With an appraisal emphasis, however, Berlyne's (1975) behaviorist emphasis is supplanted by an emphasis on subjective cognitive judgments. For predicting the experience of interest, perceptions of an object's complexity rather than the object's "objective complexity" are central.

As noted earlier, an inverted-U function requires two dimensions. If the first appraisal for interest is whether an event is new, what is the second appraisal? Coping potential is a plausible candidate. *Coping potential* refers broadly to estimates of resources, power, abilities, and control in relation to an event (Bandura, 1997; Ellsworth & Scherer, 2003; Lazarus, 1991; Scherer, 2001a). Judgments of coping potential appear in the appraisal structures of many emotions (Ellsworth & Scherer, 2003). For interest, coping potential probably refers to people's appraisals of whether they can understand the ambiguous event. Upon appraising something as unfamiliar, complex, and ambiguous, people probably appraise the likelihood that the poorly understood event will become coherent and clear.[2]

The simplest appraisal structure of interest, then, involves two appraisal components: an appraisal of novelty, broadly defined; and an appraisal of one's coping potential in relation to comprehending the obscure event. Some appraisal theories synthesize the set of components into an abstract theme (Lazarus, 2001). The events that people find interesting can probably be described thematically as events that are not understood but understandable. Like other emotions, the experience of interest may change or end depending on continuing appraisals of the situation. Interest may end through the reappraisal of either appraisal component. The person may eventually understand the event—upon reappraising the event's novelty (broadly construed), the person would no longer judge the event as new or complex. Similarly, reappraising coping potential will affect interest. An initially interesting movie, for example, can become uninteresting when the viewers feel unable to form a coherent understanding of the narrative. Conversely, a confusing text can become interesting if its hidden meaning is revealed.

Empirical Evidence

Past research on interest is consistent with an appraisal perspective on the cause of interest. For example, differences in appraised ability translate into differences in interest. Experts in art and music prefer relatively complex images and melodies, whereas novices prefer relatively simple images and melodies (Francès, 1976; Hare, 1974; Hekkert & van Wieringen, 1996). In one experiment, for example, experts rated abstract art as more understandable and as more interesting (Millis, 2001, Study 3). Adults and children show a similar difference—adults prefer relatively more complex images and music (Bragg & Crozier, 1974). Walker's (1980) "hedgehog theory" of complexity and preference predicts that people

---

2. Although new in the study of emotional feelings of interest, the suggestion that perceptions of ability affect interest has been widely studied in vocational psychology. A huge literature shows that a person's self-efficacy regarding a vocation predicts interest in the vocation (Lent, Brown, & Hackett, 1994). This is an intriguing bridge between apparently distinct areas of the psychology of interest; we'll return to this topic in chapter 7.

prefer activities of higher complexity as their experience increases. These findings fit the hypothesis that the appraisal structure of interest involves appraisals of coping potential. Experts relative to novices, and adults relative to children, should have higher appraised ability to understand art and music.

A second body of work, also in the study of aesthetics, examines the effects of meaningful information on emotional responses to art. Several experiments show that titles enhance positive emotional responses to art by making art more comprehensible. Providing titles for abstract paintings increases the viewer's appraised ability to understand the paintings (Russell & Milne, 1997). In turn, people enjoy the art more, especially when the titles promote elaborated representations (Millis, 2001). Providing extensive information about a painting, such as the artist's biography and the context of the work, has a large effect on understanding and on emotions (Russell, 2003). Taken together, these experiments show how emotional responses can be enhanced by increasing appraisals of coping potential.

Past research thus fits an appraisal position on interest: variations in appraisals of ability to understand affect feelings of interest. But it is never surprising when past research is consistent with a new hypothesis. After all, past research preceded the hypothesis. Congruent evidence from past studies offers indirect support at best. Several new experiments were conducted to test the predictions of an appraisal perspective (Silvia, 2005c). In the first study, people provided self-reports of trait curiosity, openness to experience, and appraisals of their ability to understand complex and abstract art. People then viewed random polygons that ranged from simple (4 sides) to complex (160 sides). Their viewing set was manipulated: One group picked the "most interesting" polygon; the second group picked the "most enjoyable" polygon. Appraisals of ability to understand significantly predicted the complexity of the most interesting polygon. As people felt more able to understand complex art, they picked highly complex polygons as being the most interesting. Only appraisals of ability predicted polygon choice; individual differences in curiosity and openness to experience were unrelated, showing discriminant validity for appraisals. Consistent with the interest–enjoyment differences reviewed in chapter 1, the most interesting polygon was significantly more complex than the most enjoyable polygon. Moreover, appraisals of the ability to understand predicted the level of complexity that people found interesting but not the level that people found enjoyable, thus dis-

FIGURE 2.6 "The Whitest Parts of the Body"—Scott MacLeod

such daring against men
with a throat so big
separated by a hundred years
full of misfortune: the bloody
flux. taken by a fit of madness
prone to eating human flesh
and measured, in due course,
by naturalists

in older individuals it almost
disappears, rather forbidding,
even repulsive [it is a
pelagic species] just as
troublesome in other
parts of the world

(smashed or upset and their occupants
cast into the water)

in a state of sexual activity
are more irritable, more aggressive
but this only attracted more

and hood of shining white

it carries out terrible ravages
lost, and usually permanently
lost, amongst whom, wringing her hands
and crying out
to heaven,
was the girl's mother

Source: Reprinted from *The Life of Haifisch* by Scott MacLeod (1999), published by Broken Boulder Press, with permission from the author and publisher.

criminating between the appraisal structures of different positive emotions (cf. Ellsworth & Smith, 1988).

A second study manipulated coping potential. People read a complex poem, presented in figure 2.6. In a control condition, people read the poem, appraised their ability to understand it, and reported their feelings of interest. In a high-ability condition, coping potential was increased by giving information that unlocked the poem's meaning. Before reading, people in this group learned that the poem was about killer sharks. As expected, people in the high-ability group found the poem more interesting than did people in the control group. Mediation analyses indicated that appraisals of ability to understand fully mediated the effects of the manipulation on interest. The extra information about the poem's meaning increased perceived ability to understand the poem; understanding, in turn, increased feelings of interest.

A third experiment illustrated the joint role of appraisals of novelty–complexity and coping potential. People viewed simple and complex pictures taken from books of modern visual art. For each picture, they gave ratings of interest and ability to understand the picture. As expected, interest depended on both complexity and coping potential. For simple pictures, ratings of ability to understand were unrelated to interest. For complex pictures, however, ability strongly predicted interest—interest increased as appraised ability increased. These relations remained after controlling for possible confounds, such as trait curiosity and positive affectivity.

In a fourth experiment, appraisals predicted behavioral expressions of interest. People viewed random polygons, ranging from simple to complex, on a computer screen. Their appraised ability to understand complex art had been measured earlier in the semester. People could view each polygon for as long as they wished; when the image became boring, they could press a key to move to the next image. Consistent with the appraisal model, appraisals of ability interacted with the polygons' complexity to predict viewing times. People spent the most time viewing an image when they felt able to understand complex art and the image was highly complex (see fig. 2.7). In addition to illustrating the joint role of the two appraisal components, this experiment shows that the effects of appraisals on interest are not limited to self-reports.

Another experiment examined within-person relationships between appraisals and interest (Silvia, 2005a). Appraisals should predict interest at the within-person level (Scherer, 2001a), but most appraisal research

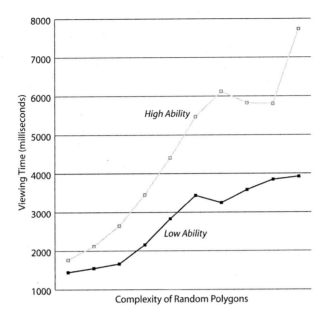

FIGURE 2.7 Effects of appraised ability and complexity on time spent viewing images

assesses between-person relationships between appraisals and emotions (Reisenzein, 2000). In a within-person analysis, people viewed over 30 pictures of abstract visual art. They rated each image for interest and for appraisals of complexity and of ability to understand the image. The large numbers of responses per participant enabled an analysis of the within-person covariance of appraisals and interest. Both appraisals strongly and significantly predicted interest, thus providing a within-person confirmation of the appraisal predictions. Moreover, these appraisals positively predicted interest for each person in the sample—no negative relations between appraisals and interest were found. Thus, there was no variance in the direction of the effects of appraisals on interest.

The Promise of Appraisal Theories for Interest

Appraisal theories were developed to tackle some of the difficult problems faced by the psychology of emotions (Roseman & Smith, 2001): Why do people have different emotions in response to the same event?

Why does the same person experience different emotions to similar events? How do emotions change over time? Appraisal theories have done a good job of explaining between-person and within-person variability in emotional experience (Scherer, 2001b). If interest is an emotion, then its origins should be explicable with constructs and processes that apply to all emotions. The appraisal structure of interest proposed here is admittedly simple. Nevertheless, it can address the issues that a model of interest must explain. By connecting interest to appraisals of novelty and coping potential, broadly defined, an appraisal model of interest can explain why people don't find the same things interesting, why interest changes dynamically over time, and why feelings of interest vary in response to similar events. Moreover, its explanation is rooted in a theoretical tradition that has clearly advanced the study of emotion.

What about the venerable inverted-U? An appraisal approach to interest implies that the inverted-U function should be laid to rest for two reasons. First, the effects of events on emotions do not stem from objective qualities of the events but from subjective interpretations of the events. As a result, it is misleading to assert a general law of stimulus intensity and emotional response independent of the type of stimulus. Second, the inverted-U pattern conflates at least two independent appraisals. The inverted-U curve might describe an empirical relationship, but the appraisals explain the relationship. Analyzing the sources of interest is easier when independent appraisals, such as appraisals of novelty and appraisals of coping potential, are separated.

Chapter Summary and Conclusions

The question that guides this chapter—What is interesting?—is deceptively simple. In reviewing the long history of thought on interestingness, we have encountered an eclectic group of theories. By now, it should be clear that past theories have not fully succeeded in explaining interest. They did a good job of explaining why some things are interesting to nearly everybody; most proposed something akin to Berlyne's family of collative variables. But explaining variability—particularly why people respond differently to high levels of complexity—has been harder. After reviewing many past theories of interest, this chapter developed a new analysis rooted in appraisal theories of emotion. Explaining interest in terms of the "interestingness" of events obscures the cognitive dynamics that generate the emotion of interest. Instead of attributing the cause of interest to inherently interesting features of events, the appraisal approach explains interest in terms of the person's cognitive processing of events (Lazarus, 2001).

The following chapter examines research on *text-based interest*—qualities that make a text more or less interesting to a reader. Researchers have suggested around 20 factors that affect the interestingness of a text, such as coherence, vividness, concreteness, prior knowledge, personal relevance, and comprehensibility. The ideas reviewed in this chapter can help integrate the sprawling literature on text-based interest. Perhaps the dozens of ostensible causes of interest work because they affect the appraisals that generate interest. Viewing text-based interest in terms of appraisals leads to new predictions about how and why coherence, prior knowledge, and so on affect interest. We'll also examine how interest influences learning from text. People learn more from interesting texts, but why?

3

Interest and Learning

Psychology's oldest writings about interest come from the field of education. Theorists such as John Dewey (1910, 1913) and Felix Arnold (1910), influenced by the earlier work of Herbart (1891), assigned a pivotal role to interest in thinking, learning, and motivation. At that time, however, theories of interest weren't tested empirically. Scientific research on interest, learning, and education didn't emerge as major area of educational psychology until the 1980s, inspired by findings on interest's role in text processing. The study of interest's implications for learning, motivation, and academic achievement now occupies a central place in educational research (Hidi & Harackiewicz, 2000; Krapp, 1999, 2002a; Schiefele, 1999; Schiefele & Wild, 2000; Schraw & Lehman, 2001).

This chapter reviews the role of interest in learning, with an emphasis on reading. Text is one of the most common forms of imparting information to learners, so it's no surprise that the study of *text-based interest* dominates the study of interest and learning (Hidi, 2001; Sadoski, 2001; Schiefele, 1999; Schraw & Lehman, 2001; Wade, 2001). As part of the rise of research on text processing (Kintsch & van Dijk, 1978), early experiments found that interest played an important role in how people select, process, and remember what they read (Anderson, 1982; Asher, 1980; Hidi, Baird, & Hildyard, 1982). The study of text-based interest has evolved into two questions. How does interest affect cognitive processes related to learning? What makes something interesting to read? This chapter reviews what research has to say about these questions.

The study of interest and learning integrates basic and applied goals, and it thus deserves a special place in the psychology of interest. On the basic side, many fundamental aspects of interest are illuminated by the study of learning. This area examines the functions of interest in motivation and achievement (Hidi, 1990) and the cognitive consequences of interest that foster understanding (Schiefele, 1999). Furthermore, the study of what makes texts interesting is a special case of what makes things in general interesting, the question we examined in chapter 2. Research on learning thus illuminates important cognition–emotion intersections. On the applied side, there is a ready audience for scientific findings on interest and learning. Research on interest offers clear guidelines for improving education, such as how to design better textbooks (Garner, 1992; Wade, 2001) and how to create interesting classrooms (Bergin, 1999).

Just as the study of learning has much to offer the psychology of interest, other areas of psychology can inform the study of learning. For example, studies of interest and reading have proposed around two dozen sources of text-based interest (Schraw & Lehman, 2001; Wade, Buxton, & Kelly, 1999), with little consideration of what these sources have in common and why they work. The emotional appraisal perspective on interest (see chapter 2) provides an integrative way of reducing the sprawl of sources of text-based interest. Furthermore, an emotional model of interest informs some complex questions about the nature of text-based interest. Some unproductive debates—such as whether there are kinds of interest or whether interest differs from curiosity—are resolved by an emotion perspective (see chapter 8). By the end of this chapter we should have a better appreciation of the bridges between interest and learning and other areas of psychology.

Interest and Learning From Text

Intuition suggests that interest facilitates learning, and in this case intuition is correct. Many studies, far too many to review here, find that interest enhances learning from text (see Hidi, 2001; Sadoski & Paivio, 2001; Wade, 1992). In his review, Schiefele (1999) found that interest had a substantial effect on text learning (average $r = .33$). Interest improves memory for single sentences (Sadoski, Goetz, & Fritz, 1993; Shirey & Reynolds, 1988), brief paragraphs (Sadoski, Goetz, & Rodriguez, 2000), long essays (Schraw, Bruning, & Svoboda, 1995), and many text types, such as sonnets, haiku, biographies, news reports, and short stories (Sadoski et al., 2000; Sadoski & Quast, 1990; Son & Metcalfe, 2000). Furthermore, cognitive factors relevant to reading—such as intelligence, verbal ability, prior knowledge, and reading level—do not explain the link between interest and learning. Interest still improves learning when these variables are controlled (Schiefele, 2001; Schraw et al., 1995). Finally, interest mediates the effects of other variables on learning. For example, a text's concreteness, coherence, vividness, and comprehensibility improve learning, in part by making the text more interesting (Sadoski, 2001; Sadoski et al., 1993; Schraw et al., 1995).

Why does interest have such robust effects on learning? Schiefele (1998) argues, perhaps pessimistically, that "studies identifying components of the learning process that may mediate the effect of interest and learning are almost completely absent" (p. 91). Research is just beginning to uncover the mechanisms through which interest enhances learning. Three mechanisms have been proposed: interest might increase attention to text; interest might lead people to process a text at deeper levels; and interest might affect the use of reading strategies. We'll review this emerging literature, draw some conclusions, and consider directions for future work.

Attention and Interest

Interest and attention have been conceptual cousins since early theories of interest and education (Arnold, 1910; Dewey, 1913). If people pay more attention to interesting texts, then learning should increase. In this case, empirical research fails to support intuition: attention doesn't mediate the effects of interest on learning. In one study (Anderson, 1982), fourth-graders read single sentences on a computer screen and rated them for interest. Attention was measured by response times to a second task. A tone would sound during some sentences; the readers pressed a key upon hearing the tone. If attention is intensely focused on the text, then it should take the readers longer to respond to the second task. A recall test was given after the children finished reading the sentences. Interest significantly improved recall, consistent with many other experiments. Interest also significantly increased the attention devoted to a sentence. But attention didn't mediate the effect of interest on recall. Heightened attention and better recall were independent effects of interest (Asher, 1980).

An alternative, counterintuitive view suggests that interest *reduces* the amount of attention devoted to text. Hidi (1990, 1995) argues that interest elicits spontaneous, automatic allocation of attention. This frees up resources for a flexible and rapid processing of the text. Boring material, however, requires more reader self-regulation. Similarly, McDaniel, Waddill, Finstad, and Bourg (2000) suggested that "with less interesting text, the reader is forced to use resources to keep attention focused on extracting meaning" (p. 500). This view suggests an intriguing prediction: people should pay less attention to interesting texts.

The notion that interest promotes spontaneous, effortless engagement has its roots in John Dewey's (1913) writings on interest. The problem of education based on discipline and self-control, he thought, was that people devote their attention and energies to self-regulating, to simply persisting with the tedious task. Any attention that remains will be spent on irrelevant yet more interesting thoughts, such as what to do once the task is over. People thus engage with boring activities on a concrete level. He suggested that a function of interest in learning is to unify the person and the activity, and thus to stimulate thoughtfulness. Instead of trying to stay focused on a boring task, people can experience activities at abstract, flexible, and conceptual levels.

To see if people pay less attention to interesting texts, Shirey and Reynolds (1988) asked college students to read single sentences on a computer screen. Time spent reading each sentence and response times to a secondary task were the measures of attention. People spent less time reading interesting sentences, and they responded faster to the secondary task when reading interesting sentences. Despite this, people remembered more interesting sentences than boring sentences. This study replicated the effect of interest on learning, but it showed the opposite effect of interest on attention (Reynolds, 1992; Shirey, 1992). In a study of short stories, college students read stories that varied in overall interest (McDaniel et al., 2000, Study 1). Attention was measured by response time to a secondary task. The tone signaling the secondary task would sound during either the first or second half of the story. While reading the first half of the story, people paid equal attention to the interesting and the boring stories. While reading the second half of the story, however, people paid less attention to the interesting stories.

Levels of Processing and Interest

If interest doesn't enhance learning because of heightened attention, then how does interest affect learning? Research suggests that *depth of processing* might be responsible. Text processing, according to van Dijk and Kintsch (1983), can occur at three levels. At the *verbatim* level, readers process the text's superficial structure. At the *propositional* level, readers process the meaning of the propositions constituting the text. This level contains the text's specific meaning (a microstructure) and general meaning (a macrostructure). And at the *situational* level, the deepest level of text processing, readers build a situation model of the text's characters, events, facts, and analogical information. The situation model extends beyond the text. Extra-textual information can enhance a situation model, such as when readers elaborate the text's meaning and connect its ideas to personal experience and prior knowledge.

To the chagrin of educators, readers can process texts at deep levels but they usually don't (Entwistle, 1988). Instead of deeply processing the text's meaning and situation, many readers engage in rote rehearsal of specific facts without placing the facts within the text's broader meaning. For example, a student reading a psychology textbook might try to remember verbatim the book's definition of *psychoanalysis*. But if the reader doesn't process the meaning of *psychoanalysis*, develop a situation model (represent Freud's life, the reception of his ideas, and so on), or relate psychoanalysis to personal experience, then he or she is left with a shallow representation of the text. Representing a text superficially leads to an incoherent organization of the text's main points and a lack of connections between the text's ideas and the reader's prior knowledge.

Perhaps interest leads people to process text more deeply. In turn, deeper processing leads to better comprehension and recall of the text. Many experiments support this position (see Schiefele, 1999). In an early study, college students read an essay and completed a measure of processing levels; their interest in the topic had been measured several weeks earlier (Schiefele, 1992, p. 169). People with low interest in the topic represented the text at the superficial verbatim level. People with high interest, in contrast, represented the text at the deeper propositional and situational levels. In a later study (Schiefele, 1996), high school students read essays about television and prehistoric people, and then they completed a comprehension test assessing levels of text processing. People with high interest in the topic processed at the propositional level of the text—the level of the text's meaning. People with low interest, in contrast, showed greater verbatim level processing—they focused more on superficial and factual aspects of the text.

Schiefele and Krapp (1996) assessed the effects of interest on depth of processing using a free-recall measure. After reading an essay about the psychology of communication, students tried to write down the text's contents as completely as possible. The free recall of the text was coded for the number of idea units recalled, the number of main ideas recalled, and the number of new ideas. Generating new, unrelated ideas indicates deeper processing—people are connecting the text's contents to prior knowledge and elaborating its meaning. People with high interest in the topic recalled more of the text's main ideas and more ideas overall. They also contributed more new ideas in the free recall, indicating deeper processing of the text. Finally, people with high interest were more likely to recall the main ideas in their correct sequence, reflecting a more coherent representation of the text.

The effects of interest on processing strategies extend beyond laboratory studies (see Krapp, 1999, pp. 29–30). During the semester, college students rated how interesting they found their classes, how much time they spent studying for their classes, their learning strategies during studying, and their extrinsic motivation (e.g., desire for good grades). Students' interest in a class at mid-semester predicted the amount of time they spent studying and their learning strategies. Consistent with the laboratory research, interested students used more deep-level strategies. They were more likely to think critically about the material while studying and to form connections between the material and their prior knowledge and experience. Interest was unrelated to using superficial strategies such as rote rehearsal; extrinsic motivation, in contrast, predicted using rote rehearsal.

To show causal claims about the roles of interest and processing depth in learning, researchers conducted an experiment that manipulated the reader's level of processing and the text's interestingness (McDaniel et al., 2000, Study 2). College students read interesting or boring stories. In a control condition, people simply read the stories. In a second condition, letters were deleted from many of the text's words. This should orient the reader to the text's superficial structure and thus promote superficial verbatim processing. In a third condition, the sentences were presented in a random order, and the reader needed to unscramble them

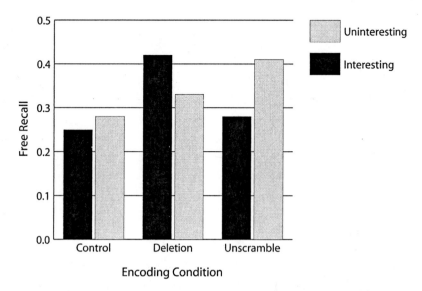

FIGURE 3.1 How interest and depth of processing affect recall
Source: Adapted from McDaniel et al. (2000).

to read the text. This should orient the reader to the relationships between the text's propositions, thus promoting a deeper level of processing. If interest promotes processing the organizational and relational features of the text, then people who read interesting texts should benefit
from enhanced processing of individual propositions (the deleted-letter
condition). Likewise, if boring stories promote processing the text's individual propositions, then people reading boring stories should benefit
from enhanced processing of the text's relational features (the scrambled
sentence condition). These predictions were supported; figure 3.1 displays the findings. For interesting texts, recall was enhanced by superficial processing. For boring texts, recall was enhanced by deeper processing.

Learning Strategies and Interest

A final way that interest affects learning is by affecting learning strategies
and educational choices. Interest affects what people choose to study and
how much time they spend studying it. When faced with many tasks
and little time to study—a perennial student dilemma—students must

divide their time strategically. In several experiments, students read different texts (biographies, haiku, and sonnets), judged the difficulty of learning those texts, and rated their interest in the texts (Son & Metcalfe, 2000). Interest predicted how long the students spent reading each text, even when people knew they would be tested on all of the texts. In turn, increased study time improved performance on a subsequent memory test. A longitudinal study of German public school students (Köller, Baumert, & Schnabel, 2001) shows how such choices affect learning over time. Interest in math during 10th grade predicted math achievement in 12th grade. Students interested in math were more likely to choose advanced math classes. Taking advanced classes, in turn, fostered higher achievement in math.

In a comprehensive study of interest and learning (Ainley, Hidi, & Berndorff, 2002), students were presented a set of texts on diverse topics (e.g., X-rays, body image). The students differed in how interesting they found these topics. Students could read the texts in any order, and they could stop reading and switch to another text if they wanted. Emotional experience was measured online by inserting brief measures of affect into the text. At the end of the study, students took tests of learning and comprehension. Structural models suggested that interest in the topic led to positive affective experiences while reading. Positive emotions increased persistence, measured as the amount of time people spent reading the text. Persistence, in turn, promoted better scores on a measure of learning. Interest's effect on learning was thus distal, mediated by what people chose to read and how long they spent reading it.

Interest's intriguing effects on learning strategies deserve more research. In particular, it seems likely that interest could have complex, and possibly detrimental, effects on learning by leading people to adopt ineffective learning strategies. Interest is sometimes a poor basis for deciding what to study—an introductory class that is easy and interesting may deserve less study time than an advanced class that is hard and tedious. Interest may also bias judgments of how well something has been learned. If interesting material is vivid and easy to process, it may exaggerate people's confidence that they can remember the material later (Rawson & Dunlosky, 2002).

Summary

Interest appears to promote learning through several mechanisms. Intuition to the contrary, interest doesn't seem to increase attention. Early experiments found that interest increased attention to text (Anderson, 1982; Asher, 1980); recent experiments found that interest reduced attention (McDaniel et al., 2000; Shirey & Reynolds, 1988). A second mechanism, depth of processing, has received stronger support. The interested reader approaches and processes text differently from the uninterested reader. Interest promotes focusing on the text's meaning and building a propositional representation, whereas boredom promotes focusing on the text's superficial aspects (Schiefele, 1999, 2001). Finally, learning strategies are another mechanism of interest and learning. People devote their limited study time to interesting topics (Son & Metcalfe, 2000), and they spend more time reading things they find interesting (Ainley et al., 2002). Interest thus fosters learning by affecting decisions about what to study and how long to study it.

Research on interest and reading is going in the right direction by examining the mechanisms of interest and learning. The three mechanisms reviewed here clearly deserve more research. Despite some discouraging findings, the role of attention shouldn't be written off. Although several studies found that interest reduced attention (McDaniel et al., 2000; Shirey & Reynolds, 1988), they have not explained why earlier studies found the opposite effect (Anderson, 1982; Asher, 1980). Furthermore, the notion that interest reduces attention is hard to reconcile with research on depth of processing and reading time. If interest motivates spending more time reading a text (Ainley et al., 2002) and processing the text more deeply (Schiefele, 1999), then in one sense interest affects attention to the text.

Seductive Details: When Are Texts Too Interesting?

John Dewey (1913), criticizing the prevailing models of education, argued against "trying to make things interesting." He suggested that such attempts divided the student's attention between the task itself and its interesting periphery—trying to arouse interest might be counterproductive. Dewey's ideas resurfaced decades later in the study of *seductive details* (Garner, Brown, Sanders, & Menke, 1992; Wade, 1992). Spicing up a boring text by adding interesting details might backfire. If the interesting material is irrelevant to the text's main points, then the reader might remember the interesting details at the expense of the important themes—the interesting details seduce attention from the main ideas.

The seductive details hypothesis has provoked controversy (Goetz & Sadoski, 1995a, 1995b; Wade, Alexander, Schraw, & Kulikowich, 1995) and stimulated a lot of research (Alexander & Jetton, 1996; Sadoski, 2001; Schraw & Lehman, 2001). It's probably the most intriguing idea in the study of interest and reading. After all, a lot of research shows that interest enhances learning from text. It seems paradoxical that interest could impair learning by leading people to learn the wrong things, the peripheral details of a text. If this hypothesis is true, then writers would need to reconsider the educational value of the vivid pictures, cartoons, and images that populate most textbooks (Garner, 1992).

Much of the controversy over seductive details probably stems from disagreements about how to define a seductive effect of details. One version of the seductive details hypothesis states that "information that rates high in interest but low in importance to the main ideas or themes of a text is recalled more often and receives more attention than its importance would seem to warrant" (Wade et al., 1995, p. 513). Or, as Garner (1992) frames it, "The vivid details are recalled, but the important pieces of information (often abstract, general points) are not" (p. 54). This defines the seductive details effect as the recall of the *seductive details themselves*, both absolutely and relative to the main ideas. If people recall too many seductive details, or if people recall more seductive details than main ideas, then we infer a detrimental effect.

Goetz and Sadoski (1995a) offer a refined hypothesis: "In order to provide evidence of a seductive detail effect, it is essential to show that readers are being seduced away from important but uninteresting information *that they otherwise would have learned and remembered.* This requires contrasting the recall of the important information presented in passages with and without seductive details" (p. 507, emphasis in original). If reading a text with interesting details reduces recall of the main ideas relative to reading the same text without the details, then we can infer an effect of seductive details. Unlike the first version, reduced recall of the *main ideas* indicates a seductive effect. This hypothesis is easily tested because it includes a comparison standard: recall of the main points is compared for a text with and without seductive details. Focusing the hypothesis on the main points also better fits with the view that seductive details are detrimental (Garner et al., 1992; Wade, 1992). After all, the details are seductive only if they lure the reader away from the important main points.

A strong form of Goetz and Sadoski's hypothesis involves an extra criterion: the effects of *uninteresting* details. Adding irrelevant details disrupts the text's structure and reduces its coherence (Bradshaw & Anderson, 1982; Mohr, Glover, & Ronning, 1984). The seductive details effect presumably stems from the interestingness of the details (Garner et al., 1992; Wade, 1992). If tedious details—boring, unimportant details—and seductive details have the same effect, then disrupted coherence, not seductive interest, is the cause of poor recall (Sadoski, 2001).

The weak and strong forms of the seductive details effect imply the necessary elements of an experiment. To test the weak form, a study must manipulate the presence of seductive details within a text. Without a "no seductive details" control group, we can't know if the details affected remembering the main ideas. To test the strong form, the study must also manipulate the presence of tedious details. This shows whether a seduction effect stems from a detail's interestingness or concreteness. If seductive and tedious details have the same effects, then interest per se would seem unimportant.

Reviewing the Evidence

In the first study of seductive details, adults read a three-paragraph essay about insects (Garner et al., 1989). A different group of adults had rated the information in the essay for importance and interestingness. Some people read a version of the essay without any seductive details; others read a version of the essay—longer by nearly 40%—with several seductive details. People in the seductive-details conditions remembered fewer main ideas, consistent with the weak form of the seductive details hypothesis. A second study, however, failed to replicate this effect. When seventh-graders read the same essays, seductive details didn't affect recall of the main points. Both experiments lacked a tedious-details condition. Expanding the insect essay by 40% with uninteresting details might have had the same effect on recall.

In other experiments, people read an article about Stephen Hawking's Grand Unification Theory that contained seductive details (Garner et al.,

1991). The details were presented either as an aside or as part of the regular text. Some versions of the essay were made "generally interesting" by starting the essay with a paragraph of vivid, personal details about Hawking's life. Other "generally uninteresting" versions lacked this paragraph. These studies do not test either the weak or strong form of the hypothesis because they didn't manipulate the presence of seductive details. Everyone received seductive details, so the study lacks a comparison condition. A later experiment manipulated the presence of seductive details (Garner & Gillingham, 1991), but contrary to predictions, this did not affect recall of the main ideas.

A series of studies on biographical texts also lacked control conditions (Wade & Adams, 1990; Wade, Schraw, Buxton & Hayes, 1993). People read a long text about the life of Horatio Nelson. The sentences within the text were categorized according to their importance (high vs. low) and interestingness (high vs. low). Interest had a bigger effect on recall than did importance; sentences that were uninteresting but important tended to be recalled least often. Because the presence of seductive details wasn't manipulated, we don't know whether recall of the main points would be higher in the absence of seductive details (Goetz & Sadoski, 1995a).

Experiments involving science texts manipulated the presence of seductive details in the form of text and pictures (Harp & Mayer, 1997, 1998). In the control condition, people read a six-paragraph essay about the causes of lightning strikes. In the seductive-details condition, the essay was expanded by 30% with information about the effects of lightning strikes. People in the seductive-details condition recalled fewer main points (the causes of lightning) relative to people in the control condition (Harp & Mayer, 1997, Study 1). Later experiments manipulated aspects of the text, such as whether the main points were highlighted or whether the seductive details appeared at the beginning or end of the text (Harp & Mayer, 1998). Overall, these experiments found that including seductive details impaired recall of the main ideas.

Sadoski (2001) argued that Harp and Mayer's manipulation of seductive details simply changed the essay's main point. Each paragraph in the modified text contained information about the effects of lightning, and over half of the first paragraph described lightning's effects. This makes "the effects of lightning" seem like a main theme of the essay. Indeed, the basic text had 9 idea units, whereas the seductive text added 12 seductive idea units. The seductive details thus became main points—one group read a text about the causes of lightning and another group read an essay about the causes and effects of lightning. Because Harp and Mayer (1997, 1998) didn't include a tedious-details condition (a 30% longer text with boring information), they can't rule out Sadoski's alternative explanation.

Schraw (1998) conducted an experiment using the biography of Horatio Nelson (Wade et al., 1993). He classified seductive details into two types. *Context-dependent* details are interesting only when read within the context of the whole text; *context-independent* details can be interesting as stand-alone text segments. One experiment manipulated the presence of different kinds of seductive details. One group read the text with no seductive details, another group read the text with both kinds of seductive details, and two additional groups read the text with only one kind of seductive detail. People in all four conditions recalled the main ideas equally well; adding seductive details—regardless of type—didn't affect recall.

Summary

Fifteen years of research offer poor support for the seductive details hypothesis. Many studies don't qualify as tests of the hypothesis (Wade & Adams, 1990; Wade et al., 1993). Among the few experiments that tested the hypothesis, several studies found no effect of seductive details (Garner & Gillingham, 1991; Schraw, 1998). Furthermore, the experiments that found an effect suffer from a troubling confound (Garner et al., 1989; Harp & Mayer, 1997, 1998). Adding seductive details increased the text's length by 30 to 40 percent, thus affecting its coherence and possibly making a qualitatively new text (Goetz & Sadoski, 1995a; Sadoski, 2001). Finally, no experiments have measured the effects of tedious details. If uninteresting and unimportant details detract from recalling the text's main points, then any detrimental effects are probably due to changes in length and coherence rather than to interest. Future work needs to test the seductive details hypothesis more conclusively.

What Makes a Text Interesting?

What makes something interesting to read? If interest enhances learning from text, then it is obviously important to know how to make texts interesting. Researchers have proposed a lot of text factors that affect text-based interest; the following lengthy list illustrates the exploratory nature of research on text-based interest. Most of these sources were derived from speculation and intuition, not from a theory of what makes something interesting (see Hidi & Berndorff, 1998; Schank, 1979; Schraw et al., 1995; Wade et al., 1999). As a result, the field has a long "laundry list" of variables that affect interest, but it lacks a theory that explains why they affect interest and how they might relate to each other. What do these variables have in common? Can they be integrated into a simpler set of variables?

Coherence
Ease of comprehension
Prior knowledge
Themes of death
Simple vocabulary
Suspense
Sexual themes
Vividness
Author voice
Concreteness
Meaningfulness
Imagery
Readers' connections
Surprisingness
Importance
Character identification
Power themes
Familiarity
Unexpectedness
Emotiveness
Engagement

Only a handful of these possible sources have been extensively tested by research. We'll review the sources of interest that have the firmest empirical support. While reading about the sources of text-based interest, it is worth keeping in mind the appraisal model of interest developed in chapter 2. There we explored two components of interest's appraisal structure: appraisals of novelty and complexity, and appraisals of ability to understand. After reviewing the major sources of text-based interest, we'll consider whether the appraisal model can illuminate similarities among the disparate sources of text-based interest.

Coherence

Coherence refers to aspects of a text that facilitate organizing and understanding the text's ideas. In their review of text-based interest, Schraw and Lehman (2001) concluded that the effects of coherence on interest were "uniformly positive" (p. 36) because all studies had found that coherence enhanced interest. Coherence was one of the strongest predictors of interest in expository texts (Schraw et al., 1995) and literary texts (Schraw, 1997). In a comprehensive study of text characteristics (Wade et al., 1999), coherence (among other factors) enhanced reader interest. The effects of coherence are consistent across these studies, but they are nevertheless correlational. Manipulations of coherence (e.g., Rawson & Dunlosky, 2002) would enable stronger conclusions about its effects on interest.

Ease of Comprehension

Ease of comprehension affects reader interest: as texts become easier to understand, they become more interesting. After reading expository and literary texts, college students gave ratings of ease of comprehension, coherence, vividness, and engagement (Schraw, 1997; Schraw et al., 1995). Ease of comprehension and coherence accounted for the most variance in interest (see Wade et al., 1999). In an experiment, college students read an abstract poem (Silvia, 2005c; see chapter 2). Manipulating the ease of comprehension—providing some students with a clue that unlocked the poem's meaning—increased ratings of comprehension and of interest. One study, however, found the opposite effect (Schiefele, 1996). High school students read texts that were below their grade level in reading difficulty. The students' verbal abilities were negatively correlated with feelings of interest and enjoyment while reading. Schiefele (1996) notes that "it is likely that the texts were somewhat easy for highly able readers and, as a consequence, they felt less enjoyment when reading them" (p. 15).

Prior Knowledge

Prior knowledge is another source of interest (Alexander, Jetton, & Kulikowich, 1995; Tobias, 1994). One body of work suggests that prior knowledge affects interest linearly. In one study (Alexander, Kulikowich, & Schulze, 1994), people were separated into groups based on their knowledge of physics. After reading passages about black holes and quarks, people rated their overall interest in each passage, rated each paragraph for interest, and underlined sentences that they found particularly interesting. Prior knowledge of physics predicted overall interest. People with the most prior knowledge also reported the most interest in the individual paragraphs. Other researchers, however, contend that prior knowledge affects interest quadratically. Kintsch (1980) suggests that extremes of knowledge and ignorance will lead to low interest. High knowledge renders the incoming information familiar and unsurprising; low knowledge prevents the reader from forming connections.

Concreteness

Texts with concrete words and titles are more interesting, easier to understand, and easier to remember. In a study of single sentences (Sadoski et al., 1993), concrete sentences were more interesting than abstract sentences. Similarly, brief essays were more interesting when their titles were concrete (Sadoski et al., 2000). These studies are noteworthy because they manipulated concreteness, thus demonstrating a causal relation between concreteness and interest. Structural models suggested that concreteness affects interest indirectly. Readers found concrete texts easier to understand than abstract texts; ease of comprehension in turn increased interest.

Vividness and Surprisingness

Vividness refers to the intensity of mental imagery during reading (Sadoski & Paivio, 2001); vivid images are lifelike and resemble actual perception. Others have defined vividness as a feature of the text, which is probably misleading. For instance, Schraw and Lehman (2001) construe vividness as "text segments that stand out because they create suspense, surprise or are otherwise engaging" (p. 31); suspense or surprise probably better capture the meaning of this definition. Many correlational studies find that the reader's ratings of suspense predict ratings of interest, in both young children and college students (Jose & Brewer, 1984; Schraw et al., 1995; Schraw, 1997). In an experimental study of surprise, Iran-Nejad (1987) manipulated the surprisingness of a story's ending and whether the surprise was reduced. Surprising stories were not necessarily more interesting than unsurprising stories—surprising stories were interesting only when the surprise was reduced. Interesting stories created incongruity and then enabled comprehension through resolution of the surprise.

An Appraisal Perspective on Text-Based Interest

The proposed sources of text-based interest can be understood in terms of the appraisal model of interest developed in chapter 2. The power of the appraisal perspective is its ability to organize diverse areas of research (Roseman & Smith, 2001). According to an appraisal view, sources of interest share the same appraisal basis. Interesting ideas, interesting films, and interesting texts are presumably interesting because they share the same appraisal structure. Stated differently, text-based interest has the same causes as interest based in anything else. In chapter 2, we suggested that the appraisal structure of interest has two appraisal components: an appraisal of novelty (Scherer, 2001a), construed broadly as novelty, complexity, uncertainty, and conflict (Berlyne, 1960); and an appraisal of coping potential (Lazarus, 2001; Scherer, 2001a), construed as appraised ability to understand the new, complex, surprising thing. The sources of text-based interest can be understood as facets of these two broad appraisal dimensions.

Many sources of text-based interest reflect the novelty–complexity appraisal, particularly vividness, surprisingness, and unexpectedness. An appraisal interpretation of these text factors is straightforward—most of them are synonyms of *novelty* and *complexity*, and they are measured like these appraisals are measured in emotion research (Schorr, 2001b). Other sources of text-based interest reflect the appraisal of ability to understand. Coherence, ease of comprehension, prior knowledge, and concreteness reflect the person's appraised ability to form a coherent understanding of the text's ideas. Congruent with an appraisal view, coherence, prior knowledge, and concreteness correlate with ratings of ease of comprehension (Sadoski et al., 2000; Schraw, 1997; Schraw et al., 1995), which is an appraisal of one's ability to understand the text. Significantly, several experiments have manipulated these text factors and measured interest. Manipulating the ability to understand a poem increased appraised understanding and interest in the poem (Silvia, 2005c, Experiment 2); appraisals of understanding fully mediated the effect of the manipulation on interest. Manipulating the concreteness of essays increased ability to understand the essays and interest. As an appraisal analysis would predict, ability to understand a text mediated the effect of concreteness on interest (Sadoski et al., 1993, 2000). Thus, based on evidence to date, it seems reasonable to presume that many sources of text-based interest affect interest by affecting the appraisals that cause interest.

Table 3.1 reorganizes the sources of interest according to the two appraisal dimensions. This speculative sorting is preliminary. Many of these sources have not been tested, and only a few—concreteness, ease of comprehension, and surprisingness—have been manipulated in experiments. Furthermore, some these sources, such as surprisingness and unexpectedness, are synonymous and could be collapsed into a single source. Nevertheless, this is an improvement on the current sprawl of sources of interest. The study of interest and reading has not examined why these sources create interest or considered what these sources have in common. Appraisal theories were designed to solve problems such as these (Roseman & Smith, 2001). An appraisal model can explain why they create interest, by virtue of the causal role of appraisals in emotions

TABLE 3.1 A Speculative Appraisal Model of the Sources of Text-Based Interest

Appraisals of Novelty–Complexity	Appraisals of Ability to Understand
Vividness	Coherence
Surprisingness	Ease of comprehension
Unexpectedness	Prior knowledge
Suspense	Concreteness
Engaging themes (death, power, sex)	Readers' connection
Emotiveness	Meaningfulness
Imagery	Simple vocabulary
Author voice	Character identification

(Roseman & Evdokas, 2004), and it can illuminate what the sources have in common by locating each source within interest's appraisal structure. Needless to say, future research should evaluate the merit of an appraisal perspective on text-based interest.

Chapter Summary and Conclusions

This chapter explored connections among interest, learning, and reading. Our first issue concerned how interest affects learning. Interest clearly promotes learning from text, but why it does so is poorly understood. One intuitive hypothesis—that people pay more attention to interesting texts—is largely unsupported. People often pay less attention to interesting texts, and attention doesn't seem to mediate the effects of interest on learning (Shirey, 1992). A less obvious hypothesis—that interest promotes deeper levels of processing—has stronger support. Interest promotes processing propositional and situational meanings of a text rather than superficial aspects (Schiefele, 1999). Finally, interest affects what people choose to read and how much time they spend reading it (Ainley et al., 2002). The mere fact of deciding to read one thing versus another (Son & Metcalfe, 2000) and spending more time studying it enhances learning. Interest thus affects learning from text by changing both the quality (type of text processing; Schiefele, 2001) and quantity (amount of time; Ainley et al., 2002) of learning processes.

We also considered whether aspects of texts could sometimes be "too interesting." Research on seductive details contends that interesting details can lure the reader away from a text's important main points. As a result, interest may paradoxically impair learning. The seductive details hypothesis has little support (Sadoski, 2001; Sadoski & Paivio, 2001). Many studies didn't test the hypothesis directly, other studies found no effects, and seemingly supportive studies have credible alternative explanations. The strong version of the hypothesis, in which the effects of interesting details are compared with the effects of tedious details, has not yet been tested.

Many continuities in the psychology of interest are obscure and unappreciated. This chapter examined some of these continuities. The study of text-based interest is divorced from the study of interest as an emotion. It is remarkable that there have been so few connections drawn between the study of what makes things interesting (chapter 2) and what makes texts interesting. We considered if the sources of text-based interest can be understood in terms of the appraisal model developed in chapter 2. Elements of text can affect appraisals of novelty, complexity, and uncertainty, and they can affect appraisals of one's ability to understand the new information. The sources of text-based interest seem to sort into these two appraisal categories. This enhances the breadth of the appraisal model and provides a simple framework for organizing the dozens of sources of text-based interest.

Another continuity is the functional role of interest in learning. Emotion psychologists contend that a key feature of an emotion is adaptive significance across the life span (Abe & Izard, 1999; Oatley & Jenkins, 1992; see chapter 1). Emotion psychology has had much to say about the adaptive functions of interest, asserting that interest improves learning, builds knowledge and skills, and promotes engagement with the environment (Izard & Ackerman, 2000). Emotion psychology, however, has not tested these assertions. In contrast, educational psychology has had little to say about the functions of interest, but it has provided a large literature documenting the constructive effects presumed by emotion psychology (e.g., Köller et al., 2001; Schiefele, 1991; Schiefele et al., 1992). Researchers in these areas could learn a lot from each other.

This chapter concludes part I of this book. Thus far we have explored interest as an aspect of momentary experience, such as emotional qualities of interest (chapter 1), theories of what makes something interesting (chapter 2), and the role of interest in learning and reading. Part II explores the psychology of interests as aspects of personality—the enduring hobbies, avocations, and caprices that characterize human motivation. Chapter 4 explores individual differences related to interest, chapters 5 and 6 consider the origins of interests, and chapter 7 reviews vocational interests, the most widely studied kind of interests.

PART II

INTERESTS
AND
PERSONALITY

4

Interest, Personality, and Individual Differences

Many years ago Kluckhohn and Murray (1948) noted that in some ways a person is like all other people, in other ways like many other people, and in still other ways like no other people. Since then, personality psychology has been a fractious discipline, full of rancor between the behaviorists and the psychoanalysts, the trait theorists and the humanists, the situationists and the dispositionists. Much of this controversy was needless, and it could have been averted had researchers remembered Kluckhohn and Murray's simple insight. In recent years personality psychology has achieved a nascent reconciliation, prompted in part by the recognition that personality can be studied meaningfully at different levels (McAdams, 1993, 1996), including universal traits, personal goals, and idiosyncratic life-stories.

In part I of this book we learned about ways in which interest is common to all people. As an emotion, interest should have some innate and universal features. In part II, we'll explore the latter two aspects of interest: aspects of interest that are common to many and aspects that are unique. Individual differences in psychological traits can be seen as qualities of personality common to many, rather than common to all. Some traits may be universal (McCrae & Costa, 1997), but the levels and manifestations of the traits are not. In this sense traits are "common to many"—they represent shared themes around which individuals deviate, not invariant universal qualities.

In this chapter, we'll see what psychologists have said about individual differences as related to interest. Researchers have proposed that people differ in curiosity, breadth and depth of interests, sensation seeking, proneness to boredom, and openness to experience. All of these individual differences involve notions of interest, albeit in different ways. We'll examine how each concept has been defined and measured, and more important, we'll see how fruitful the concept has been in enhancing our knowledge of interest. Research on individual differences, when at its best, illuminates the development and the mechanisms of psychological processes (Underwood, 1975). When at its worst, however, individual-differences research degenerates into haphazard correlations between self-report scales, with few theoretical implications and little gain in understanding (Wicklund, 1990). Such research shows that people who report differing in one way also report differing in another way, but it doesn't address the origins or meaning of the differences. We'll assess how deeply research has explored the *why* underneath each of these trait concepts and how thoroughly the measurement instruments have been applied to activity and experience rather than to other self-report measures.

The subsequent chapters in part II address aspects of interest that are unique and idiosyncratic, emphasizing the development of interests: how people acquire their hobbies and avocations. Chapter 5 presents an overview of the history of thought on the development of interests; chapter 6 presents a new theory of how interests develop. Chapter 7 reviews theoretical issues associated with vocational interests, the most thoroughly researched forms of interests. Many theories of vocational interests would fit in the present chapter because proponents assume that vocational interests are part of personality (Holland, 1999). Indeed, vocational-interest inventories are the most sophisticated measures of individual differences in interests (Fouad, 1999). Nevertheless, we'll defer discussion of vocational interests until chapter 7.

Interest and Individual Differences

The following sections review individual differences associated with interest and curiosity. Each section reviews how a concept has been defined and measured, describes research devoted to illuminating the concept, and then offers an evaluation of the research to date. The sections are ordered chronologically, with some exceptions—some criticisms and conceptual continuities are more easily appreciated by reviewing the concepts out of order. The final section briefly describes some models that are too recent to review in detail (e.g., Collins, Litman, & Spielberger, 2003; Litman, 2005; Litman & Jimerson, 2004; Litman & Spielberger, 2003) or that never generated much research (e.g., Day, 1971). The chapter concludes by evaluating the literature as a whole, isolating the most fruitful and most promising concepts, and discussing the role of research on individual differences for the psychology of interest.

State and Trait Curiosity

The most direct individual-difference approach is state–trait curiosity. In this view, curiosity is viewed as a trait, a stable disposition of the person that influences behavior. Beyond this general assertion, however, state–trait models include different assumptions about the sources and nature of curiosity. This section reviews theories by Spielberger and Starr (1994), Naylor (1981), Kashdan, Rose, and Fincham (2004), and Maw (1971). We'll review the theories and research and then consider some criticisms.

Self-Report Approaches

SPIELBERGER'S OPTIMAL AROUSAL MODEL

Spielberger and Starr (1994) proposed a state–trait model of curiosity rooted in Berlyne's (1971a) second arousal model (see chapter 2). They adopted most of Berlyne's assumptions about state curiosity. They agreed that the collative variables (novelty, complexity, uncertainty, and conflict) are the main sources of curiosity and that curiosity reflects the operation of antagonistic neural systems. Unlike Berlyne, they suggested that curiosity can be a trait, hence State (S)-Curiosity and Trait (T)-Curiosity: "High levels of S-Curiosity reflect an intense desire to seek out, explore and understand new things in the environment. The . . . T-Curiosity subscale assesses individual differences in the disposition to experience S-Curiosity when responding to novel or ambiguous stimuli. Persons high in T-Curiosity experience curiosity states more frequently and with higher levels of intensity than persons low in T-Curiosity" (p. 236). S-Curiosity involves the operation of Berlyne's primary reward system—increases in an object's collative properties lead to increases in feelings of curiosity. Curiosity is bounded by anxiety, which involves Berlyne's primary aversion system: increases in stimulation beyond a certain point evoke anxiety in addition to curiosity. The simultaneous action of curiosity and anxiety creates an inverted-U function (see chapter 2).

Based on this theory, Spielberger and Starr (1994) made intriguing predictions about how T-Curiosity and Trait (T)-Anxiety interact. They predicted that these traits interactively predict exploratory behavior—curiosity promotes exploration, and anxiety inhibits exploration. As a result, people with the same level of T-Curiosity will behave differently if they differ in T-Anxiety. When faced with uncertainty, for example, people high in T-Curiosity and low in T-Anxiety will be more curious relative to people high in both T-Curiosity and T-Anxiety. These are interesting predictions, but they remain largely untested. Spielberger has developed several measures of state–trait curiosity and anxiety; the State–Trait Personality Inventory (Spielberger et al., 1979), which contains 10-item scales for state and trait curiosity, is the most widely used.

Some interesting research has come from Spielberger's state–trait curiosity model. Peters (1978) conducted a field study of how curiosity and anxiety affect information seeking in college classrooms, using behavioral measures of exploration. She measured T-Curiosity, T-Anxiety, and whether students found the teacher threatening. Observers measured how many questions the students asked and how often students responded to questions posed by the instructor. When instructors were seen as nonthreatening, high T-Curiosity students asked five times as many questions as low T-Curiosity students. When instructors were seen as threatening, however, questions dropped to low levels regardless of T-Curiosity. T-Curiosity thus interacted with the situational variable to affect behavioral expressions of interest.

Spielberger and Starr's T-Curiosity concept surpasses many other individual-difference approaches to interest because it makes testable predictions about the underlying psychology of the trait. Anchoring the dynamics of trait curiosity in Berlyne's arousal theory enables firm predictions. Moreover, showing interactions with situational variables on behavioral measures (e.g., Peters, 1978) connects the trait to activity and experience rather than to other self-report scales. Yet not much research has been done with trait curiosity. Most of the work inspired by Spielberger's state–trait model has focused on anxiety and anger; curiosity has been relatively neglected. Perhaps this is an opportunity to rework the theory behind T-Curiosity (Berlyne, 1971a). In chapter 2, we saw that

Berlyne's model makes untenable assumptions about the biology of curiosity. Updating the underlying theory could revitalize research on T-Curiosity.

NAYLOR'S TRAIT-CURIOSITY INVENTORY

Naylor's (1981) Melbourne Curiosity Inventory is an alternative scale of state–trait curiosity. *Trait curiosity* in this model "refers to individual differences in the capacity to experience curiosity. It is presumed that persons possessing more C-Trait experience a wider range of situations as curiosity arousing than do persons possessing less. It is also presumed that those possessing more C-Trait experience greater intensities of C-State" (p. 173). This model isn't founded on a specific theory of curiosity; it simply assumes that curiosity exists in state and trait forms. Twenty items, such as the following examples, measure trait curiosity:

> I think learning "about things" is interesting and exciting.
> I am curious about things.
> I like to try to solve problems that puzzle me.

Another 20 items measure state curiosity; below are some examples:

> I want to explore possibilities.
> My interest has been captured.
> I feel involved in what I am doing.

The two scales form independent factors, and their reliability coefficients are good. Some validity for the trait curiosity measure comes from its relations to Holland's (1997) hexagonal typology of vocational interests (see chapter 7). Naylor (1981) found that trait curiosity correlated highest with Holland's Investigative type, second-highest with the Artistic type, and least with the Conventional type.

Few studies have used this scale, probably because Naylor's approach is atheoretical. Without an underlying theory that discusses the sources of curiosity and suggests when trait curiosity will and won't affect activity, it's hard to derive clear predictions for research.

THE PERSONAL-GROWTH FACILITATION MODEL

The newest model of trait curiosity comes from positive psychology, the study of human strengths, happiness, and virtues (Aspinwall & Staudinger, 2003; Seligman & Csikszentmihalyi, 2000). Kashdan and his colleagues propose that curiosity is "a positive emotional-motivational system associated with the recognition, pursuit, and self-regulation of novel and challenging opportunities" (Kashdan et al., 2004, p. 291). This model of trait curiosity is congruent with the constructive functions of interest reviewed in chapter 1 (cf. Fredrickson, 1998), but it differs from past models in key ways. Instead of tracing curiosity to arousal systems (Berlyne, 1960; Spielberger & Starr, 1994), to emotions (Fredrickson, 1998), or to cognitive motives (Schiefele, 1991; Schraw & Lehman, 2001), the personal-growth facilitation theory assumes that curiosity stems from the person's self-development projects (Kashdan, 2004). This relocates curiosity within the broad questions of personality psychology, such as the nature of organismic needs (Ryan, 1995).

Individual differences in curiosity are measured with the Curiosity and Exploration Inventory, a "dispositional measure of curiosity comprising (a) exploration or tendencies to seek out new information and experiences and (b) absorption or tendencies to become fully engaged in these rewarding experiences" (Kashdan et al., 2004, p. 292). This scale consists of 7 items, such as:

> When I am participating in an activity, I tend to get so involved that I lose track of time.
> Everywhere I go, I am out looking for new things or experiences.

This scale gives subscale scores for exploration and absorption. The overall score correlates positively with positive affect, vitality, well-being, hope, and optimism; it correlates negatively with boredom proneness, neuroticism, and social anxiety (Kashdan, 2002; Kashdan et al., 2004). A reworded version of this scale assesses state curiosity.

Research based on the personal-growth facilitation model is just getting started, but the model appears promising. By basing its measurement on a theory of curiosity, this model can make predictions about how curiosity (as measured by the scale) should and shouldn't affect activity.

Teacher and Peer Reports

Unlike other approaches to trait curiosity, Maw's (1971) model focused on curiosity differences in children. To avoid self-reports, he assessed children's curiosity with combinations of peer and teacher reports. His research measured curiosity according to a behavioral definition (Maw & Maw, 1970): "An elementary school child was said to demonstrate curiosity when he (a) reacts positively to new, strange, incongruous, or mysterious elements in his environment by moving toward them, exploring them, or manipulating them; (b) exhibits a need or a desire to know more about himself and/or his environment; (c) scans his surroundings seeking new experiences; and/or (d) persists in examining and/or exploring stimuli in order to know more about them" (p. 124). Children were sorted into high- and low-curiosity groups based on a composite index of teacher and peer ratings. Teachers received the definition of *curiosity* and ranked their students in terms of curiosity. To gather peer ratings, Maw created a "Who Should Play the Part?" instrument. This describes eight characters who display high- or low-curiosity behaviors. The students nominate fellow classmates to play the parts, presumably based on the peer's similarity to the role.

Maw then explored the personality differences among children differing in curiosity. Most of these differences were found for self-report instruments. High-curiosity children had higher self-esteem, a greater sense of personal worth, better adjustment, a stronger sense of belonging, less prejudiced and more democratic attitudes, and higher self-rated curiosity (Maw & Maw, 1970). Behavioral measures found differences in how they ask questions, find absurdities, remember unusual information, and solve mazes and puzzles (Maw, 1971). Sex differences appeared for many of these variables (Maw, 1971; Maw & Magoon, 1971).

One of the biggest correlates of Maw's measure of curiosity is intelligence. Theoretically, this makes sense. If interest promotes exposure to diverse experience (see chapter 1), then it should facilitate the growth of competence and intelligence (Raine, Reynolds, Venables, & Mednick, 2002). Conversely, intelligent children should feel more capable of understanding complex and ambiguous information, which promotes interest (see chapter 2). Methodologically, however, this is a problem: intelligence might confound the ratings of curiosity. In fact, many of Maw's findings (like memory and problem solving) reflect intelligence. To test this, Coie (1974) conducted a comprehensive study of curiosity in schoolchildren, involving teacher ratings, several measures of intelligence, and behavioral measures of exploration in different situations. He found that teachers' ratings of curiosity were heavily influenced by their perceptions of the children's intelligence. For boys, teacher ratings of curiosity predicted only intelligence. For girls, teacher ratings predicted intelligence and a few behavioral measures of curiosity. Coie didn't include peer ratings of curiosity, so it's hard to tell how problematic these finding are for Maw's research, which combined teacher and peer ratings. It seems unlikely that peer ratings were as heavily influenced by intelligence, although Maw doesn't describe how the teacher and peer ratings were combined or whether teacher and peer ratings showed diverging effects. Either way, it's clear that teacher and peer ratings of curiosity shouldn't be taken at face value.

It's a shame that Maw's approach to measuring trait curiosity has stalled—peer and observer ratings of curiosity never caught on. The other models of trait curiosity measure curiosity with people's self-reports (Kashdan, 2004; Naylor, 1981; Spielberger & Starr, 1994). A body of research based solely on self-reports is precarious, particularly when most of the dependent variables are also self-reports.

Depth and Breadth of Interests

Some researchers suggest that trait curiosity is multidimensional and should thus be split into two facets. *Depth versus breadth of interest* has been proposed as the key dimension. Langevin (1971) suggested that depth of interest is the intensity of interest and breadth of interest is the range of things found to be interesting. This fits with intuitive notions of depth and breadth. Ainley (1998), in contrast, defines depth of interest as "a tendency towards wanting to explore and investigate new objects, events and ideas in order to understand them," and breadth of interest as "a tendency towards wanting to seek varied and changing experiences in order to experience what they are like" (p. 259). In this view, depth resembles notions of trait curiosity discussed earlier (Spielberger & Starr, 1994; Naylor, 1981), and breadth resembles sensation seeking (Zuckerman, 1994).

The depth–breadth distinction was first suggested by Langevin (1971). He conducted a broad factor analysis to see how different measures of curiosity correlated. Schoolchildren completed measures of intelligence, self-report questionnaire measures of curiosity, and several behavioral measures of curiosity. Teachers also rated each child's curiosity. Overall, the measures of curiosity correlated weakly. A factor analysis of the curiosity and intelligence measures found four factors. The first consisted of scores from the intelligence scales; the second contained two questionnaire scales; the third consisted of Raven matrices scores; and the fourth consisted of two behavioral measures of curiosity. The two factors related to curiosity didn't explain much variance. Based on this evidence, Langevin proposed the breadth–depth distinction. The second factor was said to reflect breadth; the fourth factor was said to reflect depth.

This evidence for breadth and depth forms of interest is sketchy at best, especially when the two factors also differ in measurement type (self-report scales vs. behavioral measures) and administration type (classroom group sessions vs. individual testing). Indeed, Langevin (1976) later suggested that the breadth–depth distinction is specious and probably due to method artifacts. He argued that the extant curiosity scales were too poorly developed to enable reliable analyses. A factor analysis of curiosity measures found that the first factor failed to explain more than 20% of the variance; many of the scales had reliability coefficients below .60. Langevin concluded that better measures of curiosity were needed before factor analyses could be informative.

A later study of breadth and depth interests took a similar approach. Ainley (1987) factor-analyzed a broad range of curiosity and interest scales. She used only self-report questionnaires, however, to avoid the method artifacts that Langevin (1971, 1976) had encountered. The analysis found two factors, which she interpreted as reflecting breadth and depth of interest factors. Ainley's study evoked a strong reply from Boyle (1989), who contended that a state–trait model better described the data. Spielberger and Starr (1994, p. 227) suggested that this was an odd conclusion, given that Ainley analyzed only trait curiosity measures. Nevertheless, Boyle tested his alternative model by factor-analyzing a broad range of curiosity and anxiety scales. His analysis found a lot of factors, which he interpreted as supporting a state–trait model over a depth–breadth model. Precisely why a diverse factor structure supports one model over the other is unclear.

Ultimately, this approach to exploring breadth–depth interest will not be very fruitful. Factor analysis won't reveal a concept's true nature because scales are created with a certain result in mind (Allport, 1961). Finding a two-factor solution tells us little about the nature of curiosity. The factors still need to be *interpreted*, and interpretation requires some external criterion that privileges one interpretation over another. If all we have is a factor analysis—with no additional measures to provide validity—then we have a poor basis for arguing for a state–trait versus a breadth–depth conception. Researchers will ultimately need to see how the two models fare in the realm of experience, not the realm of eigenvalues. If one model explains or illuminates interest better than the other, research will show it.

The cycle of rehashing old scales to see what falls out was broken by Ainley (1998), who describes a new scale designed to measure breadth and depth of interest. People rate how much they would like to participate in 40 activities. Some activities reflect depth of interest (e.g., "Figuring out why some event happened the way it did"), whereas other activities reflect breadth of interest ("Walking into an old deserted house at midnight"). Total scores for depth and breadth can thus be obtained. This scale seems promising; it's certainly an improvement over analyzing old scales. The format, however, may pose problems. Asking people how much they would like to do different activities restricts the scale to places and groups in which the activities are plausible. If cultural or developmental differences in depth–breadth interest appear, they might say more about the activities in the scale than about actual interest differences (Loewenstein, 1994, p. 79). Also, a scale composed of lists of activities can't encompass the range of possible interests. Such scales thus underestimate the interest of people who pursue unusual interests. Plenty of people with broad intellectual interests would have no inclination to walk around in deserted houses during the middle of the night. Either way, a firm assessment will have to wait for future research, as the scale is currently unpublished.

It seems like work on the depth–breadth curiosity distinction is just getting started, despite 30 years of research and debate. Most of the research simply analyzed old scales. All we know thus far is that self-report scales of interest and curiosity don't correlate very highly with each other and that they form weak factors when factor analyzed. Ainley's (1998) depth–breadth scale is the first measurement instrument developed specifically to measure the breadth–depth of interests distinction. Future work is needed to show whether the distinction enhances our understanding of interest.

Breadth of Interest

Another research tradition focuses solely on the breadth of a person's interests rather than on breadth versus depth of interest. Jackson's conception of breadth of interest is the most clearly stated model. According to Jackson (1994):

> *Breadth of interest* denotes concerns of a more-or-less intellectual nature, rather than those involving, for example, physical activities. People scoring high on this scale would be expected to show intellectual curiosity about a diversity of topics. Low scorers, on the other hand, would be expected to be concerned with a relatively narrow range of topics. Breadth of Interest does not refer to the intensity of interest in any one area. Hence, high scorers are not necessarily "deep" thinkers, and low scorers are not necessarily "shallow" thinkers. (p. 21)

Defining trait adjectives for high scorers include *curious*, *interested*, and *involved*; defining adjectives for low scorers include *inflexible*, *narrow*, and *insular* (Jackson, 1994, p. 4).

Breadth of interest (Bdi) is one of 15 scales contained in the Jackson Personality Inventory–Revised (Jackson, 1994). The Bdi scale has 20 items answered with a true/false format. Some of the items describe a general breadth of interest, divorced from specific interest contents. Other items refer to having interests in specific areas, such as music, art, and politics. Unlike most of the breadth–depth research described earlier, Jackson's breadth of interest concept is founded on solid psychometrics. Jackson reports extensive validation research, including studies of breadth of interest in relation to other personality inventories, peer-rating studies, and known-groups validation studies.

Gaeddert and Hansen (1993) conducted an exploratory study of breadth of interests. They mailed questionnaires to large samples of engineers and public administrators. Breadth of interests was measured several different ways. First, people completed Jackson's (1994) breadth of interest scale. Second, people completed a vocational-interest inventory and were classified according to Holland's (1985a, 1997) hexagonal typology of interests (see chapter 7). In brief, Holland argues that vocational interests have a hexagonal structure. Adjacent interest categories should be most correlated; opposite interest categories should be least correlated. Having high interests in opposing categories was coded as high interest diversity (Johnson & Stokes, 2002). Third, people gave free responses of "all the hobby and/or leisure time activities they participated in during a typical year" (p. 301). These were coded according to the absolute number of activities and the diversity of the activities. Fourth, people rated themselves on scales measuring whether they felt they had more numerous, diverse, and intense interests than others. Finally, people listed the number and types of books and magazines they read and the organizations to which they belonged.

The study found that the different measures of interests were not highly correlated with each other. Jackson's (1994) Bdi scale was the best predictor—it correlated with nearly all the other measures, although the coefficients were generally low. Having adjacent or opposing Holland codes was essentially uncorrelated with everything else. Gaeddert and Hansen (1993) then formed a complicated composite score based on the variables that predicted scores on the Bdi. This composite was related to gender and occupational differences. The clearest finding from their study was that Jackson's Bdi scale was the most efficient predictor of interest diversity. It predicted scores on the other measures, whereas the other measures predicted each other poorly.

In their studies of individuality, Dollinger, Robinson, and Ross (1999) asked people to create a photo essay by taking photographs that "answer the broad question 'Who are you?' " (p. 626) and combining them into a collage. The photo essays were coded according to a standard system based on reflections of individuality; coding dimensions included repetition, abstraction, portrayal of the self in groups, unconventional portrayals, display of creative products, and use of metaphor. Individuality, as measured by this method, correlated with Jackson's breadth of interest scale in two studies. Individuality also predicted creativity, a universal nonprejudiced orientation, and expecting a culturally diverse future.

Jackson's (1994) model of breadth of interest has some limitations. Including specific interests in the scale overestimates breadth for some people and underestimates breadth for others. For instance, someone might have very broad interests but not be interested in art or politics. Jackson's Bdi scale underestimates the breadth of this person's interests because many of the items refer to art and politics. Likewise, a person interested only in art and politics would receive an inflated score. Moreover, Jackson's emphasis on "intellectual interests" like art and politics ignores common, everyday hobbies like playing sports and watching movies. These aren't big problems—all measures have error, after all.

But if we want to know the breadth of a specific person's interests, it would be nice to quantify the person's actual interests rather than to see if the person happens to be interested in the activities listed in the scale. The biggest limitation, however, is the atheoretical nature of the breadth of interest concept. It isn't clear what this concept predicts or implies about interest; this limits the contributions it can make to the general study of interest.

Sensation Seeking

Sensation seeking, according to Zuckerman (1994), "is a trait defined by the seeking of varied, novel, complex, and intense sensations and experiences, and the willingness to take physical, social, legal, and financial risks for the sake of such experience" (p. 27). Research on sensation seeking began in studies of sensory deprivation (Zuckerman, 1969) and soon expanded into virtually every area of psychology. Modern research focuses on psychobiological substrates of sensation seeking and their implications for psychopathology (Zuckerman, 1994, 1999). Several scales measure sensation seeking (Hoyle, Stephenson, Palmgreen, Lorch, & Donohew, 2002; Madsen, Das, Bogen, & Grossman, 1987). The most popular is Zuckerman's (1994, pp. 389–392) Sensation Seeking Scale–Form V. This scale has 40 forced-choice items, such as:

A. I like "wild," uninhibited parties.
B. I prefer quiet parties with good conversation.

Four subscales can be scored: Thrill and Adventure Seeking, Disinhibition, Experience Seeking, and Boredom Susceptibility. The subscales show different relations to other variables and different levels of heritability (Zuckerman, 1994).

Psychobiology of Sensation Seeking

Consistent with the prevailing views of Hebb (1955), Berlyne (1967), and Eysenck (1967), Zuckerman (1969) initially assumed that an optimal level of arousal was the physiological mechanism underlying individual differences. Research on sensation seeking eventually discarded this assumption and adopted a psychobiological perspective (Zuckerman,

1994). The psychobiological view gains support from behavioral genetics research, which suggests a heritable component of sensation seeking. In a twin study, identical and fraternal twins completed a self-report measure of sensation seeking (Fulker, Eysenck, & Zuckerman, 1980). For fraternal twins, scores for sensation seeking correlated .21 for both genders. For identical twins, scores correlated .63 (men) and .56 (women). Further analysis suggested an estimate of 58% heritability; correction for measurement error yielded an estimate of 69%. These estimates are at the high end of heritability for individual differences and close to the heritability estimates for cognitive variables (Zuckerman, 1991). An analysis of twins reared in different environments provided further evidence for heritability (Zuckerman, 1994, pp. 293–295). Scores on sensation seeking correlated .54 for identical twins and .32 for fraternal twins reared apart. A recent study with over 1,500 twin pairs estimated the heritability of sensation seeking to lie between 48% and 63% (Koopmans, Boomsma, Heath, & van Doornen, 1995).

But what is being inherited? Zuckerman (1994) argues that "genetic factors affect this personality trait through their determination of levels of activity or sensitivity of systems regulated by the catecholamines dopamine and norepinephrine, as well as neuroregulators like MAO" (p. 23). Many studies connect monoamine oxidase (MAO) enzymes and the neurotransmitters that they regulate to sensation seeking. Twin studies find that MAO levels are nearly entirely determined by genetic factors (Zuckerman, 1991). Levels of MAO negatively correlate with scores on scales of sensation seeking, and variations in MAO levels mirror variations in sensation seeking. People with low levels of MAO, for example, are more likely to have criminal convictions and to abuse alcohol, drugs, and nicotine. Age and gender differences in MAO levels also parallel age and gender differences in scores on sensation seeking. Zuckerman suggests a complex psychobiological model for sensation seeking, which we won't discuss. Here we'll only note that the interest in psychobiology of sensation seeking distinguishes it from the other traits discussed in this chapter.

Sensation Seeking and Interest

The trait of sensation seeking predicts what people find interesting. It isn't surprising that high sensation seekers are more interested in new things and unfamiliar places (Zuckerman, 1994); this in part defines the trait. More intriguing are the subtler relations between sensation seeking and expressions of interest. Studies of preferences for art, for instance, find large differences between high and low sensation seekers (see Zuckerman, 1994). Images high in complexity and conflict are more interesting to high sensation seekers. For example, high sensation seekers prefer complex polygons over simple polygons (Looft & Baranowski, 1971) and abstract pictures over concrete pictures (Furnham & Bunyan, 1988). The structural features of the art—such as its complexity and coherence—seem more important than what the picture depicts.

The sensation-seeking trait has similar effects on humor appreciation. Some models of humor categorize jokes based on uncertainty arousal and resolution (Ruch, 1992). Humor based on incongruity resolution starts with incongruity and then resolves it with a punch line. Humor based on nonsense, in contrast, creates incongruity but fails to resolve it. Nonsensical humor often creates more uncertainty and absurdity than it reduces, such as this excerpt from a comical story by David Nielsen (2001):

> The Sheriff stepped outside. There was a Pink Pig. The Pig came over to lick the Sheriff's Boot, which had Slop on it. The Sheriff wanted to Scratch the Pig with his Rake, but the Rake had been Reserved for George Washington. George Washington was not there, but if George Washington ever found out he Scratched his Pig with the Rake, he knew for certain there would be dire consequences. George Washington would Most Certainly chop his head off and Flush it down the Toilet. So the Sheriff did not Scratch the Pig with the Rake. The Chesapeake Bay was right next Door. The Sheriff looked at it. There was a Red Whale in it. It waved its Fin at the Sheriff and Spat water into the Sky. A Large Ocean Liner sailed past and it Cut the Red Whale in Half. It was Disgusting. There was an Alligator on board the Ocean Liner. It covered its Eyes because it could not Stand the Sight. It was Horrible. George Washington, however, would have None of That, and he pulled the Alligator's hands away from its Face. George Washington made the Alligator watch the Gore from the Deck of the Ship. (p. 6)[1]

1. Reprinted with permission of Broken Boulder Press.

People high and low in sensation seeking enjoy different forms of humor (Ruch, 1988). Low sensation seekers prefer conventional incongruity-resolution humor, in which their uncertainty is resolved. High sensation seekers prefer nonsensical humor, in which uncertainty is created and maintained. The excerpt from Nielsen's story, for example, would be preferred by high sensation seekers.

Boredom Proneness

Understanding boredom is important for understanding interest, yet it's hard to pin down how interest and boredom relate. It's tempting to view boredom as interest's opposite, although this would be misleading—emotions don't really have opposites. Boredom isn't simply the absence of interest because many states involve the absence of interest. Mikulas and Vodanovich (1993) define boredom as "a state of relatively low arousal and dissatisfaction, which is attributed to an inadequately stimulating situation" (p. 3). This would locate boredom in the passive–negative quadrant of affective space, diagonal to the active–positive quadrant containing interest (Feldman-Barrett & Russell, 1999). People do cite positive aspects of boredom, however, such as opportunities for reflection and planning (Harris, 2000). Moreover, while people report that boredom is generally unpleasant, they also report difficulties in regulating feelings of boredom. Often people feel unmotivated when bored, suggesting that boredom is more complex than a simple reaction to monotony (see Harris, 2000; Spacks, 1995). Finally, the arousal dimension of boredom is unclear. Berlyne (1960) argued that boredom involved high arousal and cited sensory deprivation experiments as support (see chapter 2). Vocal expressions of boredom, however, indicate reduced arousal (Scherer, 1986). All told, it seems likely that boredom reflects a constellation of motivational circumstances, uninterestedness being a primary feature.

Most of the research on boredom involves individual differences in *boredom proneness*, or how often and how easily people become bored. Farmer and Sundberg (1986) presented a unitary, single-factor model of boredom proneness, measured with a 28-item scale. This scale contains items such as:

Much of the time I just sit around doing nothing.
It takes a lot of change and variety to keep me really happy.

When I was young, I was often in monotonous and tiresome situations.

Vodanovich and Kass (1990a) later proposed that boredom proneness consists of five factors. A factor analysis of the scale found five factors, but the final three factors were weak. A later study found two major factors and some support for a third minor factor (Gordon, Wilkinson, McGown, & Jovanoska, 1997). Ultimately, as Allport (1961) argued, "nothing can come out of factor analysis that was not first put into it" (p. 330). Conflict over the structure of boredom proneness won't be settled by analyzing the original scale. An alternative theoretical model requires new measures, using the theory as a guide. Support for an alternative theory can't be discovered within an existing scale (Silvia, 1999).

Psychometrics aside, research has correlated the boredom proneness scale with a massive number of individual-difference variables. Men are more boredom prone than women (Vodanovich & Kass, 1990b), and African Americans are more boredom prone than Caucasians (Watt & Vodanovich, 1992a). People scoring high in boredom proneness are more impulsive (Watt & Vodanovich, 1992b); report more hostility and aggression (Rupp & Vodanovich, 1997); commit more crimes during adolescence (Newberry & Duncan, 2001); have more cognitive failures (Wallace, Vodanovich, & Restino, 2003); are less self-actualized (McLeod & Vodanovich, 1991); report being less satisfied with their jobs, and are less likely to show up for work (Kass, Vodanovich, & Callendar, 2001); experience less positive affect and more anxiety and depression (Vodanovich, Verner, & Gilbride, 1991); report more health symptoms (Sommers & Vodanovich, 2000); make simpler and more stable attributions (Polly, Vodanovich, Watt, & Blanchard, 1993); report less need for cognition and more self-focus (Seib & Vodanovich, 1998); and procrastinate more often (Vodanovich & Rupp, 1999). The life of the boredom-prone person seems bleak, indeed.

Boredom proneness is a promising concept that remains underdeveloped. After nearly 20 years of research, not much is known about the role of boredom proneness in activity and experience. Is boredom proneness universal? Does boredom proneness stem from biological processes? Is boredom proneness simply a facet of sensation seeking? The mechanisms underlying boredom proneness remain obscure. The scale measuring boredom proneness predicts many other things, but why it does so is unknown. Only a couple of studies have moved beyond correlational surveys to see how boredom proneness affects behavioral and experiential measures (Kass, Vodanovich, Stanny, & Taylor, 2001). Future work is needed to pin down the processes that mediate between the distal trait and momentary action. Maybe boredom proneness works because it involves low arousal, attributions for the lack of interest to the environment, or inadequate mood regulation skills. Maybe boredom proneness works via psychobiological processes, akin to sensation seeking (Zuckerman, 1994). Or maybe not—research should try to find out instead of showing more correlations with other traits.

Openness to Experience

The Big Five model—a perspective that aspires to specify the fundamental dimensions of individual differences (John, 1990; McCrae & Costa, 1999)—views openness to experience as one of the five dimensions of human personality. This factor "is a broad and general dimension, seen in vivid fantasy, artistic sensitivity, depth of feeling, behavioral flexibility, intellectual curiosity, and unconventional attitudes" (McCrae, 1996, p. 323). Of the five factors, openness to experience is the most relevant for individual differences in interest. Openness also happens to be the most controversial of the five factors. Researchers debate whether the factor reflects intelligence, experiential openness, or culture, and they question whether openness can be considered a universal trait. A special issue of the *European Journal of Personality* reviews the conflict (De Raad & Van Heck, 1994), which remains unresolved (De Raad, 1998).

Research on openness, like all research on the Big Five, follows two paths: the study of personality through self-reports, and the study of trait terms found in natural languages. We'll review these areas separately because the two methods project different images of openness to experience. Questionnaire research supports an image of the openness construct as receptivity to new experiences and ideas; the study of trait terms suggests intelligence, and it often fails to find a fifth factor.

Questionnaire Research

Many self-report scales measure openness to experience. The most popular scale is probably the *openness factor* in Costa and McCrae's (1992) NEO Personality Inventory. They define the openness factor with six facets: fantasy, aesthetics, feelings, actions, ideas, and values. Other scales measure the general dimension and do not define facets. Openness to experience correlates with a diverse set of variables, such as political values, authoritarianism (McCrae, 1994, 1996), and creativity (Feist, 1998; Wolfradt & Pretz, 2001). Curiosity seems to be a big part of openness. Kashdan (2004) presents an interesting view of how the two concepts relate:

> Curiosity is a fundamental motivational component of all openness facets. Yet high openness also entails imaginative, artistic, and unconventional sensibilities neither necessary nor sufficient for curiosity per se. Similarly, individuals can be high in openness, expressing a willingness to better understand themselves and be open-minded, yet reluctant to challenge and expand themselves. The experience of curiosity is more of a mechanism of action (cognitively, emotionally, and/or behaviorally), whereas openness is more of a psychological predisposition. (pp. 126–127)

Kashdan and his colleagues (2004) found a high correlation between their trait curiosity scale (described earlier) and a measure of openness to experience. Their analyses suggested, however, that trait curiosity has unique predictive validity beyond that conferred by the higher order openness factor (cf. Paunonen & Ashton, 2001).

Behavioral genetics research suggests a heritable component of openness to experience (Bergeman et al., 1993). Identical and fraternal twins, reared together or apart, completed an openness-to-experience scale. Openness scores were highly correlated for identical twins reared together ($r = .51$) and apart ($r = .43$). The correlations were lower for fraternal twins reared together ($r = .14$) and apart ($r = .23$). Model-fitting analyses estimated that 40% of the variance in openness scores could be explained by genetic influences. Of the remaining 60% attributable to the environment, only 6% was explained by the shared environment. Heritability estimates didn't differ according to gender or age.

McCrae and Costa (1997) have argued that openness to experience is universal, based on cross-cultural research with their five-factor inventory. Translations of the NEO-PI scales were administered in American, Chinese, German, Hebrew, Korean, Japanese, and Portuguese samples. Universality was assessed by comparing the factor structure in each culture to the factor structure in the American sample. The degree of similarity was considerable, taken by McCrae and Costa (1997) to suggest universality. Many studies, however, fail to find the Big Five factors. Usually more than five robust factors are needed to represent a broad item pool (Block, 1995). The original five factors are usually recovered, although often they are not (e.g., Benet-Martinez & Waller, 1997; Paunonen & Jackson, 1996). Other studies find that the five factors can be described with two higher order factors (Carroll, 2002; Digman, 1997), resembling self-control and ego resiliency (Block, 2001). Finally, the specific facet scales seem to be more efficient than the five broad factors themselves (Paunonen & Ashton, 2001). For research on individual differences in curiosity, for example, a trait curiosity scale may be more useful than the broad openness factor.

Lexical Research

A second tradition in Big Five research is the lexical approach, which studies relations among a natural language's lexicon of personality descriptors. This approach "shuns explicit theory" (De Raad, 1994, p. 231); instead, it lets the language speak for itself. By examining the trait structure of a language, researchers hope to gain insight into how people think about personality concepts. Researchers assume that people will develop words to describe the individual differences that are most significant to their daily lives. Complex methodological issues attend lexical research. We'll ignore these here (see De Raad, 1994, 1998) and focus on the findings.

Lexical research questions the reliability and meaning of openness to experience. Studies of trait descriptors in natural languages commonly fail to replicate the Big Five structure proposed by McCrae and Costa (1999). Instead, studies find more factors, fewer factors, or five factors with different interpretations. Openness to experience is the least stable of the five factors (De Raad, 1998). For instance, studies of trait terms in Italian (Di Blas & Forzi, 1999) and in Turkish (Somer & Goldberg, 1999) failed to recover an openness factor. When an openness factor is recovered, its interpretation resembles intelligence, imagination, or culture more than receptivity to experience (De Raad, 1994; Goldberg, 1994).

Evaluating Openness to Experience

Openness to experience seems like a house divided. One group of researchers sees it as a taxonomic category, a useful concept for organizing natural language trait descriptors (Goldberg, 1994; John, 1990). This group views openness as an umbrella category for all of the other concepts described in this chapter. Another group sees openness as a real, "in the skin" trait, with biological foundations and behavioral manifestations. But perhaps the conflict is merely apparent. The study of natural language is an interesting scientific topic in its own right, but I doubt it can challenge findings from scientific personality psychology. Does a scientific concept need to appear in a scientist's language, let alone in every world language, to be a legitimate scientific concept? German scientists studying D4 dopamine receptor genes shouldn't care whether everyday German speakers know a common word for D4DR—and they shouldn't bother asking if everyday Dutch, English, Turkish, Chinese, Italian, and Spanish speakers know a word for D4DR. No natural languages contained words related to monoamine oxidase (MAO) systems before science coined them; should scientists doubt the reality of MAO systems?

If science aspires to surpass common sense (Atkinson, 1964), then scientists need to cut the umbilical cord to natural language. The fact that Swedish identical and fraternal twins showed heritability of openness (Bergeman et al., 1993) is more relevant than whether the Swedish language has single words that capture the scientific concept of openness. Moreover, one wonders what the lexical approach wants to explain. If the goal is to learn about trait descriptors, then studying trait terms is appropriate. The real goal, however, seems to be learning whether a culture's lay psychology contains certain trait concepts, such as representations of the Big Five constructs. All researchers seem to agree that openness is not easily summarized in single trait words (De Raad, 1994, 1998; McCrae, 1994), so it seems unreasonable for lexical research to persevere on single trait words.

For our purposes, the fate of openness to experience does not rise and fall with the fate of the five-factor model. We are more concerned with whether openness is a discernable dimension and if it can enhance our understanding of interest. Some noteworthy studies on openness include the research on heritability (Bergeman et al., 1993), the stability of openness to experience over long periods (McCrae & Costa, 1990), how openness predicts emotional responses to art (Rawlings, 2000, 2003), and the role of openness in the formation of friendships and intimate partnerships (McCrae, 1996). Yet much of the questionnaire research on openness is uninspiring. Block (2001) asserts that "If only because it is an unthinking research task, the personality inventories designed for the five given factors have been related to any available criterion" (p. 99). The result, he argues, is that the Big Five literature "is a hodgepodge of reports, signifying almost nothing of central importance to the study of personality." Indeed, few studies address the origins and functions of openness in activity and experience. Most studies of openness to experience simply correlate an openness scale with some other scale (McCrae, 1994, 1996). Such research can carry a construct only so far.

Miscellaneous Models

Thus far we've covered the most prominent models of individual differences in interest, curiosity, and intrinsic motivation. In this section we'll look at a few of the many "mini-theories" of trait curiosity. Psychometric practices have improved substantially over the last 40 years (DeVellis, 2003); most of the older measures fail to meet modern psychometric standards for reliability and validity (see Langevin, 1976). Discussions of older measures can be found elsewhere (Ainley, 1987; Langevin, 1976; Olson & Camp, 1984; Vidler & Rawan, 1974, 1975).

Hy Day's (1971) Ontario Test of Intrinsic Motivation (OTIM) measures one of the most complex models of individual differences in curiosity. The development of the scale was inspired by research on stable preferences for polygons differing in complexity (Day, 1966, 1967, 1968). Day adopts Berlyne's distinction between specific and diverse curiosity (see chapter 2), although he emphasizes specific curiosity. The OTIM contains 110 items, such as:

I read any magazine that reports new scientific discoveries.
I wish people would explain how all the different instruments in an orchestra sound so well together.

Ninety items measure specific curiosity, according to a $10 \times 3 \times 3$ cube model. The cube's first face measures the 10 vocational interest categories in the Kuder preference record (see Darley & Hagenah, 1955). The second face measures three aspects of stimulation that can arouse curiosity (novelty, ambiguity, and complexity). The third face measures ways of responding (consultation, observation, and thinking). Each of the cube's 30 cells thus has one item. Two additional 10-item scales measure diversive curiosity and social desirability. The OTIM thus yields 19 scores: 10 for the interest categories, 3 for stimulation, 3 for responses, 1 for diversive curiosity, an aggregated overall score, and a social desirability score.

Factor analyses have generally supported the distinction between specific and diversive curiosity (Olson & Camp, 1984; Olson et al., 1984). All three stimulation scales predicted endorsement of proverbs related to curiosity and exploration (Maw & Maw, 1975). Scores on the thinking subscale predicted question asking during a college class; the consultation and observation subscales did not (Evans, 1971). People who were asked to volunteer for psychology experiments were more likely to sign up for experiments related to their OTIM interest area (Day & Maynes, 1972). Some of the subscales predicted the frequency of participation and the preferred complexity level of the experiment. A danger of the OTIM, however, is its flexibility. Any inventory with 18 possible curiosity scores will nearly always provide significant correlations, given large samples (Murphy & Myors, 1998). Few studies have used the OTIM, possibly because brief, reliable alternatives appeared shortly after Day's research.

Litman has recently developed several new measures of curiosity (Collins et al., 2003; Litman & Jimerson, 2004; Litman & Spielberger, 2003). This research returns to Berlyne's (1960) distinction between epistemic and perceptual curiosity. Epistemic curiosity results from incomplete, incoherent, or uncertain knowledge; perceptual curiosity involves increasing sensory experience. These studies have developed brief scales for measuring epistemic and perceptual curiosity; each scale splits into subscales that assess specific and diversive components (Berlyne, 1960; see chapter 2). Research with these scales, while still in its early stages, clearly surpasses past work on individual differences in epistemic and perceptual curiosity (Litman, Hutchins, & Russon, 2005). In a new twist, Litman and Jimerson (2004) proposed that individual differences in curiosity can reflect either curiosity as a feeling of interest or as a feeling of deprivation. They contend that most models associate curiosity with positive emotions (e.g., Kashdan, 2004), thereby neglecting a negative experience of curiosity based on lacking information and unpleasant arousal (Loewenstein, 1994). This intriguing idea deserves more research.

In Search of the Curious Person

What has the psychology of interest learned from its search for the curious person? Early research on individual differences in interest was discouraging and unsuccessful—the measurement was unreliable and eclectic, and the theories were vague or absent (see Loewenstein, 1994). After a long hiatus, however, the field has revived. Much of the work reviewed in this chapter is recent and occasionally unpublished, particularly new models of trait curiosity (Kashdan et al., 2004), breadth and depth of interest (Ainley, 1998), epistemic and perceptual curiosity (Collins et al., 2003; Litman & Jimerson, 2004; Litman & Spielberger, 2003), and conflicting views of openness to experience (De Raad, 1998; McCrae, 1996). Even sensation seeking, a veteran among arrivistes, has recently been reoriented around psychobiological processes (Zuckerman, 1994, 1999).

The surge of new ideas regarding interest and individual differences, while a sign of a healthy research area, makes it hard to evaluate this area. We'll have to wait and see whether the newer approaches develop into fruitful, generative theories or if they fizzle out. Rather than evaluate a nascent literature, then, we'll outline the features that future work should emphasize. Above all else, future work needs to ground itself in a theory. Individual-differences research succeeds when it illuminates general issues (Cronbach, 1957; Underwood, 1975). The most informative models in this chapter tackle conceptual problems in the psychology of interest (Kashdan, 2004; Litman & Spielberger, 2003; Spielberger & Starr, 1994; Zuckerman, 1994); the less informative models simply document and measure differences between people (Ainley, 1987; Farmer & Sundberg, 1986; Jackson, 1994; Maw, 1971; Naylor, 1981). Theories maximize how much we can gain from an individual-difference concept.

When possible, future work should include behavioral measures, unobtrusive measures, and implicit measures (e.g., Litman et al., 2005). Self-report scales dominate individual-differences research, and the perils of self-reports are underappreciated (Knowles & Byers, 1996; Nicholls, Licht, & Pearl, 1982; Osberg, 1985; Schwartz, 1999). Social desirability is a dire problem when studying positive qualities like curiosity. People's strategies for maintaining favorable self-images are pervasive, subtle, and disarming (Dunning, 1999). Social desirability can't be controlled statistically by including "social desirability scales"—these only discriminate crudely between the few hard-core dissemblers and the many ordinary dissemblers. Moreover, people often lack the skills and insight necessary for accurate self-reports (Wilson, 2002). When a poor writer judges his writing more favorably than a great writer judges her writing (Kruger & Dunning, 1999), when people who fail report higher self-esteem than people who succeed (Wicklund, 1998), and when people who report positive racial attitudes show behavioral racism (Biernat & Crandall, 1999), we get sobering lessons in self-report measurement.

Chapter Summary and Conclusions

Individual differences in emotional dispositions are the most common bridges between emotions and personality. This chapter reviewed individual differences related to interest, curiosity, and intrinsic motivation. Individual differences are aspects of interest that are common to many, the broad psychological themes around which people vary in intensity and quality, in pattern and expression. This area seems poised for a renaissance—I expect that the next decade will bring new ideas and enhance our understanding of the dynamics of interest at this level of analysis.

The next two chapters explore aspects of interest that are wholly unique. As Allport (1961) asked, "Is it reasonable to assume that all people do in fact possess the same basic constitution of personality? Must the units of organization in all lives be the same? Must the factors, except for their differential weighting, be identical?" (p. 329). We thus turn from individual differences to personality. We'll look at how people develop their unique, arcane, and occasionally bizarre hobbies and interests. Chapter 5 reviews past theories of how unique interests develop. Chapter 6 presents a new theory, based on theories of emotional knowledge and causal attribution (Duval & Silvia, 2001; Heider, 1958; Weiner, 1986). Chapter 7 looks at vocational interests—peoples' interests associated with the modern world of work.

5

Interests and Motivational Development

Why do one person's motives differ from another person's motives? If people aren't born with their adult preferences, goals, and interests, then how do these develop? The study of *motivational development* is the study of these questions. During the days of the grand theories of personality and motivation, behaviorists, humanists, and Freudians alike suggested answers to the problems of motivational development: motives transformed from other motives; motives developed through secondary reinforcement; motives emerged from deeper needs, instincts, and drives. Yet during this period hypotheses outnumbered studies; few psychologists tested their theories of motivational development.

Those in modern psychology, while enthusiastic about research on motivation, seem unconcerned with the problems of motivational development. Research on human motivation usually emphasizes universal motives—such as organismic needs (Deci & Ryan, 2000), evolved social motives (Baumeister & Leary, 1995), or basic cognitive motives (e.g., Dunning, 1999; Silvia & Duval, 2001a, 2004)—thus obviating questions of how people develop unique personal motives. Although the rise of research on idiosyncratic motives—personal strivings, personal goals, and current concerns (Emmons, 1999)—has moved unique aspects of motivation into the spotlight, even these theories have little to say about how personal motives develop and change (see Emmons, 1999; Klinger, 1971).

The development of interests is a special case of motivational development. Researchers in this area ask how a person acquires some interests and not others, and how different people come to have different interests. Not surprisingly, the study of the development of interests parallels the study of motivational development. The early period is mostly theoretical, full of untested hypotheses and unresolved arguments; the modern period is mostly unconcerned with how interests develop. Vocational research stands out as an important exception; theories of the origins of vocational interests have been tested extensively (Holland, 1997; Lent, Brown, & Hackett, 1994; Savickas, 1999). We'll examine vocational interests in chapter 7.

In this chapter we'll see how past theories explain the development of idiosyncratic interests. Nearly all theoretical orientations have offered explanations for how interests develop. We'll thus consider an eclectic bunch of ideas, ranging from sordid sexual drives to reinforcement to inherited instincts. Our first goal is to review the theories, showing the diversity of thought on the problem of how interests develop. Our second goal is to illuminate some of the broad continuities common to these theories—apparent differences can conceal fundamental similarities. Our third goal is to pave the way for presenting a new theory of how interests develop, described in chapter 6. By the end of this chapter, we should have a better appreciation of the history of thought on motivational development.

Theoretical Themes

Two major themes characterize the theories described in this chapter. The first dimension of similarity among our theories is the structure of their explanation for the development of interests. The most common explanatory structure is the Motivation × Connection model. According to these theories, idiosyncratic motives develop through the interaction of two processes. The motivation aspect refers to processes that instigate and reward activity; the connection aspect refers to processes that link motivation to specific activities. Without motivation the person lacks a basis for acting at all; without connection the person lacks a way of forming preferences for specific activities. One could view motivation as the intensity aspect and connection as the direction or selectivity aspect. Although their specific claims vary, many theories described in this chapter adopt this Motivation × Connection structure. Some view motivation in terms of basic emotions; other theories propose basic drives. Some suggest that connections come about through repeating activities; others study the contiguity of neutral activities with preferred activities.

A second dimension that describes these theories is whether interests stem from intrinsic or extrinsic motivation. Many theories assume that interests develop from intrinsic motivational sources, such as emotional feelings of interest or curiosity instincts. Interests, in these theories, represent "for its own sake" motivation. Other theories assume that interests stem from extrinsic motivational sources. In these theories, interests operate in the service of other motives, such as tension-producing drives or erotic and aggressive instincts (Freud, 1923; Hull, 1952). Some extrinsic theories argue that intrinsic interests can result from transformation of extrinsic motives (e.g., Allport, 1961).

Our review organizes the theories according to the developmental process emphasized by the theory. One class of theories argues that interests develop from similar motivational sources. A second class of theories argues that interests develop from a transformation of extrinsic motives into intrinsic motives. Finally, a third class of theories argues that interests stem from deeper psychological needs and act as mechanisms of need gratification. We'll find that the theories don't always sort easily into exclusive categories and that the theories share similarities that cut across this system. Nevertheless, the categorization can give us a foothold as a means into the sprawling diversity of thought on this topic.

Interests Developing From Similar Motives

One class of theories describes how new motivational structures develop from qualitatively similar sources. In this class, interests are amplified or articulated products of some similar motive. Yet, despite differences in articulation, interests retain the ancestral structure's core motivational nature. These theories do not posit that the extrinsic becomes intrinsic, for example, or that the external becomes internal: the original and resulting motive retain a core qualitative continuity. In each case, interests ultimately stem from some interest-like source of motivation. For example, enduring interests might be based in a general curiosity instinct or in an emotion of interest. We'll consider three theories: McDougall's theory of the curiosity instinct, Tomkins's script theory, and Prenzel's theory of the selective persistence of interest.

The Curiosity Instinct

William McDougall (1908/1960) posited a set of pan-cultural and evolved motivational systems known as *instincts*. Unlike other theorists, who defined *instinct* as an inflexible action program under stimulus control, McDougall defined *instinct* as having cognitive, affective, and conative properties. He felt that "every instance of instinctive behaviour involves a knowing of some thing or object, a feeling in regard to it, and a striving towards or away from that object" (p. 23). The cognitive and behavioral aspects change through experience as people learn a broader range of events that instigate the instinct and develop ways of responding to the event. The affective aspect, in contrast, remains invariant in its subjective character and motivating function.

Instincts and their emotions are the raw materials of motivational development. Each instinct enables the development of a *sentiment*, "an organised system of emotional dispositions centred about the idea of some object" (McDougall, 1908/1960, p. 137). While varying in complexity, degree of organization, and abstraction, all sentiments share a reference to some object and the invariant affective quality of the instinct, which provides the conative urge for the sentiment. The parental instinct, for example, enables the development of an attachment to a child. The instinct's affect—"tender emotion"—motivates interaction and nurturing. The sentiment associated with the child is a new motive that arose from the instinct and continues to rely on the tender emotion for motivation.

The *curiosity instinct* was the instinct associated with exploration and learning—"its impulse is to approach and to examine more closely the object that excites it" (McDougall, 1908/1960, p. 49). *Wonder* was the emotional quality of an aroused curiosity instinct. McDougall had little to say about the curiosity instinct relative to the other instincts. In fact, he argued that this instinct became progressively weaker in advanced animals like humans. Modern psychologists make the opposite argument, noting that advanced animals rely more on learning and hence need stronger mechanisms of knowledge seeking (Fredrickson, 1998).

Interests, in McDougall's view, are sentiments derived from the curiosity instinct and its emotion of wonder. Consistent with the heyday of associationism, McDougall thought that sentiments developed through simple repetition. A single encounter with an object that arouses the curiosity instinct creates a rudimentary sentiment. Repeated encounters would eventually create an articulated and powerful interest sentiment that energized activity relevant to the sentiment. If the person were deprived of later encounters, the sentiment would diminish. McDougall's curiosity instinct theory is thus a good example of a Motivation × Connection theory. The curiosity instinct provides the motivation to interact with an object, and repetition strengthens the connection between the motivation and the specific object.

Script Theory

Silvan Tomkins's (1976, 1979, 1987, 1991) script theory of personality may be the most complicated model of motivational development. Script theory addresses how emotional experiences develop (and fail to develop) into integrated guiding motives. The theory's basic unit is the scene. Tomkins (1991, p. 74) defines a *scene* as "the basic element in life as it is lived. The simplest, most primitive scene includes at least one affect and at least one object of that affect." A scene is a slice of emotional life, as subjectively perceived. Many scenes in a life remain completely isolated. People have experienced, for example, many distinct scenes in which they laughed at a joke or cursed at another driver. These transient scenes remain largely disconnected from other experiences; they thus have little impact on the structure and functioning of personality. But sometimes scenes become interconnected and develop into *scripts*, or sets of rules for predicting, interpreting, responding to, and controlling scenes. A script in this sense resembles conventional concepts of scripts and schemas (Schank & Abelson, 1977). Scripts are *selective*, in that they refer to certain types of scenes; *incomplete*, because it is impossible to specify what might happen in a scene; and more or less *accurate*. As a consequence, scripts are subject to constant revision from ongoing experience.

Script theory, then, conceives of life as a series of emotional scenes. Some scenes are combined into scripts, which are ways of understanding past and future life scenes. The key question is thus how scripts develop from scenes. This is the phenomenon of *magnification*, or the "connecting of one affect-laden scene with another affect-laden scene" (Tomkins, 1991, p. 75). Magnification is a cognitive process in which scenes are assembled into groups based on shared features. Perceiving the similarities among scenes enables them to be magnified into a script. The script's meanings are then extracted from the category of scenes.

To clarify these processes, consider how a simple "addiction script" could develop through magnification. A person who has been feeling depressed goes to a party and gets drunk. The alcohol reduces the negative affect and creates enjoyment. Here is a simple scene in which an object (alcohol) replaces negative affect with positive affect. This single scene could generate a script if the affect involved were extremely powerful. The more likely route is that similar scenes occur and combine. If the person again relieves negative affect with alcohol, these additional scenes will be sufficiently similar to combine into a nascent addiction script. In the second aspect of magnification, meaning is extracted from the scenes. In this example, the addiction script suggests that alcohol is a good way to reduce suffering. Transient emotional experiences have thus been consolidated into a stable, guiding idea.

At first scenes determine the development of scripts. Scripts later determine the course of scenes—they impose their interpretive lens over experience and influence the selection and creation of environments. When a person with an addiction script feels anxious, for example, the script specifies effective ways of dealing with anxiety, how and where to procure those ways, the likely outcomes, and so forth. The script thus magnifies additional scenes that are script relevant. Including additional emotional scenes can enlarge the script, which might eventually become monopolistic within the total set of scripts.

How does script theory explain interests? Although Tomkins never specifically addressed interests, they would fall under the category of *affluence scripts*, "which address neither the damages, the limitations, the contaminations, nor the toxicities of the human condition, but rather those scenes which promise *and* deliver intense and/or enduring positive affects of excitement or enjoyment. These script the sources of the individual's zest for life" (Tomkins, 1991, p. 107). Affluence scripts specify what the person will find to be fun and interesting. As with all scripts, they begin with a single scene involving an emotion and an object. An interest would develop when an activity arouses the interest affect—perhaps a high school student happens to watch a TV show on forensic science and is interested in how fiber evidence can catch untidy criminals. At this point it's impossible to know if an interest script will develop, unless the experience was so overwhelming as to form a script in itself. But perhaps the person runs across the same show the next week and is interested in how forensic scientists analyze questioned documents. Here we have the rudiments of script. These two experiences will cohere, given their core similarities, and be magnified by the emotional

feelings of interest. A simple meaning emerges from this nascent script—
"forensic science is fun," perhaps.

The person can now predict and anticipate circumstances that will
create interest—the script influences scenes. Should the student feel
bored, for example, the script specifies forensic science as a promising
possibility for interest and enjoyment. And, of course, this script can
expand into a broader, more guiding script if more emotional scenes are
added. The student might experience interest while reading a book on
criminal profiling—this set of experiences would be assimilated and further magnify the script. The script might eventually become strong
enough to influence major life decisions; the high school student might
apply to colleges with good programs in forensic science. If these years
of scenes continue to create interest and enjoyment, the script will influence career selection. But if they don't, then the script will change, either
by being demagnified (incorporating scenes with relatively minor affect)
or by including scenes with opposing affects.

Script theory is a general theory of personality. Tomkins's ideas are
much more complicated than our brief discussion suggests: he posits
different kinds of scripts, different aspects of similarity among emotional
experiences, and differences between scripts based on positive and negative affects (Carlson, 1981; Carlson & Carlson, 1984). At its core, however, script theory has a simple structure. Like McDougall's theory of the
curiosity instinct, script theory assumes that motivational development
depends on the intensity of motivation and the strength of connections.
In script theory, emotions provide the source of motivation, and the magnification process provides connections between the emotion and an object. As emotional experiences of interest are experienced more intensely,
and as the number of similar experiences of interest accumulate, the interest script becomes stronger. Script theory thus represents another Motivation × Connection theory.

The Selective Persistence of Interest

Almost anything can be interesting once. Only a few things ever become
endlessly fascinating, and nothing is endlessly fascinating for everyone.
A group of people, for instance, might be motivated by curiosity to attend
a lecture on F. Scott Fitzgerald. Most of them may simply enjoy the
lecture and never have anything serious to do with Fitzgerald again. Yet

some people might later read Fitzgerald's books; a few might dip into the critical literature, read a biography, and eventually develop a lasting interest in Fitzgerald and his work. Such situations are the starting point of Prenzel's (1992) theory of interest development. In his view, the essence of an interest is the freely chosen interaction with an object over several points in time. The key question is why people sometimes return to a previously interesting activity and other times never pursue it again.

As Prenzel (1992) notes, his theory "attempts to explain which of the processes and events that occur while a person is engaged with an object lead the person to (a) take up that object later (persistence), and (b) use certain actions to center activity around a certain aspect of the domain (selectivity)" (p. 79). *Cognitive conflict*, a key concept in Prenzel's theory, resembles Berlyne's collative variables (see chapter 2). Cognitive conflict occurs when an activity or object violates aspects of existing knowledge, creates uncertainties, poses novelties, or seems complex. Prenzel assumes that an initial attraction to an object (considered here broadly) leads the person to a first encounter. During the course of this encounter, certain experiences affect the likelihood of future persistence: resolving cognitive conflict; feeling interest, enjoyment, and flow; and perceiving "remaining potentially resolvable cognitive conflicts" (p. 84). Selectivity of future encounters—engaging with some objects and not others—stems from previous feelings of interest and enjoyment, and from perceptions of "unresolved, but resolvable, discrepancies between object schemata and the interest object" (p. 84). This theory can be seen as a neo-Berlyne model of interest development. People persist in an activity when the activity has enough conflict to be interesting. What motivates subsequent encounters is the conflict resulting from unresolved discrepancies. At the second encounter, the earlier conflict might be resolved. If no new conflict is created, then the person probably won't seek a third encounter.

Two things increase the likelihood that a person will develop a long-term interest in—that is, repeatedly interact with—an object. The first is the person's configuration of knowledge. Interacting with an object generally promotes elaborated knowledge of the object. As a person's knowledge becomes richer and more detailed, the capacity for conflict increases because there is more raw material for conflict. Someone new to Freud's ideas, for example, wouldn't be especially curious about a book entitled *Sigmund Freud and the Jewish Mystical Tradition* (Bakan, 1958)—it wouldn't conflict with anything. Yet someone familiar with Freud's anti-religious rationalism would experience conflict upon hearing of Freud's ideas in relation to ancient Kabbalistic texts. An interest can thus sustain itself by promoting the complex knowledge needed to ensure continued conflict.

The second aspect is the nature of the interest area. Many enduring interests have no ceiling on the amount of possible conflict. Few concrete objects can continually produce new cognitive conflict—this is why people rarely develop interests in single objects. A person might find a new computer interesting for a while, but it's hard to develop and sustain a long-term interest in a single computer. The computer's properties would become increasingly familiar, comprehensible, and predictable. Computers in general, however, are a possible interest because the evolving of technologies provides novelty, complexity, and uncertainty. A strength of Prenzel's view, then, is that it addresses why interests sometimes wither and die. When the person no longer experiences cognitive conflict, the area will cease to be interesting.

Interests Transforming From Different Motives

A second class of theories describes how new motives arise from ancestral motives that differ in some significant way. In our first class, nascent states of interest develop into full-fledged interests, and interests remain connected to their motivational origins. A curiosity sentiment, for example, remains connected to the curiosity instinct (McDougall, 1908/1960). In this second class of theories, interests develop from different motivational sources. The motive's qualitative nature is transformed; interests developing from different motives are no longer functionally connected to their origins. Three transformation perspectives will be considered: John Dewey's (1913) theory of direct and indirect interests, Gordon Allport's (1937, 1961) functional autonomy principle, and cognitive dissonance theory (Festinger, 1957).

Direct and Indirect Interests

In his slim volume *Interest and Effort in Education,* John Dewey (1913) examines two models of learning motivation. The *effort model* argues that learning requires rigid self-control and exertion of the will. The *interest model* argues that learning tasks need to be surrounded with fun or interesting trappings. Dewey rejected both positions because each assumes

that learning tasks are external to the self, and as a result learning requires exertion of the will or needs to be made interesting. Moreover,
both models promote *divided activity*—the child's attention is divided between the tedious task and what he or she really wants to do, or between
the diverting trappings of the task and the task's true boring nature. True
interest, in Dewey's view, creates *unified activity*—the entirety of the interested child is devoted to the interesting activity.

Dewey argued that children will inevitably pursue their own idiosyncratic interests—known as *direct interest*—although he doesn't specify
how direct interests develop. The educator needs to create *indirect interest*,
which arises when an object's relevance for a direct interest is revealed.
Dewey felt that "anything indifferent or repellent becomes of interest
when seen as a means to an end already commanding attention" (p. 25).
The best way to teach a child to read sheet music, for example, is to wait
until the child is already interested in playing the guitar. When the child
realizes that learning to read sheet music will further the interest in guitar, he or she will try to learn to read the sheet music in a self-sustained,
unified way. The educationally legitimate use of interest, then, is to show
how a learning task is integral to the child's ongoing interests: "It is one
thing to make, say, number interesting by merely attaching to it other
things that happen to call out a pleasurable reaction; it is a radically
different sort of thing to make it interesting by introducing it so that it
functions as a genuine means of carrying on a more inclusive activity"
(pp. 42–43). Dewey believed indirect interests will transform into direct
interests. The direct interest in the guitar "suffuses, saturates, and thus
transforms" (p. 25) the indirect interest in sheet music. An implication is
that people will acquire a lot of true interests if allowed autonomy in
their learning. As indirect interests are acquired, each newly developed
interest forks into new direct interests.

In sum, Dewey felt that people inevitably have interests, although
he didn't delve into how these arise. New interests develop when a person realizes that an object furthers an existing project of interest. The
object will eventually become an interest in its own right, although again
the nature of this process isn't detailed. A limitation of Dewey's theory
is its silence concerning the mechanisms involved—Dewey was more
interested in the pragmatic implications for educational practice than in
the dynamics of motivational development. Nevertheless, Dewey was
ahead of his time in anticipating Allport's (1937) theory of functional
autonomy and later theories of intrinsic motivation.

Functional Autonomy

Gordon Allport (1937, 1961) proposed a theory of functional autonomy in an "attempt to escape the limitations of uniform, rigid, abstract, backward-looking theories, and to recognize the spontaneous, changing, forward-looking, concrete character that much adult motivation surely has" (1961, pp. 226–227). *Functional autonomy* refers to a transformation process whereby a motive splits off from an extrinsic motivational source and becomes self-sustaining. A young boy, for example, may start playing basketball to become more popular at school. Over time, however, the interest in basketball may spin off from the original motive of social acceptance—the boy may begin enjoying basketball intrinsically. The interest in basketball has thus become functionally autonomous of the initial motive.

Allport (1961) described two types of functional autonomy. The first, *perseverative* functional autonomy, occurs when "a mechanism set in action because of one motive continues at least for a time to 'feed' itself" (p. 231). The second and more significant type is *propriate* functional autonomy. Allport (1961) refers to functionally autonomous propriate motives as interests, values, and sentiments (p. 236). These motives are considered propriate because they influence the selection of information, situations, and actions, and they organize and integrate the person's style of life. An interest in education reform, for example, influences other aspects of personality and the development of future intentions and motives.

Interests, then, result from a process of functional autonomy—but how do motives become functionally autonomous? Hall and Lindzey (1957) charge that "Allport provides no adequate account of the process or mechanism underlying functional autonomy. He tells us that the phenomenon takes place but provides no satisfactory explanation of how or why it takes place" (p. 291). Allport (1961) speculates about how motives become autonomous, but ultimately he assumes that if humans develop and differentiate, then human motives should develop and differentiate as well. Moreover, the functional autonomy principle doesn't consider whether motives might be intrinsic to begin with. Allport probably wouldn't quarrel with the notion that some motives are intrinsic without being transformed, but he didn't discuss the possibility.

Functional autonomy appears in a recent theory of interest development. Todt and Schreiber (1998, p. 34) argue that specific interests can emerge after "pressure to do something for a long time." They are more specific than Allport, however, regarding how repetition might promote the development of interests. Practicing an activity, when followed by positive emotional experiences, leads to expecting that the activity will yield pleasant experiences in the future. This expectancy promotes further practice and engagement, creating a cycle in which continued positive experiences strengthen the expectancy.

Cognitive Dissonance

Cognitive dissonance theory describes how consistency motivation influences behavior and attitudes (Festinger, 1957; Wicklund & Brehm, 1976). An aversive state of dissonance arises when two cognitions are inconsistent; the negative state motivates activity aimed at restoring consistency. One cause of dissonance is investing effort or discomfort in an activity. Because negative aspects of an activity are inconsistent with the investment, people will increase the attractiveness of the activity. This prediction was demonstrated in a classic experiment by Aronson and Mills (1959). College women were asked to join a discussion group on sexuality. Some of the women had to undergo an uncomfortable procedure—reading explicit sexual material before a male experimenter—to join the group. The participants then listened to the discussion, which was designed to be tedious and boring. Participants who experienced discomfort in order to join the group rated the discussion as more interesting and enjoyable relative to those who joined the group without an unpleasant initiation (Gerard & Mathewson, 1966). Interestingness can thus result from participating in tediousness.

Another experiment had people fish for flashlights containing money or no money (Aronson, 1960). The fishing task was either very easy or quite difficult. When the task was difficult and thus effortful, people preferred the color of the flashlights that didn't contain money. This effect presumably reflects one mode of reducing dissonance. If people invest effort to get something yet receive no external reward, dissonance will be created. People can restore consistency by transforming their attitudes toward the object so that the object becomes intrinsically rewarding. While preferences are not the same as what we mean by interest, this study shows how a lack of extrinsic incentives can increase the intrinsic value of an object.

An experiment by Weick (1964) shows how dissonance can be re-duced by increasing the interestingness of an activity. When a task offers no extrinsic reward, people can justify their effort by increasing the value and interestingness of the task. This increased value should then lead to greater effort, which may validate the increased value by resulting in greater performance. Participants worked on a concept-formation task and then rated it for interestingness. One group simply completed the experiment and received their credit. The experimenter told people in the second group that he was no longer allowed to give credits because he had disregarded admonitions from the subject-pool coordinator; nearly everyone agreed to participate nonetheless. Weick found that the group without an external incentive expended more effort on the cog-nitive task, performed better on the task, set more reasonable goals, and rated the experiment as significantly more interesting, compared to the group that received the external incentive.

Interests Reflecting Deeper Needs

A third class of theories explains interests in terms of deeper needs. In these theories, interests aren't conceptually primary; rather, they reflect the operations of more fundamental motivational systems. These theories tend to focus on understanding the deeper needs rather than the inter-ests. As a result, interests sometimes seem superficial—mere by-products of more important processes. We'll consider Freudian psychodynamics, Roe's theory of early need satisfaction, and learning theories that connect interests to patterns of reinforcement.

Psychodynamics

Freud argued that two foundational motives participate in all activity. The life instinct, Eros, involves uninhibited sexual impulses and self-preservation instincts. This motive is responsible for the tendency of liv-ing things to develop, merge, and differentiate: "Eros, by bringing about a more and more far-reaching combination of the particles into which living substance is dispersed, aims at complicating life and at the same time, of course, at preserving it" (Freud, 1923, p. 38). Eros is bounded by the death instinct, "the task of which is to lead organic life back into the inanimate state" (p. 38). This motive derives from the property of living matter that causes degeneration and death (Freud, 1920; see Bakan, 1966).

Interests develop because direct instinctual expression is usually dangerous or socially unacceptable. The energy is thus shunted into more acceptable behaviors that resemble the desired action. A person's destructive impulses may be displaced into playing football or bow hunting; a desire to smear feces can be conveniently displaced into painting. Freud assumed that interests aren't enjoyed for their own sake; they're valued only because they reduce instinctual tensions. Interests are merely substitute activities: they serve other psychological functions and thus don't represent intrinsic motivation. In fact, intrinsic motivation is impossible in Freud's model because the ego depends on other sources for energy (White, 1963). As Freud (1923) wrote: "The functional importance of the ego is manifested in the fact that normally control over the approaches to motility devolves upon it. Thus in its relation to the id it is like a man on horseback, who has to hold in check the superior strength of the horse; with this difference, that the rider tries to do so with his own strength while the ego uses borrowed forces" (p. 19).

In Freud's theory we see another example of a Motivation × Connection model of motivational development. The instincts provide diffuse, general motivation for activity; the ego selects certain activities as ways of reducing tension. Rewarding feelings of tension reduction form and strengthen connections between the drive and the specific activity.

Need Gratification

Roe (1957), one of vocational psychology's pioneers, proposed that interests stem from deeper social needs for love, affiliation, and acceptance. In early childhood, needs for love can be gratified or thwarted by the parents. When the parents gratify the child's needs, the child develops person-oriented interests. When the parents thwart the child's needs, however, the child develops non-person-oriented interests, such as interests in inanimate objects, animals, or abstract ideas. Complicating matters, Roe suggested that people with thwarted needs might compensate by developing person-oriented interests, although this remained a minor and untested part of her theory.

In the first version of her theory, Roe (1957) assumed six types of parent–child relations. Loving, protecting, and demanding relations promoted person-oriented interests in the child; rejecting, neglecting, and casual relations promoted non-person-oriented interests. Research did not support this theory, however. A study of women training as nurses and research scientists found no link between retrospective reports of parent–child relations and person-oriented interests (Grigg, 1959). A study of male students in chemistry, ministry, and theology also found no relations between reported parental treatment and interests, even when maternal and paternal treatment were considered separately (Switzer, Grigg, Miller, & Young, 1962).

In a revised version of the theory, Roe and Siegelman (1964) assumed that parent–child relations were dimensions rather than types. They also suggested that inadequate measurement may have hindered past studies. A comprehensive study tested the revised theory. Male and female engineers represented people with non-person-oriented interests; male and female social workers represented people with person-oriented interests. The engineers and social workers took part in structured interviews and completed a series of questionnaires assessing their interests and childhood experiences with each parent. Parents were described on the dimensions of loving–rejecting, casual–demanding, and degree of overt attention.

The expected differences in interests appeared between the occupational groups: social workers' interests were relatively more person-oriented. But interest differences failed to correspond with perceptions of childhood experience. Engineers and social workers didn't differ on any of the three dimensions of parental treatment, even when the data were viewed according to the gender of the parent or the gender of the participant. Internal analyses found some complicated interactions. Few significant findings were found for women; several were found for men, particularly male engineers. These effects further depended on the gender of the parent.

Overall, the pattern of findings was complex and did not support Roe's theory. In retrospect, we can understand why such a study would fail to find strong links between childhood experience and adult interests. Many aspects of personality, particularly idiosyncratic goals and motives, simply aren't strongly related to early experience (Lewis, 1997; McAdams, 1996). Retrospective reports of parental treatment also involve complex biases; sometimes retrospective reports diverge completely from actual measures of parental treatment (Lewis, 1997). Nevertheless, Roe deserves credit for being one of the first psychologists to test empirically a theory of interest development.

Learning Theories

During behaviorism's heyday, simple principles of learning were invoked to explain complex patterns of personality and culture (Dollard & Miller, 1950). Although usually lumped together into learning theory, these theories usually disagreed about the mechanisms of motivation and action. Thorndike's (1935b) brand of learning theory was dynamic and receptive to subjective variables. He assumed that "thought and action occur largely in the service of wants, interests, and attitudes and are stimulated and guided by them" (p. 4). These states were conceived as primarily motivational: "The active want, interest, or attitude may be considered as a force by itself or as a fraction more or less of the total dynamic system of the person at the time" (p. 4). Interests weren't defined much more specifically than this. Thorndike often used the term loosely to mean motivation, as in "self-preservation interests" or "social dominance interests."

Thorndike argued that the law of effect was the deeper motive underlying interests and attitudes: "We now know that the fundamental forces which can change desires and emotions, directing them into desirable channels, are the same as change ideas and actions. A human being learns to react to the situations of life by such and such wants, interests, and attitudes, as he learns to react to them by such and such percepts, ideas, and movements" (1935b, p. 217). To create interests in algebra, a teacher need only surround algebra with positive stimuli and provide rewards that "attach a satisfyingness to the desired behavior" (1935a, p. 22). Thorndike also suggested that interests can be created through role playing and imitation. Simply acting interested in athletics, for example, might lead to a genuine long-term interest.

Another learning theory viewed interests as by-products of drive reduction (Dollard & Miller, 1950). The deeper motive was drive, conceived in Hull's (1943) early theory as specific drives associated with hunger, thirst, sex, and pain, and in Hull's (1952) later theory as general stimulation. Reducing drive was pleasant, so anything that reduced drive (such as food) became preferred. Through principles of secondary reinforcement, anything related to the sources of drive reduction (such as the color of a goal box containing food) could become preferred as well. Secondary reinforcement could presumably operate several steps beyond the actual reinforcer. For example, an adolescent male might enjoy soccer because he plays soccer with his dad; he likes his dad because his dad feeds him; and he likes food because it directly reduces drive. Interests are thus several steps removed from the actual source of motivation. Despite its elegance, this theory is wrong on both mechanisms. Concepts of general drive faded from motivational psychology long ago (Bolles, 1967), and research never supported secondary reinforcement as a distal source of motivation. Theories of motivational development via secondary reinforcement were mostly speculative. Experiments found that secondary reinforcement is capricious and strongly dependent on continued primary reinforcement (Atkinson, 1964).

The two learning theories differ in their models of interests. Thorndike's theory is a connection theory. He is unconcerned with why people do something in the first place. Once they do it, however, then the connection to the activity can be stamped in by positive consequences associated with the activity. Hull's drive theory, in contrast, is a prototypical Motivation × Connection theory. Drive provides the motivation underlying interests; reinforcement owing to drive reduction forms and strengthens connections between the person and specific activities.

Chapter Summary and Conclusions

This chapter reviewed theories of how people develop idiosyncratic interests. At first glance, the diversity among the theories is striking. Psychologists have suggested several distal sources of interests: instincts associated with curiosity, sexuality, and death; emotional feelings of interest; unnerving feelings of cognitive dissonance; drive reduction and need gratification; and vague notions of attraction to an activity. Furthermore, many mechanisms that connect motivation to specific activities have been proposed: habits resulting from drive reduction, repetition of an activity, recognizing similarities among emotional events, and positive emotional consequences. Perhaps it isn't surprising that modern psychology avoids problems of motivational development. Past work certainly hasn't offered a theoretical consensus or much compelling evidence in support of any given theory. Most theories remain untested; in some cases it isn't clear how the theory could be tested.

Nevertheless, the diversity of thought on the origins of interests shouldn't obscure the many theoretical continuities. Most theories have taken the same approach to explaining how interests develop: a general source of motivation interacts with a mechanism that connects the motivation to a specific activity. Throughout the chapter we have seen examples of Motivation × Connection theories, although the sources of the motivation and the types of connections have varied. Some theories have suggested that interests stem from intrinsic motivation, such as emotions of interest or curiosity instincts. Others have suggested that the source of motivation is extrinsic—such as drives or aggressive instincts—although modern theories seem to favor intrinsic motivation.

One reason for reviewing past theories of interest development was to prefigure a new theory, described in chapter 6. Like many theories presented in this chapter, our new approach involves a Motivation × Connection structure. This theory is founded on assumptions about how emotions and knowledge of emotions influence motivational development. We'll see how the development of interests involves the development of causal knowledge regarding how activities influence emotional experience. Some new research supporting the theory is presented, including experiments that manipulate the development of interests.

6

How Do Interests Develop?
Bridging Emotion and Personality

In chapter 5 we explored the problem of motivational development: the study of how motives form and change. The development of interests, as an instance of motivational development, has received a lot of theoretical attention. Psychologists have explained the development of interests with many different theories, mechanisms, and predictions ranging from psychodynamic drives to cognitive dissonance. Most of the theories remain unsupported by research, although they illustrate the variety of approaches to the problem of motivational development.

In this chapter we will consider a new theory of how interests develop. With such a substantial body of thought on the topic, it is tempting to draw eclectically from past theories (Allport, 1968)—take a few effective constructs from here, a well-tested prediction from there, and organize them into a single model. Organizing past theories under one roof might yield an interesting model, but such models tend to be noncommittal: they often fail to make new, specific predictions.[1] To develop a theory of how interests develop, we'll return to the theme that guides this book—the distinction between interest and interests, emotion and personality, transient experience and enduring psychological structures.

---

1. An earlier paper on interest and interests tried to organize past theories into a general model (Silvia, 2001b). Like most models, it couldn't function as a theory—it didn't make clear predictions that distinguished it from other theories. The theory developed in this chapter supplants past writings.

This chapter bridges emotion and personality by describing how the experience of interest influences the development of enduring interests. In brief, the theory argues that the development of interests involves the development of emotional knowledge. The capacity for meta-emotional experience enables people to make attributions for the causes of their emotions and to form expectations regarding the likely emotional effects of different actions. This theory, by emphasizing cognitive and meta-cognitive processes, breaks from past theorizing and offers new predictions about the dynamics of motivational development.

After criticizing past theories for failing to test their hypotheses empirically (chapter 5), we'll need to back up our predictions with evidence. After reviewing the basics of the emotion–attribution theory, we'll present some experiments that address the theory's main predictions. These experiments, possibly the only laboratory studies that manipulate the development of interests, offer solid preliminary support for the theory. We conclude this chapter by considering some implications for the broader problem of motivational development.

Thinking About Emotions

In spending so much time thinking about emotions, people forget that they *can* think about their emotions. People are not passive recipients of experience. Humans, by virtue of their cognitive prowess, can have *meta-emotional experience*. People can become aware of the fact that they are experiencing an emotion (Russell, 2003), they can think about this emotional experience (Seager, 2002), and they can think about their thoughts about their emotions. It is difficult to exaggerate the significance of meta-emotional experience for the psychology of emotions. The ability to think about emotions enables emotional knowledge: people can analyze the causes of the emotion, consider how other people would feel in the same situation, and form expectations about how events might affect emotional experience. This is one of the most critical differences between the emotional lives of nonhuman animals and humans. Other creatures can be afraid, for example, but they don't know they are afraid or represent their fear conceptually.

We will emphasize one particular aspect of emotions that people can think about: the causes of emotions. The process of *causal attribution* involves organizing events into cause–effect relationships (Duval & Duval,

1983; Försterling, 2001; Heider, 1958; Hewstone, 1989). Attributions are fundamental to understanding and navigating the social world. As Heider (1958) contends, "Man wants to know the sources of his experiences, whence they come, how they arise, not only because of his intellectual curiosity, but also because such attribution allows him to understand his world, to predict and control events involving himself and others" (p. 146). It's hard to imagine how people could make decisions, influence others, and develop plans without using their knowledge of the causal structure of the environment, of "what causes what." Forecasting the likely consequences of different decisions, imagining how another person will react to different influence strategies, and considering how different aspects of a plan interlock rely on knowledge of cause–effect relationships.

People make attributions for all kinds of events, including emotional experiences. Just as they can think about the causes of earthquakes, divorces, and computer crashes, people can think about why they feel the way they feel. Sometimes the attribution process is explicit and conscious (Krull & Anderson, 1997). In these situations, people consciously reason about why they feel happy, why they're in a bad mood, and why they're angry. More commonly, however, the attribution process is automatic. The automaticity of attribution is important for understanding attributions for emotional experiences. The attribution process is constructive and inferential, but people usually experience attribution as perceptual. Causal attributions can be so automatic that people subjectively feel that the causal structure of the world is apprehended rather than constructed (Heider, 1944, 1958; Schlottman, 2001). As Russell (2003) notes, "the phenomenal experience of most attributed affects fails to recognize any attribution process; instead, one subjectively experiences a simple affective reaction to the Object" (p. 159). When an emotion and a likely cause are both salient, the attribution process operates outside of awareness. When a menacing snake slithers onto the trail, for instance, people will experience fear—the attribution of the experience of fear to the snake is not usually experienced. Mere temporal and spatial contiguity can lead to the perception of a causal connection between two events (Duval & Duval, 1983).

Why should we care about attributions for emotions? How does this inform the problem of how interests develop? The relevance for our problem lies in three features of causal attributions. First, causal attributions can be inaccurate. The perceived cause of an event need not be the event's real cause. Second, attributions for past events affect expectations for future events (Weiner, 1986). Third, attributions guide action, regardless of their accuracy (Duval & Silvia, 2001; Heider, 1958). The perceived cause of an event influences responses to the event.

(Mis)Understanding the Causes of Emotions

Causal attributions would be uninteresting to psychologists if those attributions were always accurate. Indeed, the enterprise of science would be superfluous if everyday people usually made accurate attributions for physical and psychological events. Perceived causality and true causality diverge, although how much they diverge is unclear unless we know an event's true cause. The fundamental flexibility of attributions is illustrated by the diversity of attributions that people make for the same events. Was an earthquake caused by natural processes, wrathful deities, or the earth's taking revenge for humanity's pollution? Is an image of Jesus found on a grilled tortilla (Nickell, 1993) a divine message, a hoax, or an expected consequence of grilling hundreds of tortillas? Clearly, not all attributions can be right.

Furthermore, processes irrelevant to causality influence the attributions that people make. For instance, people tend to attribute causality to salient stimuli, even when salience is unrelated to the effect. For example, purely linguistic features of descriptions, such as the positions of subjects and objects in a sentence (Pryor & Kriss, 1977) or the type of verb (Rudolph & Försterling, 1997), affect causal attributions. If people can see only one of two people in a conversation, they tend to attribute causality for the conversation's outcome to the person they can see, even when randomly assigned to see one person or the other (Lassiter, Geers, Munhall, Ploutz-Snyder, & Breitenbecher, 2002). Finally, motivations influence causal attributions (Sedikides & Strube, 1997). Many experiments illustrate the tendency to make self-serving attributions for success and failure (Duval & Silvia, 2002), to blame others for one's own failure (Silvia & Duval, 2001), and to make attributions that bolster one's beliefs and attitudes (Regan, Straus, & Fazio, 1974).

People can be wrong about the causes of their emotions, just as they can be wrong about the causes of anything else. Consider a person who feels deeply unhappy. This person could make many different attributions for the negative emotional experience. Perhaps the unhappiness is attributed to an uncontrollable biological problem, to having unrealistic standards, or to several weeks of cloudy days. Perhaps the person attributes it to anxieties experienced during a past life as a clam (see Evans, 1974, p. 45). At least one of these attributions is always wrong, and the others are not correct in all instances of unhappiness.

Why are attributions for emotional experiences often inaccurate? Three features of emotions create disconnections between the true and perceived causes of emotions. First, the causes of emotions often occur automatically and outside of awareness (Smith & Kirby, 2001). Conscious appraisals of events can create emotions (Lazarus, 1991; Weiner, 1985), but unconscious and implicit appraisals play a huge role in emotional life (van Reekum & Scherer, 1997). Many of the processes involved in the generation of emotion resist introspection (Wilson, 2002); some might be inaccessible in principle (LeDoux, 1996). Indeed, some researchers argue that affective states could themselves be unconscious, although this is controversial (Berridge & Winkielman, 2003; Stapel, Koomen, & Ruys, 2002). Given the complexities of emotional processing, it's unrealistic to expect people to comprehend the causes of their feelings.

Second, people's concepts of emotions (Russell & Lemay, 2000) hinder an accurate understanding of the causes of emotions. People have "lay theories" of how emotions work. When introspecting about emotions, people can reach erroneous judgments by applying incorrect theories of emotions (Wilson, 2002). For instance, people believe that the weather strongly affects their mood, but the weather's effects on positive and negative affect are actually tiny (Watson, 2000). Similarly, the common belief in "blue Mondays"—that one's mood is worst on Monday—appears to be wrong (Watson, 2000). A person's current causal knowledge influences the plausibility of a causal explanation, and in some cases existing causal knowledge may be retrieved and applied to an event automatically (Krull & Anderson, 1997). A social group that believes that human unhappiness reflects unresolved tragedies from past lives (Evans, 1974) provides its members with a set of attributions that members of other groups lack.

Third, people make wrong attributions for their emotions because emotional states do not inherently indicate their causes. The conscious experience of emotion is not stamped with information about its true cause (Clore & Colcombe, 2003). This contradicts our subjective experience of emotions; as Russell (2003) pointed out, an emotion feels like it contains causal information. If emotional states indicated their true causes, it would be difficult to supplant the built-in attribution with a new attribution. Many experiments on *misattribution*, however, show that it is easy to manipulate attributions for emotional experiences. When provided with a plausible (but incorrect) cause for their feelings, people will attribute their feelings to the new cause. As a result, the expectations and actions promoted by the emotion change as well. The term *misattribution* is unfortunate because it implies that the true attribution is the default and that inaccurate attributions will come about only through external intervention. Nevertheless, the basic point—that attributions for emotions are flexible—has been demonstrated for many affective states.

One experiment manipulated attributions for the experience of fear (Ross, Rodin, & Zimbardo, 1969). Threats of electric shock made people afraid, but some people were led to attribute their fear to unusual bursts of noise. Changing the attribution for fear changed the behavioral consequences of fear. When people attributed fear to the shock, they preferred to work on a task that would allow them to avoid the shock. When people misattributed their fear to the noise, they preferred to work on a task that would yield money instead of the task that would avert the shocks.

In another experiment, people misattributed negative affect due to cognitive inconsistency to a placebo pill. Participants wrote an essay advocating a position that contradicted their true attitude (Zanna & Cooper, 1974). Such inconsistency creates an unpleasant affective state known as cognitive dissonance (Elliot & Devine, 1994; see chapter 5). The unpleasant state motivates attitude change in the direction of restoring congruity. Some participants took a placebo pill, which they expected to arouse unpleasant, anxious feelings. Others expected the placebo pill to create pleasant, relaxed feelings. People in a control condition did not take a placebo pill. People in the control condition changed their attitudes to match their behavior, thus replicating many other experiments. When people thought that the pill was the cause of their unpleasant feelings, however, they showed no attitude change. Furthermore, people who thought the pill should be relaxing showed amplified attitude change, relative to the control group, presumably because the experience of negative affect despite a relaxing pill implied a particularly large attitude-behavior discrepancy.

In a recent misattribution experiment (Duval & Silvia, 2001, pp. 45–47), people were told that they failed a task. Attributions for the unpleasant experience of failure were manipulated. In one condition, people were led to believe that their lack of ability was the most likely cause of failure. In another condition, people were told that the small, cramped cubicle was known to make people uncomfortable and was thus a likely cause of their negative feelings. This manipulation affected the attributions that people made for their feelings. Furthermore, the attributions in turn affected later performance. People who attributed failure to themselves tried harder to improve their performance on a second task. People who attributed failure to the cubicle did not increase their effort.

Many other misattribution experiments could be described, including misattributions for feelings of empathy (Coke, Batson, & McDavis, 1978), anxiety (Dutton & Aron, 1974), general arousal (Schachter & Singer, 1962), and positive and negative mood states (e.g., Cooper, 1998; Gendolla, 2000; Keltner, Locke, & Audrain, 1993; Ottati & Isbell, 1996; Schwartz & Clore, 1983). Misattribution is clearly a robust finding. Taken together, these experiments make an important point: attributions for emotions are not "built in" to the emotional experience. The flexibility of attributions for emotions can explain why similar emotions can lead to different expectations and behaviors.

Effects of Attributions on Expectations

Attributions are significant because they influence the formation of expectancies. "Through attribution," Heider (1958) argues, "an experience leads to further beliefs important for prediction and control" (p. 162). By analyzing the causes of current and past events, people can form predictions about the likely outcomes of future events. The reason, according to Heider (1958), is simple. The process of attribution involves the identification of stable features of the environment. People impute dispositional properties to objects and persons. Locating dispositions enables predictions about what the objects and people will do. For example, if someone attributes a mean remark to another person's "aggressiveness," then the person would expect the antagonist to be mean in the future—unfriendly behavior follows from possessing a disposition of aggressiveness. Understanding the causal structure of the environment thus enables people to predict and control future events. If the effect Y is attributed to cause X, then people can expect that bringing X about will entail Y. If I attribute another person's warm smile to a joke I just told, then I expect that I can evoke future smiles by telling jokes.

A vast amount of research, reviewed by Weiner (1986, chap. 4), demonstrates that attributional information influences the formation of expectations. Consistent with Heider's reasoning, the perceived *stability* of a cause seems particularly important in expectancy formation. If people attribute success to a stable personal characteristic, then they expect to succeed again later on. Conversely, if people attribute failure to a stable personal characteristic, then they expect future failures. The same principle applies to attributions for the actions of other people (Weiner, 1991, 1995, 2000). Attributing someone's tardiness to a stable property, such as laziness, leads to expecting the person to be late in the future. Attributing tardiness to an unstable event like car trouble does not lead to expecting future lateness.

Naturally, attributions for emotions follow the same principle. Attributing an emotional state to an object influences expectations about the object's future effects on emotions. Consider a young man who sees a foreign film for the first time and experiences interest and happiness. The person can make various attributions for the causes of these emotions. He can attribute them to the foreign movie: the movie induced the positive emotional feelings. Perhaps he attributes the feelings to his companion, a woman he snuggled with during the movie. The expectations created by these attributions diverge. If he perceives that the movie caused his positive emotions, then he would expect to enjoy similar foreign movies and expect that similar people (such as his friends) would like the movie, too. If he perceives that his companion caused the positive emotions, then he would not necessarily expect to like similar movies or expect his friends to like the movie. Instead, the person would expect to like more or less any movie viewed with the same companion.

Many attribution theorists have pointed out a resemblance between everyday attribution processes and the rigorous methods of scientific inference (Heider, 1958; Kelley, 1967, 1973; Weiner, 1986).[2] Scientists also seek the stable causes of events—for example, appraisals influence interest (chapter 2), the coherence of a text influences text-based interest (chapter 3), and self-efficacy beliefs influence the development of vocational interests (chapter 7). When an experiment suggests that an inde-

2. Of course, scientists and the general public differ fundamentally in how they test their predictions and the types of evidence that are considered relevant. This is why scientific predictions about the natural and social world are more accurate than common-sense predictions (Sagan, 1995).

pendent variable affects a dependent variable, then scientists expect (1) that similar instances of the independent variable will have the same effect on the dependent variable, and (2) that the same instance of the independent variable will have the same effect on different instances of the dependent variables. For example, if viewing complex polygons affects self-reports of interest, we expect that complex music, complex paintings, and complex texts will also affect self-reports of interest. Furthermore, we expect that viewing complex polygons will affect different measures of interest, such as self-reports, looking time, choices of what to view, and so forth. Fulfilling these expectations gives validity to the theory's cause–effect predictions.

The attribution-expectation scenario can thus be recast in research terms. In predicting whether or not seeing a second foreign movie would be fun, our dependent variable, the person could consider two independent variables: the type of movie and the presence or absence of his date. If the positive emotions were attributed to the movie—most of the variance in enjoyment was explained by the type of movie—then the "type of movie" variable would be seen as critical. He would expect to enjoy a second foreign film, independent of the presence or absence of his date. If the emotions were attributed to the date, however, then the "presence of date" variable would be seen as critical. He would not expect to enjoy another foreign movie alone.

Perhaps a less prosaic example will reinforce the relationship between attributions and expectations. Consider an unhappy person who, after moping about the house all day, goes to a religious service and feels much happier (Proudfoot & Shaver, 1975). Attributing the positive emotions to divine intervention will lead to one set of expectations: solitary prayer could increase happiness. Attributions to a change of scene will lead to other expectations: going anywhere, religious or otherwise, could increase happiness. Attributions to the social contact involved in the service will lead to yet another set of expectations: meeting people, religious or otherwise, could increase happiness. Each explanation for the change in emotional experience implies different ways of repairing a negative mood in the future.

Inaccurate attributions are a major source of inaccurate expectations. When people misunderstand the causes of their feelings, their inaccurate causal model will yield inaccurate predictions of future events. Research on *affective forecasting* shows that people's predictions of how they would feel in a situation differ substantially from their actual feelings when placed in the situation (Gilbert & Wilson, 2000). The wrong expectations stem from incorrect ideas about how emotions work (Gilbert, Pinel, Wilson, Blumberg, & Wheatley, 1998). For example, people believe that having control over a decision will make them happier with the outcome of the decision, when in fact having control can breed regret owing to thinking about what could have been (Gilbert & Ebert, 2002). Because control does not necessarily cause greater happiness, expectations formed from this causal belief can be unreliable.

Effects of Attributions on Actions

Thus far we have learned how attributions affect expectations; now we'll consider how they affect actions. Causal knowledge has a special status in the psychology of action and self-regulation. If people lacked causal knowledge, the world would be baffling, mysterious, and intractable. Knowledge of the environment's causal structure, of what causes what and why, enables people to predict future events and to exercise control over the environment (Heider, 1958). Attributions for the cause of an event imply ways of promoting or preventing future occurrences of the event. People thus use attributions to guide their plans, intentions, and actions because attributions illuminate the relationship between ends and means, between goals and ways to achieve them.

For example, consider people who attribute their unhappiness to unresolved tragedies from past lives as clams (Evans, 1974). This attribution influences expectations about future unhappiness (Weiner, 1986)—the cause is stable and internal, and thus it is likely to persist unless something is done about it. What can be done about it? Knowledge of the cause aids in developing plans for action. If unhappiness is attributed to woes during clamhood, then those woes are the target for action. Special therapies for past lives will then seem plausible as a means to reach the end of alleviating unhappiness. Attributions do not furnish all of the means–end information needed for planning, but they provide the essential clues about what is causing the problem and how it might be changed.

We have already seen some examples of the role of attributions in guiding actions. The experiments on misattribution show how attributions for emotions affect responses to the emotions. Attributing fear to shock increases attempts to avoid the shock instead of gaining money;

attributing fear to something else increases a preference for gaining money instead of avoiding the shock (Ross et al., 1969). If people attribute negative affect to a discrepancy between their attitudes and actions, then they change their attitudes to match their actions. If they attribute the negative affect to a pill, then they do not change their attitudes (Zanna & Cooper, 1974). People who attribute feelings of empathy to a victim's plight offer to help the person (Coke et al., 1978, Study 1); people who attribute empathy to a pill volunteer to help less often. Attributing the experience of failure to oneself promotes attempts to improve one's skills; attributing the experience to the cramped research cubicle does not increase practice (Duval & Silvia, 2001, p. 45).

Many other examples of attributional effects on actions can be found. When people attribute their poor performance to a lack of effort, they change their effort by trying harder on a second trial. When people attribute failure to an unrealistic standard, they change the standard to be more moderate, and, critically, they do not try harder on a second trial (Duval & Lalwani, 1999). The perceived cause of the problem—one's effort or one's standards—determines what people try to change in response to the problem. All of these findings illustrate direct effects of attributions: identifying an event's cause implies ways of changing, maintaining, or recreating the event.

Attributions can affect activity indirectly through attributional effects on expectations. In decision making, for example, people forecast the likely emotional consequences of choosing various decision alternatives. Decision affect theory assumes that people use expected emotions as guides to choice (Mellers, 2000; Mellers & McGraw, 2001). Based on their causal knowledge of emotions—which events arouse which feelings—people estimate how different outcomes will make them feel. A student planning to study abroad, for example, may face a decision between studying in Australia or in Germany. Her expected emotions associated with each option—perhaps enjoyment from learning a foreign language versus conversing in English, the pleasantness of each country's weather, and the interest and enjoyment from quick trips to neighboring countries—will guide the eventual decision. Expectations about the emotional effects of decisions predict the decisions people make better than classic theories of decision making based on subjective utility (Mellers, Schwartz, & Ritov, 1999). This research thus nicely shows how causal beliefs about emotions affect action by affecting expectations.

Summary

We have reviewed three important features of attributions for emotions. Attributions can inaccurately represent the causes of events; attributions provide expectations for future events; and attributions guide actions. Taken together, these features make causal attribution one of psychology's profound, foundational processes (Heider, 1958; Hewstone, 1989). While reviewing the basics of attribution, we've seen hints of attribution's significance for the problem of motivational development. Now is the time to delineate the role of emotions and attributions in the development of interests.

Emotions, Attributions, and the Development of Interests

People do not experience emotions passively—they think about their emotions. Cognitions about emotions, such as causal attributions, as well as metacognitions about emotions, such as expectations and plans based on attributions, collectively form the basis of emotional knowledge. The development of interests, according to the emotion–attribution theory, involves the development of emotional knowledge regarding the emotional experience of interest. Attributions for the experience of interest inform people *why* they feel interest and *what* made them feel interested, and by influencing expectations and providing means–end knowledge, *how* they could create feelings of interest in the future. In this theory, cognitive and metacognitive processes form the bridge between momentary experience and enduring aspects of personality. The theory, while straightforward and simple, is nevertheless innovative in its approach to the development of interests.

The emotion–attribution theory of interest development makes specific predictions about how to manipulate the development of interests. Interests require (1) emotional experience, and (2) emotional knowledge. We'll review each component in turn.

Emotional Experience

Emotional experience consists of the momentary feelings that characterize subjective experience: discrete emotions such as interest, happiness, anger, and fear; general positive and negative moods; and diffuse, undifferentiated feelings of affect (see chapter 1). Emotional experience is essentially conscious, although people are not always conscious of their conscious experience of emotion. Emotions can be consciously experienced without being consciously represented (Russell, 2003; Seager, 2002). The experience of fear, for instance, can pervade conscious experience, but people may realize that they are afraid only after the fearful event has passed.

Among the emotions, interest and happiness are central to the development of interests. The role of feelings of interest in the development of interests should be obvious. Experiencing interest and attributing it to an activity leads to expecting that activity to arouse interest in the future. Happiness plays a role as well by rewarding the resolution of incongruities and the achievement of understanding. Interest and happiness, according to Tomkins (1962), serve different functions (see chapter 1). Interest engages people with new, complex, uncertain, and inconsistent activities; happiness engages people with familiar and simple activities. Although seemingly opposing, interest and happiness work together. Interest ensures that people will seek out and learn new things; happiness ensures that people will not neglect what is safe, certain, and effective (Fredrickson, 1998).

Emotional Knowledge

Emotional knowledge—cognitive understanding of emotional experience—consists of *causal attributions* for emotional experience; *expectations* about the effects of events on emotions; and *means–end knowledge* about how elements of the environment affect emotional experience. We have already described causal attributions, but our earlier point deserves repeating: emotional experiences do not come with built-in attributions (Russell, 2003). The cause of an emotion may feel self-evident, given the often automatic nature of attribution (Krull & Anderson, 1997), but attributions are involved nevertheless. If attributions for emotions are flexible, then the emotional experience of interest could be attributed to many factors. To recycle an example, the young man who felt enjoyment while seeing his first foreign film could have attributed his feelings to the film or to his date.

Attributions for past emotions influence expectations about how future events will affect emotional experience. If people attribute their anxiety during public speaking to the presence of an audience, then they will expect to feel anxious when speaking in front of other audiences. If anxiety is attributed to inadequate preparation, then people would expect to feel anxious only if they are unprepared for the talk. These expectations may be inaccurate, of course, if the original attribution diverged from the true cause of anxiety. Someone who attributed his or her anxiety to inadequate preparation may have felt just as anxious at a subsequent talk, despite substantial preparation. The original attribution would change, given the lack of covariance between preparation and anxiety, toward attributing anxiety to the presence of an audience (Försterling, 2001; Kelley, 1967). As the attribution changes, the ensuing expectations change as well.

Finally, attributions and expectations influence means–end knowledge regarding emotional experience. By means–end knowledge, we mean beliefs about the contingencies between events and emotions and how the contingencies can be manipulated. For example, consider a person who attributes her lively positive mood to the triple espresso she just drank. This attribution provides expectations about the likely future consequences of imbibing triple espresso drinks, and as a result it suggests a means (espresso) to reach a certain end (happiness). Attributions form the cornerstone of means–end knowledge because they illuminate the causal structure of the environment (Heider, 1958), but attributions are not the only influence. People learn about means–end relationships vicariously, and thus they needn't experience the event to understand its emotional consequences. Likewise, attributions and expectations may not contain information about how to manipulate the contingencies. For example, people may feel happy because they feel completely connected with their environment (Csikszentmihalyi, 1975), but this attribution might not imply ways of creating a feeling of complete connection. Thus, people can understand a cause–effect relationship yet be ignorant about how to bring about the cause.

The Development of Interests

If interests arise through attributions for emotional experience and the consequences of such attributions, then we can make predictions about how to manipulate the development and change of interests. First, changing emotional experience will change the development of interests. Creating positive emotional experiences is obviously relevant, but all of the emotions play important roles in the origination of interests. Whereas interest and enjoyment facilitate the development of interests, negative emotions inhibit interest development by changng people's expectations regarding an activity's emotional consequences. If people experience negative emotions during a formerly interesting activity, they will make attributions for these emotions. Should they attribute these emotions to the activity, their expectations about the emotional consequences of the activity will shift. Expectations of interest and enjoyment will seem less plausible, and expectations of negative emotions will seem more plausible.

For example, consider someone who sees a magic show, attributes the feelings of interest and enjoyment to the activity, and then begins to dabble in sleight-of-hand magic. The initial hours of learning the basics of magic tricks may be interesting and fun, but the subsequent hours of practicing complicated feats of dexterity may be frustrating. These feelings of frustration may be attributed to the activity. If so, the nascent interest in magic may wither when the expectations of the emotional consequences of the activity change. Instead of expecting interest and enjoyment, the person will expect feelings of frustration. To avoid these feelings, the person may avoid the activity, thus bringing the hobby to an end.

Second, the development of interests can be influenced by manipulating attributions for an emotion. If ideas about the cause of an emotion affect what people expect and do, then changing these ideas will affect interests. The experiments on misattribution reviewed earlier, for example, demonstrate how providing alternative plausible causes diverts attributions for emotions to inaccurate possible causes and that activity then follows the inaccurate attribution. Furthermore, the causes of emotions can be ambiguous, such as instances of free-floating affective states and emotions evoked by processes operating outside of awareness (see Johnson-Laird & Oatley, 2000). In such cases, the role of attributions is more apparent. Attributions for an emotion may not always be easy to manipulate because the contiguity between an experience and a possible cause (Duval & Duval, 1983; Hewstone, 1989) and the salience of a possible cause (Pryor & Kriss, 1977) can be sufficient to promote an attribution. Nevertheless, attributions for emotions are in principle flexible

(Russell, 2003). As a result, we can manipulate the development of interests by manipulating the attributions people make for their experiences of interest.

Testing the Emotion–Attribution Theory

The emotion–attribution theory predicts that several processes—emotions, attributions, expectations, and means–end knowledge—jointly influence the development of interests. Thus far, two experiments have tested the theory's central predictions about the role of attributions for emotions in interest development (Silvia, 2004). The basic structure of these experiments involves creating feelings of interest, manipulating attributions for the emotional experience, and then measuring beliefs and actions that reflect the development of emotional knowledge.

In the first experiment, people viewed a video of magic tricks. In a magic attribution condition, people responded to open-ended questions that promoted attributions of their positive emotional state to the magic tricks. In a misattribution condition, people wrote about other factors that could have influenced their current feelings (e.g., positive events during the last week, the presence of other people in the room, positive events prior to the experiment). In a control condition, people simply watched the video. Attributions for emotions had the expected effects on markers of interest development. People in the misattribution condition expressed the least desire to learn more about magic tricks and to receive a free booklet describing simple card tricks. They were also the least likely to volunteer for a later study related to magic tricks.

In a second experiment, people viewed interesting asemic poems—improvised writing at "an infra-verbal level" (Gaze, 2000, p. 1)—on a computer screen. In a misattribution condition, people were told that positive images had been subliminally presented in between the asemic poems. After showing them the ostensible positive images (e.g., smiling babies), the experimenter said that the subliminal images probably influenced their mood (see Gilbert & Gill, 2000). Relative to people in a control condition, people who attributed their positive mood to subliminal influence reported less interest in asemic poetry and less desire to learn more about that style of writing. Furthermore, people in the misattribution condition were less likely to volunteer for a related study or to take a free booklet of asemic poems.

Taken together, these experiments support the basic assumptions of the emotion–attribution theory. The development of interests depended on causal attributions for the momentary experience of interest and happiness. Attributions during the experiment predicted wanting to learn more about the topic, volunteering for related studies, and taking home information about magic or poetry. When attributions were diverted to other factors, such as aspects of the environment and subliminal pictures, then the experience of interest during the experiment did not predict indicators of interest development. These experiments stand out from other studies of the development of interests. Nearly all past studies used correlational methods. Only a handful of studies have tried to manipulate the development of interests in the laboratory (see chapter 7); none of them considered attribution as the key mechanism. Additional aspects of the emotion–attribution theory certainly require empirical tests, but we can consider the findings thus far as encouraging.

Implications of the Emotion–Attribution Theory

Stability of Interests

Understanding how and why interests change is a task that all theories of interest development must face. Some theories flounder on this point. If interests are rooted in ungratified needs during childhood (Roe, 1957), for instance, why should adult interests develop, grow, and abate? The fixed experience in childhood does not seem to explain the variation during adulthood. According to the emotion–attribution theory, interests are categories of emotional knowledge. To have an enduring interest in something is to know that certain things have created interest in the past, to expect that they can create interest in the future, and to know how to bring about feelings of interest. Defining interests in terms of emotional knowledge provides a new perspective on the stability of interests.

In the emotion–attribution theory, interests change as a result of continued experience with the activity. Emotional knowledge is fundamentally dynamic, changing as new emotional experiences give rise to new attributions and their resulting expectations. In this sense, the emotion–attribution theory of interests does not view interests as "fixed," "consolidated," or "crystallized" (Swanson, 1999). Interests should be stable only to the degree that subjective experience and its interpretation remain stable. For example, consider an undergraduate student who enrolls in the course Introduction to Psychology. She may find the whole class interesting, and, after attributing interest to the course's content (as opposed to the instructor, for example), she decides to take advanced courses in psychology. Her broad interest in psychology will change as her emotional responses to specific areas of psychology diverge. If she finds social psychology tedious and attributes her boredom to the content, then her broad interest in psychology differentiates to exclude social psychology. If she particularly enjoys her class in developmental psychology and attributes enjoyment to that, then her interest becomes even more differentiated. Ultimately, she may develop an interest in specific areas of developmental psychology as her emotional responses to different areas of the field diverge. Perhaps she finds theory-of-mind research interesting and attachment research uninteresting.

Expectations are another source of differentiation in interests. A current interest can imply other potentially interesting activities. When planning their actions, people can forecast the likely emotional outcomes of a new activity by reflecting on their attributions for past activities. This metacognitive aspect of emotional knowledge enables sophisticated emotion-regulation strategies. For example, consider a young man who is invited to go rock climbing. He has never climbed rocks before, but he knows that he enjoys hiking. If he thinks he enjoys hiking because it is active and takes place outdoors, then he would expect to enjoy rock climbing. If he thinks he enjoys hiking because it affords opportunities for chatting with his friends, he may not expect to like a relatively solitary activity like rock climbing. Thoughts about attributions and expectations let people predict the emotional consequences of future events. This is not simply a matter of finding activities that resemble activities that one already finds interesting—the resemblance must be causally relevant.

Bridging Emotion and Personality

The relationship between emotions and personality is a theme that appears throughout this book. Describing the role of emotion in personality can be tricky, given the many ways in which the two intersect. The most widely known bridges between emotion and personality involve emotional traits. Trait theories seek abstract individual differences in the frequency or intensity of certain emotional experiences (Watson, 2000). Models of trait anxiety, hostility, neuroticism, and depression are good examples. Individual differences related to interest—such as trait curiosity, sensation seeking, and openness to experience (chapter 4)—are an application of this approach within the psychology of interest. Others bridge emotion and personality at the idiosyncratic level of life stories (Haviland-Jones & Kahlbaugh, 2000), such as case studies of the emotional lives of famous psychologists (Magai & Haviland-Jones, 2002). The biographical approach offers incisive analyses of the developmental consequences of emotions over the course of a life. Such studies can have problems identifying specific mechanisms common to all people, although this not always the goal of the research (Bruner, 1990; Ogilvie, 2004).

A problem with bridging emotions and personality is that emotions are brief (Ekman, 1992). Emotional experience is flexible, transient, and variable (Brehm, 1999). Identifying the mechanisms that connect transient experience and enduring aspects of the person is a challenge. We can find a bridge between emotion and personality by recognizing that people think about their transient experiences and that these guiding ideas can persist across situations. Representing emotions circumvents the essential transience of emotional experience. In reflecting on their emotions, people seek to understand the causes of their experience as well as the likely effects of emotions on their thoughts and actions. In turn, they can think about their attributions and apply their ideas to new situations and to the experiences of other people. By representing emotions, people can form stable ideas about their emotional lives. This emotional knowledge can be accessed and applied in nonemotional situations.

Motivational Psychology's Repetition Compulsion

We have placed the development of interests within the broader question of motivational development. Interest affects interests through the mechanisms of attributions and expectations. Associationism offers an alternative mechanism of motivational development. This perspective assumes that psychological concepts can be connected and that these connections can vary in strength. Motivational theorists working from this position, such as McDougall, Allport, Thorndike, and Hull, assumed that repetition was the key to associative strength (see chapter 5). These approaches connect experience to dispositions through repetition: as an experience is repeated, it accrues some quality of permanence. As an experience is repeated, the resulting motive became "crystallized," "canalized," or "consolidated," much as a dirt path eventually develops a deep rut.

Repetition as a mechanism of motivational development outlived similar associationist concepts, like habit strength and drive reduction. Modern theories still invoke repetition to explain how interests develop. Some educational psychologists, for example, propose that momentary feelings of interest influence the development of interests through repetition and prolonged exposure. They contend that *situational interest* (momentary feelings of interest) creates *individual interest* (enduring interests) through repetition and duration. (The distinction between situational and individual interest, analyzed in chapter 8, roughly resembles our distinction between interest and interests.) If situational interest is repeated often enough, individual interest will develop. This idea appears in many writings (e.g., Hidi, 1990, 2000; Hidi & Berndorff, 1998; Krapp, 1999, 2002b; Schraw & Lehman, 2001), but it remains untested.

The emotion–attribution theory, in contrast, sees motivational development as cognitive, active, and reflective. People don't passively encounter events. They think about their experiences and about their thoughts about their experiences. The mere iteration of experience is less important than the inferences and expectations related to the experience. People render their world meaningful by trying to understand the causes of events. Attributions for interest let people understand why they felt interested, and they thereby influence expectations about what will arouse interest in the future. If repetition affects the development of interests, it does so by affecting attributions. Indeed, attribution theories easily explain the effects of repetition: a consistent covariance of the interesting activity and emotional feelings of interest promotes an attribution of interest to the object (see Försterling, 2001). Repetition doesn't affect interest development through some metaphorical canalization or building of associative strength. Instead, it affects how people understand the causes of their experience. The resulting emotional knowledge, not the repetition of the event, influences the development of interests. This alternative understanding of repetition, like the repetition approach, has not been tested. Nevertheless, it illustrates how the emotion–attribution theory can reinterpret past theories and make new predictions about the dynamics of interest development.

Relation to Other Theories

The core difference between the emotion–attribution theory and past theories is its emphasis on cognitive and metacognitive processes. This theory does not assume that people inherently know the causes of their emotions. Emotions require the interpretation that attributional processes provide. Interests emerge from these interpretations. Furthermore, people can think about their attributions and expectations when planning action. A metacognitive understanding of emotions enables sophisticated emotion-regulation strategies and contributes to the growth and differentiation of interests. No other theories of motivational development emphasize cognitive and metacognitive processes to this degree, nor do they make specific predictions about how these processes promote the development of interests.

The emotion–attribution theory most resembles script theory (Tomkins, 1979), which we described in chapter 5. Script theory argues that interests are scripts that emerge when discrete experiences of interest are magnified by cognitive processes. Like script theory, the emotion–attribution theory views the development of interests as a dynamic, continuous process founded on cognitive aspects of emotional experience. Unlike script theory, the emotion–attribution theory is specific about the cognitive processes involved and thus makes testable predictions about when emotional experiences of interest will influence the development of interests. Script theory's central mechanism—magnification—is difficult to measure or manipulate; as a result, the theory's predictions are difficult to pin down.

Prenzel's (1992) theory of the selective persistence of interest is another similar theory. Both theories trace the development of interests to the momentary experience of interest. Prenzel, however, is not specific about the mechanisms that cause an interest to persist. He proposes that people first engage with an object because of features that render the object interesting (Berlyne, 1960). If the engagement creates novelty, then people will be motivated to engage with the object again. Interests thus pull people along via expanding conflict, novelty, uncertainty, and complexity. This mechanism, while intriguing, makes the process of interest development seem passive, inasmuch as the person is goaded from encounter to encounter by unresolved conflict. Furthermore, this approach obscures the more fundamental cognitive processes involved in repeated engagements. People try to understand why they feel curious and interested in the object. If people don't attribute the interesting conflict to the object, then they would have no reason to return for a second engagement. Instead, they would act based on whatever they did see as causing the feelings of interest. Moreover, if people didn't expect that an additional engagement with the object would be interesting—an expectation that can be provided by prior attributions—then they would be less motivated to persist in the activity. The processes emphasized by the emotion–attribution theory thus seem more specific and basic than the processes involved in the selective persistence theory.

Chapter Summary and Conclusions

In this chapter we proposed a theory of the development of interests. We reframed the issue of interest development in terms of emotional knowledge, the understanding of the causes and consequences of emotional experience. Unlike past theories, which emphasize association, repetition, and unconscious motivation, the emotion–attribution theory focuses on the cognitive and metacognitive processes involved in emotional understanding. By breaking with past theories, the emotion–attribution theory offers new predictions about the dynamics of interest development. New experiments support the theory's basic predictions. Attributions for emotions predicted several activities that reflect a developing interest. The experimental evidence elevates this theory above past theories that have fared poorly in the face of research and theories that remain untested.

Chapter 7 explores the psychology of *vocational interests*, or a person's interests related to the world of work. Vocational psychology has devoted decades to studying interest and interests, including some problems that other areas have not yet considered. But the study of vocational interests remains segregated from the mainstream psychology of interest (Tinsley, 2001), despite its novel ideas and sophisticated body of research. We will review the major theories and themes in the study of vocational interests in the hope of illustrating its contributions to the broader study of interest. We'll also illuminate some continuities between vocational interests and other areas of the psychology of interest.

7

Interests and Vocations

For better or worse, most people in modern economies need to have a job. And if we must work, we may as well search for interesting, fulfilling work. Over 80 years ago, psychologists suggested that people can use their *vocational interests* as guides to finding satisfying places in the world of work. Vocational interests have proved easy to study but hard to define. Savickas (1999) contended that "definitions of interest . . . seem disparate and generally fail to distinguish interest from other motivational constructs" (p. 19). Many researchers define vocational interests vaguely—such as "individual difference variables that express preference" (Crites, 1999, p. 164)—or operationally rather than conceptually, such as "patterns of likes, dislikes, and indifferences regarding career-relevant activities and occupations" (Lent, Brown, & Hackett, 1994, p. 88).

In previous chapters, we remarked on the dearth of empirical research on interest. In this chapter, we have the opposite problem—the literature on vocational interests is massive. In fact, vocational-interest research probably makes up most of the total research on the psychology of interest. In its long history, vocational psychology has contributed new ideas and tools to the psychology of interest. Starting with Strong's (1943) pioneering work, psychologists have developed diverse and sophisticated ways of measuring interests, ranging from complex inventories to simple card-sorting tasks (Hartung, 1999; Prince & Heiser, 2000). Most importantly, while many psychologists theorize about the development of interests (see chapter 5), vocational psychologists test their theories through extensive research (Holland, 1997; Savickas & Spokane, 1999).

The study of vocational interests straddles basic and applied goals. Some of the research focuses on theoretical issues, such as the structure of interests, how interests develop, and how interests influence career decision making, satisfaction, and achievement (Holland, 1997; Savickas & Spokane, 1999). Other research focuses on exporting theories to applied contexts, particularly vocational counseling. Vocational research has a ready market. Millions of people take vocational interest inventories each year, so there is a need to understand practical aspects of interests. A lot of research on vocational interests thus emphasizes assessment of interests, the validity of various interest inventories, and whether interest assessment should be qualified by gender, ethnicity, and cultural background.

The lucrative industry of interest assessment has been a mixed blessing for the study of vocational interests. On the one hand, theories of vocational interests find a wide audience beyond the usual academic circles. On the other hand, theoretical problems do not receive enough attention (Walsh, 2001); the validity of a scientific theory can be overshadowed by the validity of specific inventories and assessment tools. Savickas (1999), for example, argued that "the accumulated literature on vocational interests is more empirical than conceptual" (p. 19). The scientific side of vocational psychology appears to be waning (Gottfredson, 2001; Tinsley, 2001). In a survey of 260 graduates from doctoral programs in counseling psychology, only 1% self-identified as researchers (Krebs, Smither, & Hurley, 1991).

In the present chapter, we'll see what vocational psychologists have said about vocational interests. Our main goal is to review the prominent issues, problems, and theories in the study of vocational interests. We'll focus on two theoretical problems associated with vocational interests. First, do vocational interests form a coherent structure? Do interests form categories, and if so, how are the categories organized? Second, how do vocational interests develop? Why do people form interests in some occupations but not in others? The mechanics of interest assessment will be reviewed, but not in much detail. Interest inventories are complex, and other sources offer good introductions (Prince & Heiser, 2000; Savickas, Taber, & Spokane, 2002).

Structure of Vocational Interests

Are vocational interests organized? Do vocational interests form some sort of structure, or are they a "laundry list" of unrelated interests? Research on vocational interests has always sought basic dimensions and types of interests, but not all research has taken the extra step of exploring how the interests relate to each other (Rounds & Day, 1999). Early studies took a factor list approach. This research, lacking a theory, relied on factor analysis to derive basic interests (see Darley & Hagenah, 1955). Strong (1943), for instance, used "dustbowl empiricism" for his pioneering work on the Vocational Interest Blank (Campbell & Borgen, 1999). A classic study by Guilford took a similar approach (Guilford, Christensen, Bond, & Sutton, 1954). They applied factor analysis to a set of 1,000 items; 18 interest factors appeared, many of them arcane, such as "aggression," "physical drive," and "adventure vs. security."

Modern research, in contrast, specifies theoretically based structures of interests. This approach has come to dominate vocational psychology. In fact, structural theories of interests may be vocational psychology's biggest contribution to the psychology of interest. We'll review three structural models: Holland's (1997) influential RIASEC model, Prediger's (1982, 1996) dimensional model, and the spherical model of interests (Tracey, 2002b; Tracey & Rounds, 1996b). Less prominent models (e.g., Gati, 1979, 1991; Roe & Klos, 1969) are described and evaluated elsewhere (Rounds & Day, 1999; Tracey & Rounds, 1993, 1994).

Holland's RIASEC Model

John Holland's RIASEC model has dominated vocational psychology for several decades (Holland, 1973, 1985a, 1996, 1997). His theory is complex; we'll discuss only the parts dealing with vocational interests. Holland's first assumption is that most people can be classified into one of six personality types: Realistic, Investigative, Artistic, Social, Enterprising, and Conventional, or the acronym RIASEC. Each type represents an abstract cluster of self-beliefs, skills, values, and, most significantly, interests (see Holland, 1997, pp. 21–28, for detailed descriptions).

- *Realistic* people enjoy working with tools, machines, and their hands. They prefer concrete things, traditional values, and practical solutions to problems. Occupations preferred by Realistic types include mechanic and electrician.

- *Investigative* people value intelligence, scholarship, logic, and learning. They enjoy abstract ideas and innovative solutions to problems. Scientific jobs (researcher, science writer, and technician) exemplify careers preferred by Investigative types.
- *Artistic* people value self-expression and imagination. They view themselves as liberal, intuitive, and creative. Musician, artist, and author are common occupations for Artistic types.
- *Social* people enjoy informing, training, and helping other people. They see themselves as helpful, and they prefer interacting with other people rather than with machines and tools. Counselor, teacher, and social worker are common careers for Social types.
- *Enterprising* people value leadership, persuasion, ambition, and personal success. They value gaining positions of power and influencing other people. Careers in business, sales, and management are associated with Enterprising types.
- *Conventional* people enjoy structured, systematic activities. They view themselves as organized, reliable, and skilled at clerical tasks. Careers that involve working with and organizing concrete information—accounting, banking—appeal to Conventional types.

Holland's RIASEC types emerged from vocational research several decades ago (Astin, 1999), before the rise of modern typologies of personality structure. The Big Five model, described briefly in chapter 4, aspires to form a comprehensive taxonomy of individual differences in personality (John, 1990). This approach focuses on five broad traits: openness to experience, conscientiousness, extraversion, agreeableness, and neuroticism (McCrae & Costa, 1997). Many studies have explored how Holland's six types correspond with the Big Five traits (Costa, McCrae, & Holland, 1984; De Fruyt & Mervielde, 1997; Tokar & Swanson, 1995). A meta-analysis of these studies found that some RIASEC types reliably correlated with some Big Five traits (Larson, Rottinghaus, & Borgen, 2002). Many of the relations were unsurprising: conscientiousness predicts Conventional interests; openness to experience predicts Artistic and Investigative interests; extraversion predicts Social and Enterprising interests. Yet the analysis also found regions of independence. Realistic types did not correlate appreciably with any of the Big Five traits. Similarly, neuroticism was generally unrelated to the RIASEC types.

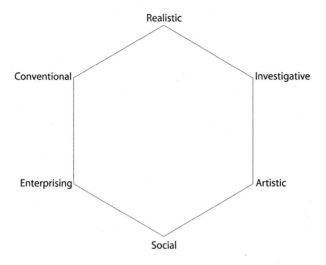

FIGURE 7.1 Holland's RIASEC hexagon of vocational interests

Holland (1997) argued that the six RIASEC types form a coherent spatial structure, namely a hexagon (Cole, Whitney, & Holland, 1971). Holland's hexagon has become an icon for vocational interest research; a hexagon even appears on the cover of *Journal of Vocational Behavior*. Figure 7.1 depicts the hexagonal arrangement of the six types. Holland assumes that the circular order of types—R, I, A, S, E, C—is fixed. Both the hexagonal structure and the order of types are invariant. Different cultures, groups, or genders should not have different orders—E, R, I, C, A, S, for instance. Furthermore, the hexagon specifies the relatedness of the types. Adjacent types should be more similar than alternate types; opposite types should be least related. For example, someone who scores highest as a Social type should score fairly high on the adjacent types (Artistic and Enterprising), lower on the alternate types (Investigative and Conventional), and lowest on the opposing type (Realistic).

The hexagonal structure is remarkably robust. The RIASEC hexagon emerges in many different interest inventories (Savickas et al., 2002). It doesn't seem to matter whether interests are measured with preferences for occupational titles, college majors, or lists of activities (Fouad, 1999). Likewise, the hexagon appears regardless of whether RIASEC types are measured with continuous scores or with a single "high point code" denoting the most preferred of the six types (Tracey & Rounds, 1992). The RIASEC hexagonal structure also replicates across several cultures, although it fits better for some than for others (e.g., Einarsdóttir, Rounds, Ægisdóttir, & Gerstein, 2002; Rounds & Tracey, 1996; Tracey, Watanabe, & Schneider, 1997). Ethnic and gender differences in interest structure fail to appear in large-sample studies and in meta-analyses (Anderson, Tracey, & Rounds, 1997; Day & Rounds, 1998; Day, Rounds, & Swaney, 1998).[1]

Holland (1997) offers a twist on the structure of vocational interests by arguing that work environments have a hexagonal structure as well. His theory suggests that environments should be classified according to RIASEC types, based on the types of people who populate the environment. An Artistic work environment, for example, would have mostly Artistic people and afford opportunities for Artistic activities. Holland proposed that job satisfaction and achievement increase when the personality type and environment type match. A Realistic person will thrive in a Realistic work environment—one filled with other Realistic people, tools, and activities—but flounder in a Social environment. In short, satisfaction and achievement are not merely issues of interest and skill but also of interactions between interests and contextual factors. Few studies explore the environmental aspect of Holland's model so the "congruence hypothesis" remains controversial (Spokane, 1985; Tinsley, 2000).

Prediger's Dimensional Model

Prediger (1982, 1996; Prediger & Vansickle, 1992) proposes an intriguing reformulation of Holland's hexagon. He contends that the RIASEC hexagon fails to represent the core structure of interests. The fundamental structure of interests, in his view, involves two dimensions that underlie the six types, not the six types themselves. Whereas Holland's theory is founded on a typology, Prediger's dimensional model makes no assumptions about discrete types. In Prediger's view, interests blend into each other as one moves across different values of the two dimensions. Hol-

1. Differences in the *structure* of interests should not be confused with differences in *levels* of interest. Many studies find gender and ethnic differences in degree of interest. Women are more likely than men to match the Social type, and men are more likely to match the Realistic and Investigative types (Fouad, 2002). The RIASEC structure, however, doesn't differ between men and women (Anderson et al., 1997).

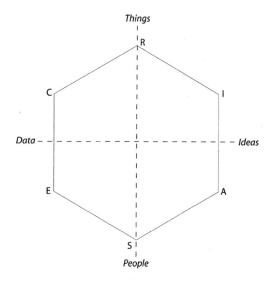

FIGURE 7.2 Prediger's dimensional representation of the RIASEC hexagon

land contends that a hexagon is the primary structure of interests; Prediger contends that the two independent dimensions are primary.

Figure 7.2 depicts the placement of these dimensions relative to Holland's six types. The first dimension is *people versus things*. This dimension refers to the preference for working with other people versus working with tools, objects, and machines. The *people* pole corresponds to the Social type; the *things* pole corresponds to the Realistic type. The second dimension is *data versus ideas*. This dimension refers to preference for working with concrete data versus abstract concepts. The *data* pole falls between the Conventional and Enterprising types; the *ideas* pole falls between the Investigative and Artistic types. Because these interest dimensions are bipolar, scoring high on one end implies scoring low on the other end. People interested in working with data, for instance, should be uninterested in working with abstract ideas.

Prediger's model complements Holland's model more than it contradicts it. Like Holland, Prediger assumes that the RIASEC types form a coherent two-dimensional structure. Both models agree on the order of the RIASEC types. If Holland's ordering of types were invalidated, Prediger's dimensional model would become invalid as well. Each model specifies the same interest structure, namely a set of interests arranged around a two-dimensional circle (Rounds & Tracey, 1993). The *data–ideas* and *people–things* model forms a simple representation of the interest circle, whereas the RIASEC types form a more differentiated representation of the circle. Whether one prefers a RIASEC description or a dimensional description may depend on theoretical and practical goals (Tracey & Rounds, 1995).

The Spherical Model

The spherical model is the most recent theory of vocational interest structure (Tracey, 2002b; Tracey & Rounds, 1995; 1996a, 1996b); it may be the most complicated as well. Tracey and Rounds challenge the core of Holland's theory—the assumption that vocational interests form six types in the shape of a hexagon—and offer a new structural model as an alternative. They contend that the RIASEC types are "arbitrary abstractions that constitute only one of an infinite number of possible representative points on the circle of vocational interests" (Tracey & Rounds, 1996b, p. 36).

What pattern of findings would indicate the arbitrary nature of the RIASEC types? The test, according to Tracey and Rounds (1995), is whether interests distribute evenly around a circle or cluster into six nodes. Holland's theory predicts that measures of vocational interests should form clusters—that is, the items in a scale should cohere into six interest types. Many studies, however, find that measures of interests form a uniform circular distribution—interests disperse evenly in a circular pattern, forming a circumplex (Tracey & Rounds, 1995, 1996b). In short, the structure of interests resembles a circle, not a hexagon.

Holland (1997) views this as a trivial issue: "Some questions and their statistical answers have no bearing on either the statement of or the usefulness of the [RIASEC] typology," including "many questions about the hexagon" (p. 159). Among these irrelevant questions, according to Holland, is "Is it a hexagon or a circle?" Yet perhaps Holland dismissed the issue prematurely—theoretical implications follow from a circular structure. Circles have an infinite number of points, so they can be sliced in many justifiable ways. Holland has a circle with six sections, but one could legitimately posit four sections (such as Prediger's model), eight sections, or any other number. If the circle itself is the core structure of vocational interests, then theorists can legitimately emphasize any number of slices. Hexagons imply that six is the ideal number of types; circles do not imply an optimal number of types.

Now we see why the spherical model challenges Holland's RIASEC model. If interests form a circle, then what's important about the RIASEC types is their *order*, not the types themselves. The six types are one of many ways of dividing the interest circle. So long as a model preserves the circular structure of interests, its divisions of the circle are legitimate. For theoretical purposes, then, all ways of slicing the circle are equally arbitrary. For applied purposes, however, pragmatic goals can influence how differentiated the circle should be viewed. For instance, counselors working with people who lack knowledge about the world of work might find a simple representation of the circle (such as Prediger's four slices) most useful. When working with people who have specific career aspirations, counselors might adopt a differentiated circle that carves out many distinctions within each RIASEC type.

If Tracey and Rounds supplant the hexagon with a circumplex, why is their theory called the "spherical model" rather than the "circular model"? Tracey and Rounds argue that the interest circle—whether it is described as six types or as two dimensions—fails to capture *occupational prestige*, a critical aspect of vocational interests. People differentiate jobs based on prestige level (Plata, 1975; Rounds & Zevon, 1983) and account for prestige in their occupational aspirations (Gottfredson, 1996). Yet prestige has not been integrated into models of vocational interest structure. Tracey and Rounds propose that the prestige dimension is perpendicular to the interest circle. When this third dimension is added, the circle becomes a sphere.

Figure 7.3 displays the spherical model of interests, which contains 18 interests (see Tracey, 2002b, p. 120). The interest circle defines the equator of the sphere—this circumplex contains the six RIASEC types and Prediger's two dimensions. To offer a more differentiated view, the spherical model slices this circle into eight interests. In a spherical structure, the interest circle becomes less differentiated as one moves toward the extremes of prestige. The upper half of figure 7.3 shows the higher prestige hemisphere; the lower half shows the lower prestige hemisphere. The interest circle shrinks from eight interests to four interests as one moves from the equator toward one of the poles. At the north and south poles of the sphere, the interest circle condenses into a single interest defined by high or low prestige.

Proposing a spherical structure is more controversial than it might

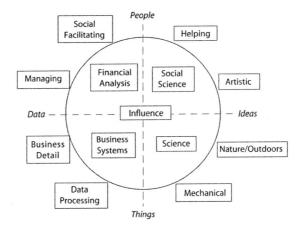

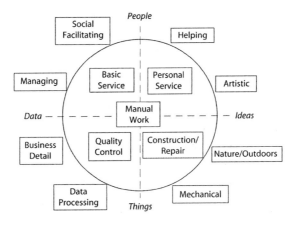

FIGURE 7.3 The spherical model of vocational interests

Note: The top part depicts the high prestige half of the interest sphere; the bottom part depicts the low prestige half of the interest sphere. As interests move from the equator toward the poles of the sphere, they become less differentiated.

Source: Reprinted from *Journal of Vocational Behavior,* 60, Terence J. G. Tracey, "Personal globe inventory: Measurement of the spherical model of interests and competence beliefs," pp. 113–172, 2002, with permission from Elsevier.

seem. A sphere isn't the only possible three-dimensional representation of vocational interests. A plausible alternative structure is a cylinder (see Tracey & Rounds, 1996b). In a cylindrical model, the interest circle would exist at all levels of prestige. For instance, the RIASEC types (or any other representation of the circle) could be observed at any cross-section of the cylinder, regardless of the level of prestige. A cylindrical model thus allows for interests in prestigious Social occupations, nonprestigious Social occupations, and any level of prestige in between. In contrast, the spherical model argues that the interest circle condenses at the extremes of prestige. Research to date shows that spherical representation fits the interest space better than do some alternative three-dimensional structures (Tracey & Rounds, 1996b). The RIASEC types, for example, merge into smaller categories and ultimately collapse into a single interest as one moves toward the poles of prestige. As a result, classic theories of interest structure, such as Holland's theory, may apply only at moderate levels of prestige (Harmon, 1996).

The Personal Globe Inventory contains scales for measuring the spherical model of interests (Tracey, 2002b); this inventory grew from several preliminary scales (Tracey, 1997; Tracey & Rounds, 1996b). The spherical structure seems reliable. Preliminary scales found that the spherical model fit well for American and Japanese samples, although it fit somewhat better for the American sample (Tracey et al., 1997). Research with the revised scales found no gender or ethnic differences in spherical structure (Tracey, 2002b), and the structure replicates in Chinese samples (Long, Adams, & Tracey, 2005). Furthermore, a sphere appears when people rate their preferences for occupational titles, how much they enjoy different activities, and their competence to do various activities (Tracey, 2002b).

Summary of Interest Structure

The study of vocational interests has come a long way since early research on interest structure, which sought lists of "basic interests" rather than representations of how interests interrelate (Darley & Hagenah, 1955). In the search of the best model of interest structure, researchers have tried hexagons, circles, dimensions, nested hierarchies, cones, and most recently, spheres as candidates for the structure of interests (Rounds & Day, 1999). This research program could be a role model for less systematic areas within the psychology of interest.

So what can we conclude? What is *the* structure of interests? The dust hasn't quite settled in the debate between Holland's (1997) RIASEC model and the spherical model (Tracey & Rounds, 1996a, 1996b). Some vocational psychologists argue that the spherical model "is a weak edifice to replace the hexagonal structure that has served the fields of vocational behavior and career counseling so well for more than two decades" (Borgen & Donnay, 1996, p. 43). Few studies have tested the spherical model beyond the preliminary research that appraised a spherical representation of interests (Tracey, 1997; Tracey & Rounds, 1996b) and developed an inventory to measure the sphere (Tracey, 2002b). Nevertheless, these few studies are compelling. They suggest the need to rethink the structure of interests, and they indicate the viability of circular and spherical structures. The spherical model may emerge as a stronger edifice as more research assesses its validity.

Although it's hard to predict the fate of the spherical model, we would expect researchers interested in the basic scientific problems of vocational psychology to favor it. The spherical model is simply more general than other structural models. It contains the RIASEC model and the data-ideas/people-things dimensions as special cases of the interest sphere. The spherical model doesn't claim that the RIASEC types are invalid. Instead, it claims that they are only one of many legitimate ways to describe the circle of interests, which itself is only one part of the broader interest sphere. Furthermore, the spherical model contributes new ideas, makes new predictions, and has strong implications for how the science of vocational psychology views vocational interests (Harmon, 1996).

Vocational interest structures highlight the field's dual identity as a basic and an applied discipline, as well as the tension that such an identity creates. Vocational psychologists expect a theory of interest structure to advance both basic and applied goals. To gain acceptance, a new theory of interest structure must make a scientific contribution—solve conceptual problems and contribute new ideas—as well as provide a practical basis for career counseling. New scientific ideas can encounter resistance from those in applied aspects of the field. Models that are primarily basic may not catch on because they don't surpass the prevailing theory's usefulness for counseling practices.

Holland's (1997) theory currently dominates both basic and applied aspects of vocational psychology. In the basic arena, the theory inspires research on interest structure, the role of interests in vocational choice and satisfaction, and interactions between interests and work environments. In the applied arena, many counselors use the hexagonal model as a basis for career counseling, and all major interest inventories measure the RIASEC types. The spherical model, in contrast, emphasizes scientific issues over practical issues—it clearly stems from vocational psychology's theoretical tradition. Many critics believe that the model may never prove useful for applied purposes. Hansen (1996) suggests that "although the sphere presented by Tracey and Rounds is intriguing from a scientific and possibly a theoretical vantage point, it probably exceeds the degree of complexity that clients can comprehend about the world of work" (p. 75). Borgen and Donnay (1996) agree, arguing that the "spherical model of vocational interests may have heuristic value for theory and research, but it seems to have relatively little potential for use in practical applications" (p. 50).

It is unfortunate that applied relevance can temper the field's enthusiasm for new theories. That a theory should revolutionize both science and practice is expecting too much. Ultimately, theories must be judged on their scientific merits. Many invalid theories are easy to apply and helpful to a lot of people. For instance, therapies based on pseudoscientific theories (such as therapeutic touch or past-life regression) are easy to learn and helpful to at least a few people (see Lilienfeld, Lynn, & Lohr, 2003), but psychological science doesn't view this as a barrier to forming better theories. The scientific side of vocational psychology should flow downstream into fruitful applications.

Measurement of Vocational Interests

Researchers typically assess vocational interests through self-report instruments known as *interest inventories*. Of the dozens of interest inventories, no more than a handful are commonly used for research. The major inventories converge, despite differences in item type, scaling, and response formats (see Savickas et al., 2002). Responses to interest inventories predict eventual job choice and discriminate among people in different occupations (Fouad, 1999). Mismatches between interests and occupations predict job dissatisfaction and the likelihood of career change (Holland, 1997). Interest inventories also discriminate among different college majors, with a hit rate of 66% (Hansen & Tan, 1992).

The RIASEC types are commonly measured by inventories developed by Holland. The Vocational Preference Inventory (Holland, 1985b) presents occupational titles that represent the different interest types. The Self-Directed Search (Holland, Fritzsche, & Powell, 1994) presents lists of occupations, activities, and abilities related to the six types. As Holland's model became prominent, established inventories included measures of the RIASEC types (Campbell & Borgen, 1999). Now all major measures of vocational interests offer RIASEC scores (Prince & Heiser, 2000).

Tracey's (2002b) Personal Globe Inventory (PGI) is the most recent interest inventory, and it promises to become a major research tool. Unlike other inventories, the PGI is modular. The inventory's scales can be reconfigured to represent several models of vocational interests. Responses can be combined into scores for RIASEC types, scores for the eight interest types proposed as an alternative to RIASEC (Tracey & Rounds, 1996b), scores for Prediger's data-ideas and people-things dimensions, and scores for the full interest sphere. This makes the inventory unusually versatile and ecumenical.

Card-sorting tasks are a fun variation on self-report inventories. Many card-sorting tasks measuring vocational interests are available (see Hartung, 1999). The most direct is the Career Interest Card Sort (Athanasou & Hosking, 1999; Hosking & Athanasou, 1997). For this task, people read and sort seven cards. Each card has a label for a vocational interest category on the front side (outdoor, practical, scientific, creative, business, office, people contact) and a description of the category on the back side. People simply sort the seven cards in order of preference. This quick, simple card-sorting task appears effective: the scores are reliable, and the rankings replicate findings from lengthy interest inventories (Athanasou & Cooksey, 1993; Cooksey & Athanasou, 1994).

Some studies measure vocational interests through *expressed interests*, or responses to open-ended questions like "What occupation do you intend to pursue when you leave school?" (Crites, 1999). Expressed interests have been surprisingly controversial. Expressed interests predict job choice much better than responses to vocational interest inventories (referred to as *measured interests*). This disparity has been a source of chagrin, leading to speculation about why two measures of interests would show such different results (Borgen & Seling, 1978; Dolliver, 1969; Spokane & Decker, 1999). This problem, however, seems chimerical. *Expressed interests* measure intended actions, not interests; *measured interests* measure what vocational psychology conventionally means by interests. It shouldn't be surprising that statements of intended job choice predict job choice better than measures of general interests. Using parallel labels for different concepts implies more similarity than is warranted (Silvia, 2001a).

Origins of Vocational Interests

How do vocational interests develop? The major theories of vocational interests are silent about the origins of vocational interests (Holland, 1997; Strong, 1943, 1955). Holland (1997) has a lot to say about the RIASEC types, but he has few specific predictions regarding how people come to resemble one type rather than another. Other major theories emphasize the structure and assessment of interests (Strong, 1943, 1955) or make general claims that are hard to test (Super, 1949). Vocational psychology's emphasis on the structure of interests might be responsible for the relative inattention to how interests develop. None of the major structural models have much to say about why people develop interests in some things but not others (Holland, 1997; Prediger, 1982; Tracey & Rounds, 1996b).

As a result, vocational psychology has separate bodies of research on interest structure and interest development. Historically, the study of interest development has been less successful than the study of structure. Theories of interest structure make clear statements about how interests relate—conflicting predictions are thus easily tested (e.g., Tracey & Rounds, 1993, 1994). Theories of interest development, in contrast, are less precise. As Savickas (1999) comments, "hypotheses and theories about the origins and development of vocational interests seem riddled with cliches that lack content and cannot be scientifically examined" (p. 19). As a result, making clear predictions and testing competing hypotheses have been difficult.

The study of the origins of vocational interests, like the study of interest structure, pursues basic and applied goals. How vocational interests develop is an intriguing scientific question. The basic approach forms theories and tests their predictions about the causes of interest development (Lent et al., 1994; Nauta, Kahn, Angell, & Cantarelli, 2002). The applied approach develops assessment tools and translates the basic research into interventions and counseling practices. Closing gender differences in vocational interests, especially math and science interests, is a common applied goal of research on interest development (Betz, 1999; Hoffman & Häussler, 1998).

Ability and Interests

An intuitive model of vocational interests is that people are interested in what they can do well. Not surprisingly, the relationship between abilities and interests is the oldest approach to interest development (see Strong, 1943). Yet one of the "things that we know," according to Walsh (1999), is "surprisingly, interests and abilities are not that highly correlated" (p. 374). After intensive study, early researchers concluded that interests and abilities are only modestly associated (Darley & Hagenah, 1955; Super, 1949). A recent meta-analysis of modern studies confirms this pessimism; it found a small correlation ($r = .20$) between ability and interest (Lent et al., 1994, p. 110). We'll take a new look at this issue by considering different definitions of ability, discussing biases in self-reports of ability, and considering whether the ability–interest question is still fruitful.

WHAT IS AN ABILITY?

Many studies of abilities and interests neglect an important starting point: what is an ability? Abilities are usually viewed as dispositions or potentials that enable a certain level of performance, such as solving math problems or putting golf balls accurately. This is essentially the lay psychology view of ability (Heider, 1958). Nevertheless, ability is a relational concept that describes a person's relationship to a particular activity. *Ability* implies reference to some task and its difficulty, just as a *task difficulty* implies reference to levels of ability. Ability and task difficulty are two ways of expressing the same point. To be labeled an "ability" in everyday parlance, a skill must be socially distinctive (Jones & Davis, 1965). An ability ceases to be called an ability when everyone has it. For example, hundreds of millions of native English speakers are experts in producing sentences, quickly recognizing words, and understanding spoken English despite diverse accents. When we say someone has high artistic ability, then, we are only partially describing a property of the person. If we surround the able person with a new group of more skilled people, and if everyone performs equally well, then no one would be attributed "ability."

APPRAISING ABILITIES

To study links between ability and interest, researchers must assume that people can report their ability reasonably accurately. Research on self-assessment, however, shows that people rarely judge their abilities accurately (Sedikides & Strube, 1997; Silvia & Gendolla, 2001). Instead, people usually make flattering, self-enhancing judgments of their personal qualities. The *better-than-average effect* appears when people rate themselves as above average on all sorts of skills and traits—such as driving, leadership, sociability, writing, and kissing—undeterred by the statistical improbability of everyone being above average (Kruger, 1999).

Biases in ability judgments run deeper than seeing oneself as better than average. High ability is a prerequisite for judging ability levels accurately. According to Kruger and Dunning (1999, 2002), one consequence of incompetence is ignorance of what indicates competence. People who are bad at something don't always know that they're bad because people can't judge themselves as substandard unless they know the standards. Bad writers, for example, not only write poorly but are also unable to discern good writing from poor writing. As a result, they can't judge their own writing as bad. Good writers, in contrast, can judge their ability more accurately because they know the standards of good writing. A result of this disparity is that good and bad performers may judge themselves similarly, but only the good performers are judging themselves accurately.

Several experiments show that accurate self-assessment of ability depends on actual ability (Kruger & Dunning, 1999). In one study, people took an objective test of their humor appreciation. After taking the test, they estimated their ability relative to their peers as a percentile rank. Overall, people judged their ability as at the 66th percentile, thus showing a better than average effect. Yet people's actual ability—measured by scores on the humor test—moderated the accuracy of ability judgments. People who performed in the upper quartile of the humor test judged their percentile rank fairly accurately. People in the lower quartile, however, made wildly inaccurate judgments. Although their actual average score was at the 12th percentile, they judged their humor ability to be at the 58th percentile. In a second study, people took a standardized test of logical reasoning and then judged their ability. People scoring in the lower quartile on the test ranked their logical reasoning ability at the 68th percentile, despite actually performing at the 12th percentile. People scoring in the upper quartile underestimated their ability; they scored at the 86th percentile, but they judged their rank to be at the 74th percentile.

In sum, people's judgments of their abilities are usually inaccurate (Sedikides & Strube, 1997). People tend to take rosy views of their abilities and traits (Kruger, 1999). Worse yet for the study of interest and ability, actual ability is required for making accurate judgments of ability. When people lack competence, they lack the knowledge of what denotes competence in themselves and in others (Kruger & Dunning, 1999). As a result, ability judgments are systematically inaccurate—incompetent people vastly overestimate their ability. This poses a problem for studies of ability and interest that rely on self-reports of ability.

Self-Efficacy and the Development of Vocational Interests

Self-efficacy theory (Bandura, 1977, 1997; Maddux & Gosselin, 2003) entered vocational psychology in the 1980s. Research found that low self-efficacy impeded the career development of women (Betz & Hackett, 1981; Hackett & Betz, 1981), suggesting a role for self-efficacy in the development of vocational interests. Two decades later, self-efficacy stands as one of vocational psychology's dominant concepts (Betz, 2000; Betz & Borgen, 2000). The study of vocational interest development is nearly synonymous with the study of self-efficacy and vocational interests. Prior models of interest development—such as the study of ability and interest—have been eclipsed, assimilated, or ignored.

The study of self-efficacy and vocational interests follows two traditions. The first approach, which is relatively applied, explores relationships between self-efficacy and vocational interests. Developing inventories to measure self-efficacy (Betz, Harmon, & Borgen, 1996), distinguishing between vocational interests and self-efficacy (Donnay & Borgen, 1999), and integrating self-efficacy information into career counseling (Betz, 1999) fall under this approach. One prominent line of research within the applied tradition has been the development of RIASEC self-efficacy scales (Betz & Gwilliam, 2002). The Skills Confidence Inventory, for example, measures self-efficacy for the six RIASEC types (Betz, Borgen, Kaplan, & Harmon, 1998; Betz et al., 1996). Self-efficacy for a RIASEC type correlates highly with interest in the type—for instance, high Artistic self-efficacy predicts high Artistic interests—implying (but not demonstrating) some sort of causal connection.

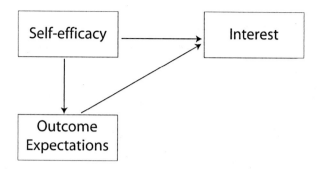

FIGURE 7.4 How self-efficacy and outcome expectations influence interest

The second approach emphasizes theoretical aspects of self-efficacy and vocational interests. Lent et al.'s (1994) social-cognitive career theory seeks to establish causal relationships between self-efficacy and vocational interests, organize existing findings, and make new predictions for future research. Their theory is probably the leading one on vocational interest development. Rooted in Bandura's (1986, 1997) social-cognitive theory, social-cognitive career theory addresses a broad range of issues beyond interest development, such as career choice and performance. We'll focus on the theory's model of interest development.

The theory assumes that "people form enduring interests in activities in which they view themselves to be efficacious and in which they anticipate positive outcomes" (Lent et al., 1994, p. 89). Figure 7.4 depicts the theory's model of interest development. Self-efficacy affects interests directly and indirectly, according to the theory. Self-efficacy expectations directly enhance vocational interests, although precisely why is not addressed by the theory. Self-efficacy further affects interests by affecting outcome expectations. When people expect an activity to yield positive outcomes, interest in the activity should increase.

Research generally supports the theory's predictions about interest development (Rottinghaus, Larson, & Borgen, 2003). According to a small meta-analysis (Lent et al., 1994), vocational interests correlate with self-efficacy and outcome expectations, which in turn correlate with each other. In a study that tested the full model (Lopez, Lent, Brown, & Gore, 1997), high school students completed measures of self-efficacy and interest in math and science. Among algebra students, self-efficacy significantly predicted outcome expectations, which in turn predicted interest. Self-efficacy did not directly predict interest in this sample. Among geometry students, the full model was demonstrated: self-efficacy affected interest directly and indirectly.

Earlier we saw that the study of ability and interest never went far because it lacked a guiding theory. The social-cognitive career theory offers a new analysis of ability and interests. Self-perceptions of ability are one source of self-efficacy expectations (Bandura, 1997). Perhaps perceptions of ability *indirectly* influence the development of interests: abilities influence self-efficacy, which in turn influences vocational interests. A recent study supported this prediction (Brown, Lent, & Gore, 2000). People completed self-report measures of abilities and interests, along with a measure of self-efficacy for RIASEC activities. Congruent with the theory's predictions, self-efficacy mediated between ability and interests. Ability no longer predicted interest when self-efficacy was included in the analysis.

CAUSAL EFFECTS OF SELF-EFFICACY

Most of the research on self-efficacy is correlational (Bandura, 1997); research on self-efficacy and interest is no exception. High correlations between interest scales and self-efficacy scales and the left-to-right path diagrams of "causal models" tempt researchers to make causal inferences, but only experiments can establish whether high self-efficacy causes increases in interest. The few experiments that have manipulated self-efficacy have found mixed effects, but overall they show that self-efficacy causes changes in interest. Campbell and Hackett (1986) asked men and women to work on a mathematics task, which was manipulated to be easy or difficult. People who completed the easy task expressed more self-efficacy and more interest in the task relative to people who completed the difficult task. This experiment shows that performance affects both self-efficacy and interest.

In a study of preschool children, Barak, Shiloh, and Haushner (1992) manipulated *cognitive restructuring* while children played with toys. During some activities, children were asked to repeat sentences that emphasized feelings of competence and enjoyment ("I am very talented in [name of relevant activity], I am doing very well in it, and I am enjoying [name of relevant activity] very much"; p. 492). The restructuring manipulation involves more than self-efficacy, but it contains feelings of confidence as a component (see Barak, 1981). During other activities, children were given extrinsic rewards for playing. Two weeks later, the children indicated their preferences for the activities. Cognitive restructuring increased preference for the play activities, whereas extrinsic rewards decreased preference for the activities (cf. Deci & Ryan, 2000).

Another experiment appraised an intervention intended to increase math and science interests among undecided college students (Luzzo, Hasper, Albert, Bibby, & Martinelli, 1999). First-year undergraduates were invited to participate if their math scores were above average and if they were undecided about their career choices. The experiment manipulated two sources of self-efficacy. One group of students received a vicarious-learning induction. They watched a 15-minute video in which two former students described how their math and science successes during college prepared them for careers related to math and science. A second group received a performance-accomplishments induction. They worked on a math task designed to create perceptions of success. A third group received both the vicarious-learning induction and the performance-accomplishment induction. Students in a control group received an introduction to their university's career center.

Before and after the intervention, people rated their self-efficacy for math and science as well as their interest in math and science. Four weeks later, people completed more measures of self-efficacy and interest, noted the courses they planned to take the following quarter, and indicated any career decisions that they had made. The courses and career decisions were coded for relevance to math and science. Neither manipulation of self-efficacy influenced interest immediately following the intervention. Four weeks later, however, people who had experienced a performance accomplishment (success on the math task) expressed higher interest in math and science. The courses they planned to take the following quarter were more related to math and science as well. Vicarious learning had little effect on interest by itself, although people who experienced both inductions of self-efficacy had particularly high interest four weeks later. These effects are striking in light of the brief manipulations of self-efficacy.

Betz and Schifano (2000) designed an intervention to increase Realistic self-efficacy among college women. Women with low Realistic self-efficacy but average Realistic interests were selected for the experiment. Women in the experimental group received a 7-hour intervention; they visited construction sites, rewired lamps, learned to use tools, and built shelves. Women in the control condition discussed their attitudes toward recent movies. Two weeks later, they completed measures of self-efficacy for Realistic tasks and Realistic interests. The intervention was partially successful: Realistic self-efficacy increased in the experimental group, but levels of Realistic interests remained the same. A few items related to Realistic interests—the items directly related to the tasks in the intervention, such as interest in rewiring lamps—did show increases, indicating some task-specific effects of self-efficacy. Overall, however, changing self-efficacy did not translate into changes in vocational interests.

DOES INTEREST CAUSE SELF-EFFICACY?

The convergence of correlational and experimental research supports one part of the social-cognitive career theory's model of interest development: self-efficacy, measured or manipulated, predicts interest. Yet perhaps interest also affects self-efficacy. In earlier chapters, we learned how the emotion of interest enables the development of competence (see Chapters 1 and 2). Motivated by curiosity, people will expose themselves to diverse situations and persist longer at activities (Fredrickson, 1998; Rathunde, 1998; Sansone & Smith, 2000a). In turn, enriched knowledge and skills should promote feelings of competence and expectations of successful performance. Bandura (1997) argues for reciprocal effects on similar grounds: "social cognitive theory posits a reciprocal but asymmetric relationship between perceived self-efficacy and occupational interests, with efficacy beliefs playing the stronger determinant role" (pp. 424–425).

Only recently has research explored whether vocational interests and self-efficacy have reciprocal effects. These studies, although correlational, assess interests and self-efficacy longitudinally. In a study of children's interests (Tracey, 2002a), fifth-grade and eighth-grade students completed measures of RIASEC interests and competence perceptions over the course of a school year. Extensive analyses suggested that the best model was a reciprocal model: self-efficacy influenced the development of interests, and interests influenced the development of self-efficacy. Furthermore, the reciprocal effects were equally strong, challenging Bandura's (1997) suggestion that self-efficacy's effect on interest exceeds interest's reciprocal effect.

Similar patterns appear for the vocational interests of undergraduates (Nauta et al., 2002). College students completed measures of RIASEC interests and self-efficacy for the RIASEC interests at three points in an academic year. Vocational interests at the start of the study predicted self-efficacy at the middle of the study. Self-efficacy at the start, however, did not predict interests midway through the study. For the first phase, then, no reciprocal effects were found: interest predicted self-efficacy, but self-efficacy didn't predict interest. Reciprocal effects appeared between the midpoint and the end of the study. Interests midway predicted self-efficacy at the study's end; self-efficacy predicted interests as well. As in Tracey's (2002a) study, interest and self-efficacy had equally strong effects. A model of the full time period (Time 1 to Time 3) was weak, but it suggested reciprocal effects of interest and self-efficacy.

By demonstrating reciprocal relations between interests and self-efficacy, these studies suggest that the social-cognitive career theory's model of interest development should be revised. Self-efficacy may not deserve the emphasis it receives if interests affect self-efficacy as strongly as self-efficacy affects interests. Nevertheless, we should be cautious about drawing strong conclusions from two studies. Longitudinal models give a tempting glimpse of causation, but experimental research is needed to determine whether interests can cause changes in self-efficacy.

NONLINEAR EFFECTS

A final issue for the social-cognitive career theory is the possibility of nonlinear effects. The theory frames its predictions in terms of linear effects (Lent et al., 1994, p. 114), yet there are good reasons to suspect that high self-efficacy can lead to boredom. Activities are boring when they lack novelty and complexity (see chapter 2). People with extreme self-efficacy may feel completely certain about the outcome of an activity—the lack of uncertainty could make the activity boring. Experiences that promote high self-efficacy—such as practice and learning—also reduce the novelty and complexity of an activity (Walker, 1980, 1981), further contributing to the possibility of boredom.

John Dewey (1913) was the first person to argue for nonlinear effects of self-efficacy on interest: "It is not too much to say that a normal person *demands* a certain amount of difficulty to surmount in order that he may have a full and vivid sense of what he is about, and hence have a lively interest in what he is doing" (p. 52). More recently, Bandura (1997) suggested that "at least moderate perceived efficacy may be required to generate and sustain interest in an activity, but increases in perceived efficacy above the threshold level do not produce further gains in interest. Indeed, supreme self-assurance may render activities unchallenging and, thus, uninteresting" (p. 220).

Lenox and Subich (1994) tested for curvilinear effects by measuring Realistic, Investigative, and Enterprising interests and self-efficacy. To expand the range of self-efficacy, they included equal numbers of participants at five levels of self-efficacy. Interest and self-efficacy showed linear effects for Enterprising interests and curvilinear effects for Realistic and Investigative interests. The curvilinear shape didn't fit the expectations of Dewey or Bandura. Instead of becoming bored at high levels of self-efficacy, people became more interested. At low to moderate levels of self-efficacy, interest and self-efficacy had a flat slope. At moderate to high levels of self-efficacy, interest and self-efficacy had a positive linear relation.

Correlational research is not the best way to test for nonlinear effects. First, the naturalistic range of self-efficacy may be small. How many undergraduates have "supreme self-assurance" for occupational tasks? Second, the scales used to measure self-efficacy may capture only part of self-efficacy's true range. The relation between a scale's observed range and the variable's true range is often unknown (DeVellis, 2003). For example, consider the students who scored at the top of the self-efficacy scale for Investigative interests in the study by Lenox and Subich (1994). Do these students really represent the upper limit of self-efficacy? Professional scientists would have higher self-efficacy than these students: scoring at the top of a scale's range (such as 10 on a 10-point scale) differs from scoring at the top of a variable's naturalistic range.

This issue, like other theoretical issues in vocational psychology, is best settled with experiments. Manipulating self-efficacy enables control over the range of self-efficacy. If the range is extended further, perhaps inverted-U patterns will appear. Two recent experiments indicate that high self-efficacy can reduce feelings of interest (Silvia, 2003). In the first experiment, people indicated their self-efficacy and interest for a series of activities. The activities ranged in difficulty, from low ("walk into a store and buy a can of soda") to moderate ("drive eight hours in one day") to high ("learn to speak five foreign languages"). Self-efficacy decreased as difficulty increased; interest increased from low to moderate difficulty, but decreased from moderate to high difficulty. In a second experiment, people tried to score a bull's-eye by throwing Velcro-covered Ping-Pong balls at a felt dartboard. Three levels of difficulty were created. In an easy condition, people threw the balls from 3 feet away; in a moderate condition, people played from a distance of 8 feet; and in a difficult condition, people played from 18 feet away. As expected, self-efficacy decreased as difficulty increased. Interest, in contrast, increased from the easy to the moderate condition, and then decreased from the moderate to the difficult condition. Both experiments, then, show that self-efficacy can reduce interest when people feel extremely confident about the likelihood of success.

FUTURE DIRECTIONS FOR SELF-EFFICACY AND VOCATIONAL INTERESTS

The development of self-efficacy RIASEC scales for the venerable Strong Interest Inventory (Betz et al., 1996) signaled that self-efficacy had become one of the major constructs in vocational psychology. Why did self-efficacy catch on? Vocational psychology has not had many testable theories of interest development, let alone testable theories that seem to work (see Savickas, 1999). The social-cognitive career theory is easy to test, and its main predictions have been supported. Our review of recent research shows that the theory should expand to deal with new evidence about the complexities of self-efficacy and vocational interests. The causal role of self-efficacy needs more attention. Self-efficacy clearly correlates with interest, and a few experiments suggest that it causes changes in interest. Furthermore, few studies have appraised self-efficacy's indirect route through outcome expectations (see Figure 7.4). In contrast to correlational findings (e.g., Lopez et al., 1997), the only experimental test failed to find an effect of outcome expectancies on interests (Diegelman & Subich, 2001). Finally, reciprocal effects of interests on self-efficacy need more attention. One study found that self-efficacy and interest affected each other (Tracey, 2002a); another study found complex reciprocal relations (Nauta et al., 2002). Experiments are needed to isolate the mutual influences of self-efficacy and interest.

Summary

What can we conclude about the origins of vocational interests? The study of ability and interests has fizzled out, despite occasional attempts at resuscitation (e.g., Randahl, 1991). Without a clear theory that predicts how and why abilities and interests should relate, it's hard to design incisive studies. Recent research subordinates the study of ability to the study of self-efficacy (Brown et al., 2000), arguing that ability affects interests indirectly by affecting self-efficacy (Lent et al., 1994). Although more research is needed, this is a clear causal hypothesis that can provide structure for future research.

Self-efficacy remains a fertile topic. Lent et al.'s (1994) social-cognitive career theory, the prevailing model of vocational interest development, demonstrates how a clearly stated theory can motivate systematic research. Among theories of interest development (see chapters 5 and 6), the social-cognitive career theory is probably the most thoroughly tested. Much of the research broadly supports the theory, but a few issues need sorting out. The causal relations appear to be more complicated than the theory predicts. If interest and self-efficacy have reciprocal effects (Nauta et al., 2002; Tracey, 2002a), the theory would need to be expanded. Likewise, nonlinear effects of self-efficacy on interests (Lenox & Subich, 1994; Silvia, 2003) and indirect effects of self-efficacy (Diegelman & Subich, 2001) should receive more attention.

Theories of development and structure remain disconnected in vocational psychology. One set of theories explains how interests are organized; another set explains how interests develop. Can these areas be integrated? Roe (1957) offered a theory of interest structure connected with a theory of interest development, but research has not supported either component of her theory. Her model of interest structure appears inaccurate (Tracey & Rounds, 1994), and her hypotheses regarding early childhood experience and adult interests have not fared well (Roe & Siegelman, 1964; see chapter 5). Studying how vocational interest structures develop, as opposed to how levels of interests develop, appears to be one possible integration of structure and development (Tracey, 2001; Tracey & Ward, 1998). Tracey (2002a) finds that structures of interests in early childhood don't resemble adult structures, such as RIASEC. The co-development of interest structures and self-efficacy beliefs may be a way to connect issues of structure and development.

Chapter Summary and Conclusions

In this chapter, we explored vocational psychology's contribution to the psychology of interest. This work is marked by sophistication, an eclectic approach to theorizing, and an emphasis on issues that other areas of psychology have not addressed. Vocational psychology is the only part of the psychology of interest to explore the structure of interests, to develop elegant tools for measuring interests, and most notably, to conduct systematic research on the origins of interests. Given the field's new models of interest structure and research on interest development, one wonders what the vocational psychology of interest will look like in 10 years. To venture some guesses, I imagine that Holland's (1997) RIASEC model will fade in prominence, displaced by alternative structural models. The social-cognitive career model will expand as more research illuminates effects of interest on self-efficacy. And, I hope, more researchers will test their theories with simple experiments instead of complex correlational studies.

Lately there has been much pessimism about the scientific future of vocational psychology (Gottfredson, 2001; Savickas, 1999; Walsh, 2001). Fewer graduate students seem interested in the field's basic research side (Krebs et al., 1991), and some people feel that the field may become a marginal part of counseling psychology, its historical home (Tinsley, 2001). My impression, as an outsider, is that vocational psychology is as theoretical as it has ever been. The emergence of new models of interest structure (Tracey & Rounds, 1996b), the development of clear theories of interest development (Lent et al., 1994), and the testing of theoretical problems (Nauta et al., 2002; Tracey, 2002a) indicate a fertile scientific discipline.

Nevertheless, researchers in vocational psychology could enhance its scientific side by distancing themselves from the industry of assessment. The road to riches and the road to knowledge may converge at points, but they end at different places. Psychological science requires good measurement, but there is too much money to be made in vocational interest assessment. When people who profit from an interest inventory publish research on the inventory's validity without noting their financial interests, outsiders might get the wrong idea about the field's scientific credibility. When researchers report that they had to compromise on a smaller sample (e.g., Lenox & Subich, 1994; Nauta et al., 2002) because they couldn't afford the cost of measuring interests, vocational psychology affords a sober look at the real difference between basic and applied goals.

PART III

EXTENSIONS
AND
CONCLUSIONS

8

Comparing Models of Interest

By this point, we've explored nearly all of the psychology of interest. To keep our travels from becoming travails, we ignored some technical points and avoided some complicated issues. This chapter opens the closet doors and analyzes whatever skeletons may lie therein. This book has developed a simple view of interest and interests. More complicated models have been proposed, and we have not yet considered these models. Educational psychologists, for example, have distinguished between situational interest and individual interest for some time (Hidi, 1990). Others propose that interest is better understood in terms of cognitive interest and emotional interest (Harp & Mayer, 1997). What does research say about the validity of these models? Should we replace our simple interest–interests distinction with a more complex framework? Some have suggested that interest is merely importance or that interest is simply attention. Are these viable ways of viewing interest? Finally, interest is often described as a source of intrinsic motivation. What is "intrinsic motivation," and is interest it? Analyzing these contrasting models will enhance our understanding of how people have thought about the state of interest and its relationship to enduring aspects of personality.

Situational and Individual Interest

The distinction between interest and interests serves as the organizing theme for this book. In the first part of the book we reviewed research on interest as an emotion and its implications for learning. In the second part we considered the role of enduring interests in personality, particularly the development of interests. Our model of interest and interests resembles an earlier model that we have not yet discussed. Suzanne Hidi (1990), in a seminal article for the psychology of interest, developed a distinction between *situational interest* and *individual interest* (cf. Hidi & Baird, 1988). Her distinction gave structure for research on interest and deserves credit for the surge of interest research in educational psychology during the 1990s.

These distinctions—interest–interests, and situational–individual interest—are a lot alike. They're motivated by similar concerns and they share similar assumptions. Why should we adopt new terms? In this section, we'll argue that the differences between the interest–interests approach and the situational–individual interest approach are technical and subtle but important nevertheless. We'll see that the situational–individual interest distinction is more complicated than it seems, as researchers expanded and modified Hidi's (1990) approach. Now is the time to unravel these technical issues and analyze the diverging ways of organizing interest and interests.

Situational, Individual, and Actualized Interest

The model of situational and individual interest posits three types of interest (see Krapp, Hidi, & Renninger, 1992). The first type—*individual interest*—is a dispositional tendency to be interested in a certain domain (Renninger, 2000). This concept represents individual differences in what people find interesting. When someone with an individual interest encounters an activity relevant to the interest, a second type of interest—*actualized interest*—arises. The latent dispositional interest becomes manifest as a momentary state of interest. Both of these types differ from a third type—*situational interest*—which is a state of interest caused by external aspects of activities and objects. Situational interest is caused by complexity, novelty, uncertainty, and conflict, as well as by inherently emotional content such as sex and violence (Hidi, 1990; Hidi & Anderson, 1992).

Like the interest–interests model, the situational–individual interest model distinguishes between dispositional and momentary aspects of interest. At this general level, the two approaches are identical. Unlike the interest–interests model, however, the situational–individual interest model proposes two types of momentary interest. The first, situational interest, arises from external factors, such as when people encounter new and complex things. The second, actualized interest, arises from dispositional interests, such as when someone whose hobby is sleight-of-hand watches a magic show on TV. The terms do not merely refer to different causes of interest: this model argues for two different states of interest, not simply one state with two origins. For example, Krapp et al. (1992) argue "although the state of interest, in the sense of an actualized individual interest, seems closely related to the experiential state of situational interest, it has not been demonstrated that the psychological processes and the effects of the two states are identical, or even comparable" (p. 10). Likewise, Hidi and Anderson (1992) state that "one important question that has not been considered is how a psychological state of interest that is due to situational factors differs from one that is due to individual predispositions" (p. 219).

In other writings, it's unclear if situational and actualized interest represent different types. Baumert and Köller (1998), for example, offer a similar model of situational and individual interest. In their view, individual interests, when active, create the state of actualized interest: "during interest-driven actions, the latent disposition (trait) becomes the actualized interest (state)" (p. 242). They then state that "actualized interest must be distinguished from situational interest, which is also conceptualized as a state phenomenon. In contrast to actualized interest, however, situational interest is generated by external stimuli—the interestingness of the situation or object" (p. 242). The two types of state interest—situational and actualized—are said to have different sources, but it isn't made explicit if they are different types of interest.

Schraw and Lehman (2001) offer the most complicated taxonomy of situational and individual interest. Figure 8.1 depicts their model. Individual interest, which they call personal interest, is composed of latent and actualized interest. Latent interest has feeling-related aspects (such as feelings of flow and competence) and value-related aspects (the personal significance of an activity). Actualized interest is a momentary "topic-specific motivational state" (p. 30). Their review of research concluded that "qualitatively different kinds of interest exist. Personal

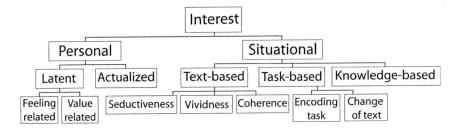

FIGURE 8.1 A complex model of situational and individual interest

Source: Reprinted from *Educational Psychology Review, 13*(1), 2001, Gregory Schraw and Stephen Lehman, "Situational interest: A review of the literature and directions for future research," Figure 1, p. 28, with kind permission of Springer Science and Business Media.

interest is stable, is based on previous experience, and is topic-specific. Situational interest is short-lived, context-dependent, and easier to manipulate" (p. 41). Like Baumert and Köller (1998), Schraw and Lehman distinguish between actualized interest and situational interest. Both are momentary motivational states, in their view, but situational interest is determined primarily by external features of the interesting object. In their discussion, it seems that the types differ in their causes rather than in their nature.

Recently, Hidi (2000, 2001) suggested the *psychological state of interest* as a new term. "The psychological state of interest," she notes, "has also been referred to as the actualized state of individual interest (e.g., Krapp et al., 1992). However, because I believe that this state can be the outcome of various forms of interest, I prefer to use the term psychological state of interest" (Hidi, 2000, p. 311). Replacing actualized interest solves the problem of two kinds of interest states, one for dispositions and one for situations. The new term, however, complicates the relationship between situational interest and the psychological state of interest. Stating that "situational interest" causes a "psychological state of interest" sounds odd—does one state of interest trigger another state of interest? Situational interest ceases to be "interest felt in a situation" or "interest caused by situational factors" and becomes "things that cause feelings of interest."

Evaluating the Distinction

By this point, it should be obvious why we avoided discussing situational and individual interest until now. This distinction is hard to criticize because several models of situational and individual interest appear in print. For instance, some people include actualized interest in their model and others don't (Hidi, 2000). Even when researchers use the same concepts, they often define the terms differently. Some people define *individual interest* as an enduring disposition instead of a state, and others define it as "both a psychological state and an enduring predisposition of the person" (Renninger, 2000, p. 375). Given its many variants, researchers should avoid speaking of *the* distinction between situational and individual interest.

Should we abandon this old model in favor of interest–interests? It depends on how the model is used. Something resembling a situational–individual interest distinction is needed. If the psychology of interest failed to distinguish between momentary experience and enduring dispositions, empirical research would become difficult to conduct and interpret. Viewed at a broad level, the distinction between situational and individual interest has served the field well. If we want to use the distinction at this level of generality, then it works as well as the distinction between interest and interests.

If we want to use the situational–individual interest model to make specific predictions about the nature of interest, however, it will require empirical tests. Some of the model's finer points are untenable or untested. The model's most controversial prediction—that actualized interest and situational interest are different subjective experiences—remains untested and unresolved. This is a strong claim, and strong claims require strong evidence. Negative arguments—such as "it has not been demonstrated that the psychological processes and the effects of the two states are identical, or even comparable" (Krapp et al., 1992, p. 10)—cannot substitute for positive evidence. Perhaps this point is moot. The distinction between situational and actualized interest has had no influence on empirical research; it hasn't qualified any findings or discriminated between competing theories.

The biggest limitation of the situational–individual interest model may be the implausible view of situational interest. Hidi (2000) views situational interest as caused by external factors that would make most people feel interested. Appraisal theories of emotion (see chapter 2) view this as misleading because interest does not come from situations—emotions are caused by interpretations of events, not events themselves (Lazarus, 2001). The diversity of emotional responses to the same event is a basic datum of emotion psychology. It's hard to find an event that makes nearly everyone sad, happy, or interested. Appraisal theories easily explain this diversity by referring to differences in the patterns of thought that give rise to emotions (Roseman & Smith, 2001). Calling the interest "situational" and ascribing it to external factors obscures the role of appraisal factors in the generation of interest (see chapter 2).

The situational–individual interest model makes different assumptions about the nature of interest. Viewing interest as an emotion implies many features that interest ought to have: appraisal structure, facial and vocal expressions, early appearance in infancy, universality, cross-species similarities, experiential qualities, and functional and motivational properties. Disparate definitions of *situational interest* appear (see Hidi, 2000; Krapp, 1999; Schraw & Lehman, 2001), but none of them emphasizes interest's emotional qualities. Such views of interest do not predict the emotional features that interest has (see chapters 1 and 2).

Furthermore, the interest–interests approach enables continuities between interest and other emotions. The terminology is convenient for describing how emotions participate in the development of idiosyncratic motives (see chapter 6). "Situational fear" and "situational happiness," for instance, would be cumbersome but tenable. But "actualized fear" versus the emotion of fear and "actualized happiness" versus the emotion of happiness are different issues. No theories or findings in emotion psychology justify splitting an emotion into "situational" and "actualized" aspects. Applying the situational–individual distinction to other emotions is at best premature, given the lack of evidence for differences between actualized and situational interest. The distinction between situational interest and the psychological state of interest (Hidi, 2000, 2001) is equally awkward when applied to other emotions. For example, stating that "situational fear" causes the "psychological state of fear" makes situational fear sound like it means "the things that make people afraid."

An Alternative

The distinction between interest and interests is a simple, general alternative to the confusing state of the situational–individual interest distinction. The original distinction between situational and individual interest (Hidi, 1990; Krapp et al., 1992) clarified some murky problems and thus advanced the study of interest and learning. Years later, however, the distinction has evolved into a class of related variants, each with a slightly different set of concepts. Furthermore, many of the model's early claims—such as the difference between actualized and situational interest—have been ignored by research or modified in later writings (e.g., Hidi, 2000). This state of affairs will not advance research on interest much further. For these reasons, a reorientation around the simpler interest–interests model may be needed.

Table 8.1 shows how interest and interests organize and supplant past terms. The simple term *interest* replaces "psychological state of interest" (Hidi, 2000), "actualized interest," and "situational interest" when it refers to a state (Krapp et al., 1992; Schraw & Lehman, 2001). The simple term *interests* refers to a person's enduring interests in activities; it replaces "individual interest" (Krapp et al., 1992) and "personal interest" (Schraw & Lehman, 2001). No replacement is needed when people use "situational interest" to refer to the causes of feelings of interest (Hidi, 2000). Simply stating "the causes of interest"—or, better yet, specifying the appraisal processes that generate feelings of interest—suffices.

TABLE 8.1 Reframing Situational and Individual Interest in Terms of Interest and Interests

Old Term	New Term
Psychological state of interest	Interest
Situational interest (as a state)	Interest
Actualized interest	Interest
Individual interest	Interests
Personal interest	Interests
Situational interest (as the causes of a state)	The causes of interest

Interest and Curiosity

The distinction between interest and curiosity is tricky and controversial. Some researchers suggest that interest and curiosity are distinct motivational states with different emotional consequences. Reeve (1996), for example, suggests that interest is a positive state motivating approach, whereas curiosity is an aversive state motivating its own reduction, an epistemic itch to be scratched. Litman and Jimerson (2004) proposed a similar distinction between two kinds of trait curiosity. Curiosity as a feeling of interest involves activation and positive emotional experiences; curiosity as a feeling of deprivation involves aversive feelings of uncertainty (Litman, 2005). In the study of reading, Hidi and Berndorff (1998) suggest that interest and curiosity have much in common, but that interest is aroused by a broader set of factors.

Other researchers view *interest* and *curiosity* as synonymous. Berlyne, for example, often used the terms interchangeably, and he measured curiosity with questions referring to interest and boredom (e.g., Berlyne, 1949, 1974d). For better or worse, most researchers implicitly equate interest and curiosity by lumping together research on interest and curiosity (e.g., Kashdan, 2004; Sansone & Smith, 2000b). In this book, for example, we have discussed research on curiosity throughout. In fact, much of the work relevant to the psychology of interest has been conducted under the label of curiosity, such as research on trait curiosity (chapter 4) and research on the causes of interest (chapter 2).

Are interest and curiosity the same? When confronted with conflicting points of view, the first thing to do is to consult the evidence. Has research supported a distinction between interest and curiosity? Despite the many claims of differences between interest and curiosity, a look at the evidence shows that there is essentially no research on this topic. Thus far, statements about differences between interest and curiosity have been theoretical and speculative. Researchers who have argued for a difference between them have yet to shore up their position with research. An exception is Litman and Jimerson's (2004) studies of two kinds of trait curiosity. This research, however, does not illuminate whether the subjective experience of interest differs from the experience of curiosity.

A recent experiment is a cautionary tale to theorists who view curiosity as aversive despite a lack of evidence. Wilson, Centerbar, Kermer, and Gilbert (2005) provided an example of how intuitive ideas about curiosity can be incorrect. Their study is part of a line of research that illuminates why people's ideas about emotions are often wrong (Gilbert & Wilson, 2000). People's predictions about how they *would* feel in a situation usually differ from how they *actually* feel when placed in the situation. To explore expected and actual reactions to uncertainty, the researchers asked the participants to take part in a bogus impression-formation task (Wilson et al., 2005, Experiment 3). People interacted with several fictional people over a computer; one of these fictional people picked the participant as a "best friend" for the study. The researchers manipulated the uncertainty of the situation: in one condition people knew who had picked them, and in another condition people didn't know who picked them and were thus curious.

Which condition should feel the happiest? All groups were equally happy immediately after learning they had been picked as a best friend, but people who remained uncertain were significantly happier 15 minutes later. Positive affect declined over time when people knew who had picked them, but it remained stable when people were uncertain. This clearly shows, lay beliefs to the contrary, that people enjoyed being curious. A different group of participants was asked about which situation would make them feel happier. Ironically, virtually everyone said he or she would prefer to know who had picked each of them. Although people apparently agreed with theorists who contend that curiosity is aversive, they felt happier when placed in the situation that promoted curiosity.

The interest–curiosity distinction may be based on the different uses of interest and curiosity in everyday speech. People often use *curiosity* to refer to events that have yet to happen or knowledge they have yet to acquire. *Interest*, in contrast, is often used to refer to ongoing events or to describe events in the past. People say they are curious to see a new movie, but they say they found the movie interesting after having seen it. Yet linguistic differences don't always reflect psychological differences—everyday language can lead science astray. The challenge for research is to identify real differences in appraisal structure, subjective qualities, and motivational consequences. To date, no evidence suggests differences between interest and curiosity, so equating them is justified.

Cognitive Interest and Emotional Interest

Are there types of interest? Thus far we have assumed that the emotion of interest is unitary. Emotions retain core qualitative characteristics independently of the specific things that induced them (Ekman, 1992; Tomkins, 1962). People might feel interest in some situations and not in others, but ultimately the emotional nature of interest is the same. This is one reason for our skepticism of different states of actualized interest and situational interest (Krapp et al., 1992), described earlier.

Kintsch (1980) proposed a distinction between cognitive interest and emotional interest within the context of reading. He suggested that cognitive interest results from organizational aspects of stories: "A story may be interesting because of the intricate pattern of events that are described, because of the surprises it holds, or because of the way it is being told" (p. 88). Emotional interest, in contrast, follows from a story's "direct emotional impact" (p. 88), such as portrayals of violence, sex, and arousing themes. Although his discussion emphasized cognitive interest, Kintsch did not stress the distinction too heavily. He emphasized that interesting stories involve both types of interest. Without emotional elements, a tightly organized story would be boring; without a coherent representation of the characters and events, emotional elements would seem meaningless. Furthermore, Kintsch's discussion implies that the typology reflects different causes of interest rather than different types of interest itself, although this isn't explicitly stated. Hidi and Baird (1986) elaborated on this point, proposing that cognitive and emotional interest differ in the information involved in creating interest. Cognitive interest comes from information contained in a story, such as its structure and the expectations it forms; emotional interest requires prior background knowledge, such as general life themes. Both sources cause the same state of interest.

Kintsch's distinction didn't catch on, although a few researchers have used it to make broad claims about interest. Harp and Mayer (1997, 1998) contend that the two types of interest have opposite effects on comprehension: cognitive interest enhances learning, and emotional interest impairs learning. This is a striking claim, given the research on interest and learning discussed in chapter 3. If researchers have been confounding two opposing types of interest, we wouldn't expect so many replicable relationships between interest and learning. What evidence supports this hypothesis?

In the only experiment on cognitive and emotional interest, Harp and Mayer (1997, Study 2) evaluated whether people discriminate between cognitive and emotional interest when reading texts. College students read a science text that explained the causes of lightning. Several elements were added to this basic text. First, summary illustrations bolstered the main ideas by depicting the process of lightning. Second, seductive elements—interesting but unimportant details, such as vivid pictures and entertaining anecdotes—were added (see chapter 3). The readers rated each element for cognitive interest and for emotional interest. Cognitive interest was measured with two items: "How much does this material help you to understand the process of lightning?" and "How helpful is this material for organizing the steps involved in the process of lightning?" Emotional interest was measured with two other items: "How interesting is this material?" and "How entertaining is this material?"

Before describing the results, we should consider what these items say about the constructs of cognitive and emotional interest. The measure of emotional interest captures what most researchers mean by interest: it addresses the reader's positive affective response to the material. The measure of cognitive interest, in contrast, has nothing to do with affective responses. Cognitive interest, as measured, is merely the person's judgment of how relevant material is to the causes of lightning. If readers rate an illustration as high in cognitive interest, they are saying simply that the illustration helps them understand the process of lightning; they aren't describing an internal state evoked by the illustration.

When the implicit definitions of cognitive and emotional interest are clarified, the experiment's results appear trivial and circular. First, material that explained the causes of lightning (the basic text and the summary illustrations) was rated higher in cognitive interest than in emotional interest. Restated, people felt that the material about lightning's causes helped them understand lightning's causes. Second, material that conveyed entertaining information (irrelevant but entertaining pictures and anecdotes) was rated higher in emotional interest than in cognitive interest. Restated, material that was unrelated to lightning's causes was seen as less helpful in understanding lightning's causes.

Unpacking the cognitive versus emotional interest distinction highlights the superficiality of claims about cognitive interest's superior effect on comprehension (Harp & Mayer, 1997). In one experiment (Harp & Mayer, 1997, Study 1), text elements about the causes of lightning (ostensibly sources of cognitive interest) facilitated recall better than did irrelevant but interesting elements (the ostensible sources of emotional interest). Harp and Mayer conclude that "on the theoretical level, this study provides important evidence in favor of cognitive interest theory over emotional interest theory" (p. 100). Once again, a close look at the procedure trivializes the findings. If cognitive interest is defined by the relevance of material to the text's main points, and if comprehension is measured by recall of the text's main points, then the conclusion that cognitive interest enhances recall is trivially true: emphasizing the main points facilitates remembering the main points. Labeling the processes according to opposing types of interest makes the experiments seem more complicated than they actually are.

What should we conclude about the distinction between cognitive and emotional interest? Only two experiments appraise the validity of the distinction (Harp & Mayer, 1997), and a close look at these studies reveals fatal problems. When we examine how emotional and cognitive interest are measured, we find that (1) emotional interest is simply what everyone else means by interest, and (2) cognitive interest isn't interest at all, but rather relevance to a text's main points. This research lays a rickety foundation for a theory of cognitive and emotional types of interest.

Beyond the lack of empirical support, conceptual reasons suggest limitations to this distinction. First, the cognitive and emotional interest distinction obscures other emotions. Categorizing all emotional elements under emotional interest puts sadness, fear, enjoyment, and other emotions into the same category. A complete understanding of emotion and text processing needs a more differentiated framework than "interest" (cognitive interest) and "other emotions" (emotional interest). Second, does this typology apply to all interesting things or only to interesting text? I don't think the psychology of interest is ready to commit to cognitive and emotional interest in pictures, cognitive and emotional interest in abstract ideas, or cognitive and emotional interest in academic areas and vocations. Categorizing the causes of an emotion, or the emotion itself, into cognitive versus emotional types adds complexity without yielding new predictions or insights. Finally, there was a time when psychology viewed cognition and emotion as antagonistic (Leeper, 1948), and that time has passed. Contrasting cognition and emotion seems unproductive in light of modern research on cognition–emotion intersections.

Interest and Importance

Occasionally interest has been equated with the importance of a situation. Saying that something is interesting, in this view, means only that the thing is significant to the person. Ortony and Turner (1990) take this position when arguing against interest as an emotion. They suggest that "if one returns to one's house to discover that it has been ransacked, one might well have an intense interest in discovering who did it" (p. 318). Yet there are good reasons to separate interest and importance. As Mandler (1982) suggests: "Interesting things are not always valued, and valued things are not always interesting. A square coffee cup is probably interesting without being valued, and a properly working tool may be valued without being particularly interesting" (p. 12). Interpreting interest in terms of importance is tricky. Many things that interest people are fictional, hypothetical, and fantastical, such as narrative events in film and writing (Tan, 2000). It isn't clear what importance means for such events.

Several areas of research show that interest and importance diverge. In chapter 3, we saw that interest and importance are distinct aspects of text (Alexander & Jetton, 1996; Hidi, Baird, & Hildyard, 1982; Wade, 2001). Text can contain interesting elements and important elements; interesting elements, however, need not be important. One study, for example, found that key ideas in a passage about insects were ranked as important to the exposition but not at all interesting. Conversely, novel ideas about insects were rated as interesting but not at all important to the passage's purpose, and presumably, to the reader's goals (Garner, Gillingham, & White, 1989). Experiments on text comprehension also suggest that interesting and important sentences are processed according to different strategies (Shirey, 1992). A consequence is that interesting elements may be remembered better than important elements if the two diverge (Goetz, Sadoski, Fatemi, & Bush, 1994; Sadoski & Quast, 1990).

Appraisal research also shows that interest is not simply importance. In a study of positive emotions, the appraised importance of a situation predicted the occurrence of several emotions, including surprise, confidence, and interest (Ellsworth & Smith, 1988). But importance did not uniquely predict interest. Sansone and Smith (2000a) describe a series of experiments on how people motivate themselves to work on tedious tasks. They found that manipulating the importance of a task didn't necessarily increase interest. When a boring task was important, people often used strategies to make the task more interesting. Using these strategies, in turn, increased feelings of interest.

In sum, interest and importance relate to each other in complex and intriguing ways (e.g., Sansone & Smith, 2000b; Wade, 2001), but they are clearly different constructs. Equating interest and importance obscures their interesting relationships and contradicts research from several areas of psychology.

Interest and Attention

Some writers have subsumed interest under attention. Wilson (1971), for example, argues: " 'feeling of interest' is not a set of sensations, nor a mood or emotion, nor an inclination to get or repeat pleasure, nor an impulse or habit. It is by contrast an inclination to notice something, to pay continuing attention to it and to try to enter into some active relationship with it which seems appropriate to its interesting features" (pp. 49–50). Interest clearly involves attention. In their studies of appraisal, Smith and Ellsworth (1985) found that ratings of attentiveness distinguished interest from other emotions (Ellsworth & Smith, 1988). Interest is commonly measured by visual attention (Berlyne, 1971a; Silvia, 2005c). A study of infants found that the effects of objects and faces on visual attention were mediated by facial expressions of interest (Langsdorf, Izard, Rayias, & Hembree, 1983; see chapter 1). Novelty evoked expressions of interest, which in turn predicted the duration of attention to the object.

But interest is not simply attention. Several lines of research advise against equating the two constructs. First, manipulating interest does not necessarily increase attention. Studies of interest and reading found that the interestingness of a text does not simply increase the amount of attention devoted to the text (Hidi, 1995; Shirey, 1992). In fact, some experiments show that people pay *less* attention to interesting texts relative to uninteresting texts (McDaniel, Waddill, Finstad, & Bourg, 2000; Shirey & Reynolds, 1988). If interest increases but attention decreases, then interest and attention are clearly different. Second, many emotions have relationships with attention. These relationships are some of the most interesting findings in the study of cognition and emotion. For example, happiness and sadness affect people's ability to control their attention (Gray, 2001; Kensinger & Corkin, 2003; Phillips, Bull, Adams, & Fraser,

2002), and fear affects preattentive processing of potentially threatening objects (Öhman, 2002; Öhman, Flykt, & Esteves, 2001). Overall, then, research casts doubt on redefining interest in terms of attention. The two are functionally related, but equating interest and attention seems unwarranted.

Interest and Intrinsic Motivation

The rise of research on interest was part of a broader shift in psychology. The decline of drive theories of motivation in the 1950s, caused in part by early research on curiosity and exploration (Harlow, 1953), opened the door for theories of intrinsic motivation. Half a century later, drive theory survives only in motivation psychology textbooks. Motivation psychology itself has been assimilated into other fields of psychology, particularly social, personality, and emotion psychology. Theories of intrinsic motivation, in contrast, are alive and well (Sansone & Harackiewicz, 2000). Intrinsic motivation theories are a diverse bunch, emphasizing organismic needs (Deci & Ryan, 2000), different types and structures of goals (Shah & Kruglanski, 2000), agentic self-regulation processes (Bandura, 1997), and interest (Izard, 1977; Sansone & Smith, 2000a, 2000b).

Intuitively, interest seems fundamental to intrinsic motivation. Nevertheless, connecting theories of interest and intrinsic motivation is difficult; these concepts, like many key concepts in psychology, have acquired many meanings over the years. Rather than survey all intersections of interest and intrinsic motivation, we'll focus on interest and self-determination theory (Deci & Ryan, 1985, 2000; Ryan & Deci, 2000). Apart from being the most widely studied theory of intrinsic motivation, self-determination theory makes clear claims about the role of interest in intrinsic motivation (Deci, 1992, 1998; Deci & Ryan, 2000; Krapp, 2002a). Other views of intrinsic motivation are reviewed elsewhere (Deci, 1975; Fiske & Maddi, 1961b; Hunt, 1971).

According to self-determination theory, the basic dimension of motivation is whether an activity is *self-determined.* When people feel self-determined, they "act with a sense of volition and agency, a sense of being autonomous and wholly willing to engage in some activity. It is as if the activity were an expression of who one is" (Deci, 1998, p. 147). There are two types of self-determined activity. The first type is intrinsically motivated activity. Deci and Ryan (2000) assert that "intrinsically motivated behaviors are those that are freely engaged out of interest without the necessity of separable consequences" (p. 233). Intrinsic motivation represents a broad category of self-rewarding activity based on interest, enjoyment, flow, vitality, and need satisfaction (Deci & Ryan, 2000; Nix, Ryan, Manly, & Deci, 1999; Reeve, 1989; Ryan & Frederick, 1997). Interest is thus a major part of intrinsic motivation. In fact, self-reported interest is a common measure of intrinsic motivation (Hidi, 2000).

The second type of self-determined activity is integrated regulation. In this type of action, people have fully internalized the value of an activity into the self. The task may be boring, tedious, or aversive, but people truly want to do it anyway. Integrated regulation is a form of extrinsic motivation: people are not doing the action because it's interesting or enjoyable. The action is self-determined because people feel like they are behaving in line with their true selves, as opposed to acting to satisfy someone else or to get a material reward. As Deci (1998) explains, "intrinsic motivation and integrated regulation are different in that intrinsically motivated behavior is done because it is interesting, while integrated behavior is done because it is personally valued" (p. 149).

Recent writings suggest a second aspect of interest and intrinsic motivation. Deci and Ryan (2000) contend that different processes arouse and maintain intrinsic motivation (cf. Mitchell, 1993). They propose that sustained intrinsic motivation requires that an activity satisfy organismic needs for autonomy and competence. Variables such as novelty and complexity spark interest, but only need satisfaction sustains intrinsic motivation. Experiments indirectly support this hypothesis. Reeve (1989) found that interest and enjoyment originated from different aspects of activities. The novelty and complexity of anagrams and puzzle tasks predicted feelings of interest, but they didn't predict feelings of enjoyment, congruent with our view of interest and happiness as distinct emotions (see chapter 1). Perceived competence for the activity, in contrast, predicted enjoyment but not interest. This pattern of findings supports Deci and Ryan's prediction. Novelty and complexity sparked feelings of interest; feeling competent at the activity increased feelings of enjoyment. Additional research is needed to test this intriguing prediction more directly.

Chapter Summary and Conclusions

In this chapter we covered some of the finer points related to the nature of interest. We contrasted this book's perspective on interest and interests with an older model of situational and individual interest. Taken generally, the distinction between situational and individual interest parallels our distinction between interest and interests. In its specifics, however, the model makes some improbable predictions (such as two types of state interest, actualized and situational) that have not been tested empirically. Other work suggested splitting interest into cognitive and emotional types. This distinction is not well supported by research, and it combines many positive and negative emotions into the "emotional interest" category. After examining the relation of interest to curiosity, attention, and importance, we examined the role of interest in intrinsic motivation. Research suggests that interest is one of many sources of intrinsic motivation (Deci, 1998).

This takes us to the end of our exploration of the psychology of interest. In the final chapter, we'll survey the main points of our journey and highlight important directions for future research.

9

Conclusion: Looking Back, Looking Ahead

This chapter marks the end of our exploration of the psychology of interest. After covering such diverse terrain, it's time to take stock of the trip and then think about where to go next. In this chapter, we first look back at the prominent themes that run through the study of interest. What do these areas have in common? Then we look ahead to the future of research on interest. What will—or what should—the psychology of interest look like 10 years from now?

Looking Back

The most striking thing about research on interest is its diversity. Interest has found a home in many areas of psychology, and it spans areas of psychology that have little in common—counseling psychologists who study career decision making and cognitive psychologists who study text processing rarely appear in the same book. This diversity makes the study of interest intriguing and challenging. Summarizing the sprawling body of thought on interest is hard, but a few major themes emerge nevertheless.

First, throughout this book we have seen how appraisal theories of emotion bridge different areas in the psychology of interest. Research on interest has not typically viewed interest as an emotion. Yet, when an appraisal model of interest is adopted, many new and intriguing predictions are made. Appraisal theories offer a new model of what makes things interesting (Silvia, 2005c). As a result, the appraisal model also makes new predictions about what makes text interesting (chapter 3), what makes art interesting (Silvia, 2005a, 2005b), and what makes anything else interesting. Research on appraisals and interest strengthens the case for interest as an emotion (chapter 1), handles problems that past models of interestingness have struggled with (chapter 2), and offers a new perspective on text-based interest (chapter 3). Appraisal ideas also extend to the study of vocational interests. Self-efficacy reliably predicts vocational interests; despite causal ambiguities, some research suggests that self-efficacy causes increases in vocational interests (Luzzo, Hasper, Albert, Bibby, & Martinelli, 1999; see chapter 7). As we saw in chapters 2 and 3, appraising something as potentially comprehensible increases interest in text and images. It's possible that the development of interests in vocationally relevant activities can be connected to appraisal processes as well.

Second, researchers in many areas of the psychology of interest contend that interest has a constructive functional role in motivation. Interest is thought to "do something," and this something is remarkably similar across the different areas of psychology. Emotion researchers assert that interest enhances the motivation to learn and explore (Fredrickson, 1998; Izard, 1977), and emotion research shows that interest predicts behavioral exploration and engagement (chapter 1). Researchers in motivation psychology agree; their experiments show that interest facilitates the accomplishment of goals (Sansone & Smith, 2000b). Education research shows that students learn interesting text more easily (Schiefele, 1999), perform better in interesting classes (Schiefele, Krapp, & Winteler, 1992), and make important learning choices based on what is interesting (Köller, Baumert, & Schnabel, 2001). Human-development research shows that enduring interests foster achievement throughout the life span (Rathunde, 1995, 1998). Using interests as the basis for career decision making increases the likelihood of finding motivating, meaningful work (Fouad, 1999; Swanson, 1999), and intrinsic motivation during work is characterized by feelings of interest (Fisher & Noble, 2004). The degree of agreement across independent areas of psychology is striking, thus confirming Holt's (1967) contention that "curiosity is hardly ever idle" (p. 187).

Most generally, we have seen the promise of models of cognition and emotion for bridging emotion and personality. The psychology of interest emerged from several different fields—such as education (Dewey, 1913), counseling and assessment (Strong, 1943), text processing (Hidi, Baird, & Hildyard, 1982), behaviorism (Berlyne, 1960), and emotion (Tomkins, 1962)—and distinct literatures developed. As a consequence, there has been little effort toward developing general models that cut across different areas of research. Although a "general theory of interest" may be impossible or impractical, it's clear that the different areas of research could learn a lot from each other.

Looking Ahead

The psychology of interest is poised for enormous growth. But, as Ring (1967) noted, research can expand outward instead of growing upward. To help prevent science's equivalent of urban sprawl, in which different researchers create unrelated suburbs of knowledge, this section highlights some of the important problems that deserve more research.

Emotional Aspects of Interest

Much more needs to be known about emotional features of interest. Modern theories of emotions assume that emotions consist of components—such as appraisals, physiology, facial expressions, and subjective experience—as well as a coherent organization of the components (Ekman, 1992; Scherer, 2001a). Chapter 2 reviewed the state of research on the components of interest. A particularly important direction is identifying physiological and expressive components of interest. The handful of experiments on facial expressions needs to be followed up with comprehensive studies, particularly studies that measure facial movements physiologically. The expressive components associated with interest are probably relatively subtle and thus less suitable for observer coding of videotaped expressions (e.g., Reeve, 1993).

If reliable expressive correlates of interest can be found, then perhaps they can be connected to the appraisals that generate interest. Appraisal researchers suggest that components of an expression, such as the raising or lowering of the eyebrows, have specific meanings associated with specific appraisals (Kaiser & Wehrle, 2001). For example, raising the eyebrows and upper eyelids reflects appraisals of novelty and unexpectedness (Pope & Smith, 1994). Perhaps facial actions associated with interest converge with interest's appraisals. A similar case has been made for physiological components. Specific physiological markers of emotion, such as increased skin conductance, are presumed to reflect specific appraisal components (Pecchinenda, 2001; Pecchinenda & Smith, 1996). As with facial expressions, physiological aspects of interest may reflect connections with interest's appraisal components. Apart from enhancing our knowledge of interest, this research would enhance the nascent literature on the coherence of emotion components (Bonanno & Keltner, 2004).

The appraisal approach to interest, in which the experience of interest is traced to the unfolding of a unique pattern of appraisals (chapter 2), is in its infancy. So far, research suggests that two appraisals are central to interest: an appraisal of novelty–complexity (broadly construed), and an appraisal of one's ability to understand the new, complex thing. Research to date has not examined whether additional appraisals are important, studied the inputs that modify the outcomes of these appraisals (Smith & Kirby, 2001), and examined how similar appraisal structures produce emotions within the emotion family of interest (Ellsworth & Scherer, 2003). Moreover, nothing is known about the process of these appraisals. Some theories assume that appraisals unfold in a fixed order (Scherer, 1999, 2001a); other theories assume that appraisals unfold parallel to one another or holistically (Lazarus, 2001). Research on the process of interest appraisals would have important implications for bigger problems in the study of appraisal. Interest is unusually well suited for tackling these problems because it is easily and ethically manipulated, and it has a relatively simple appraisal structure.

Interest, Reading, and Learning

Interest's role in reading and learning is one of the most intriguing intersections of cognition and emotion. Thus far, research has clearly shown that interest promotes learning from text under a wide range of conditions. The second stage of research—explaining how this process works—is one of the most important problems for research in text-based interest. The inner workings of interest and reading are just beginning to be uncovered. Thus far, research has suggested that interest affects how deeply people process text and the strategies they use when choosing what to read (Schiefele, 1999; Son & Metcalfe, 2000). These and other pathways deserve attention. In particular, it is worth examining the ways interest affects how people choose what to read. Perhaps interest could paradoxically impair learning by encouraging people to spend their studying time unwisely.

The standard method in studying what makes text interesting is to have people read a text, rate their interest in the text, and then rate the text on a broad range of dimensions (Schraw & Lehman, 2001). The features of the text—such as coherence, vividness, and ease of comprehension—are then correlated with interest. These correlational studies are important and informative, and they should be viewed as a foundation for a second generation of research. The correlational studies lack critical information about causality, and causality is especially ambiguous in the study of text-based interest. Does vividness cause higher interest, or is vividness simply a facet of interest? The few experimental studies (Sadoski, Goetz, & Rodriguez, 2000) are good guides for future research.

In chapter 3, we suggested that the sources of text-based interest may be special cases of broader principles of interestingness. Throughout part I, we considered interest as an emotion. If emotions come from appraisals, then the sources of interest can be understood in terms of a small set of appraisals. The appraisal model developed in chapter 2 suggests that interest comes primarily from appraising something as new, complex, and uncertain but also as potentially comprehensible. The many sources of text-based interest may be reduced to these two appraisal dimensions. Pursuing an appraisal model of text-based interest is worthwhile for a few reasons. First, it integrates the study of text-based interest with the broader body of work on cognition and emotion. This enriches the theoretical context of research on interest and reading. Second, an appraisal model can bring some structure to the sprawling literature on what makes text interesting. Does text-based interest really have several dozen causes? Might there be a simpler underlying structure to the sources of interest? Third, the appraisal model makes causal predictions and provides a set of methods for testing appraisal hypotheses. These can help the study of text-based interest to advance beyond correlational designs.

Researchers studying seductive details need to take a closer look at the evidence. Many studies have failed to find a seductive-details effect. Most of the ostensibly supportive studies either (1) didn't actually find support for a detrimental effect of seductive details, or (2) didn't manipulate the presence or absence of seductive details. In light of the mixed findings, it's worth rethinking the explanation for the seductive-details effect. Sadoski (2001) has pointed out that adding unrelated material to a text simply disrupts the text's coherence. Because poor coherence is known to impair memory, it's possible that poor coherence, not high interest, is making the text harder to remember. These competing explanations—interesting details seduce attention versus irrelevant information reduces coherence—are easily tested in experimental designs.

Individual Differences and Interest

Theories of individual differences related to interest, particularly models of trait curiosity, are experiencing a renaissance (Kashdan, 2004; Litman & Jimerson, 2004). The coming years will show rapid developments in how psychologists think about the curious person. The most central task for this area of research is to form process-oriented explanations for these traits. Identifying and assessing individual differences is often the first step in understanding a phenomenon (Underwood, 1975); research to date can't be faulted for not examining psychological dynamics in much detail. For the future, however, researchers should examine why these traits predict curiosity. Why are curious people more interested in things? What psychological processes connect the disposition to activity and experience?

Appraisal theories of emotion are promising for explaining the processes that underlie trait curiosity (Lewis, 2001; van Reekum & Scherer, 1997). The appraisal perspective assumes that patterns of emotions stem from patterns of appraisal (Roseman & Smith, 2001). Chronically angry people are angry because they appraise events in ways that create anger; happy people appraise their worlds in ways that create happiness. In short, individual differences in curiosity may be founded on individual differences in appraisals. In this view, trait curiosity would predict interest because curious people are more likely to appraise events (1) as new, complex, and uncertain, and (2) as comprehensible and coherent. But, on the other hand, these traits may not be rooted in appraisals, as implied by psychobiological approaches (e.g., Zuckerman, 1994). Either way, appraisals are an intriguing way of bridging cognition, emotion, and personality.

Another task for research on individual differences in interest is to assess what models of trait curiosity have in common. The past few years have seen the arrival of many new curiosity models (Collins, Litman, &

Spielberger, 2003; Kashdan et al., 2004; Litman & Jimerson, 2004; Litman & Spielberger, 2003). Such situations can arouse a sense of territoriality, leading to an exaggeration of the differences between related concepts and a reluctance to pit models against each other in comparative tests (Wicklund, 1990). It would be shame for this to happen in the study of curiosity because I suspect that what these scales have in common is what is central to interest, exploration, and motivation. Whether these assessment tools measure markedly different things is an empirical question that is easy to answer. Directly comparing these models is essential for the cumulative development of this field.

Finally, the study of individual differences should intersect with other areas of the psychology of interest. The study of traits related to interest is too restricted to the field of personality and individual differences. Much is known about how traits related to interest intersect with other traits; little is known about how these traits relate to other dimensions of interest and interests. For example, does trait curiosity offer anything to the study of text-based interest? Are curious people more likely to use interest as a basis for selecting learning materials? Can the study of vocational interests benefit from examining curiosity? What do these traits have to say about interest in art and aesthetics?

The Development of Interests

The study of the development of interests is unusual relative to other areas of the psychology of interest: it's marked by an excess of theories and a dearth of research. The need for research is probably more pressing in this area than in any other. After reviewing past theories of how interests develop (chapter 5), we considered a new theory rooted in cognition and emotion (chapter 6). The emotion–attribution model proposes that the development of interests involves the development of emotional knowledge. Based on the experience of emotions and attributions for the causes of the emotions, people will form ideas about what was interesting and enjoyable in the past, the objects and activities that can create positive emotions, and the likelihood that activities will be interesting.

An appeal of this model is its continuity with the emphasis on cognition and emotion in other areas. Throughout this book, we have emphasized how modern theories in emotion psychology can inform problems in the psychology of interest. The emotion–attribution model extends this emphasis on the interaction of emotional and cognitive processes in its contention that interpretations of emotions form the bridge between momentary experience and stable aspects of personality. More appealing, though, is that this model makes new predictions about how interests develop and change. This model can be tested experimentally, and preliminary studies have supported its predictions. Nevertheless, it remains for future work to evaluate the model more definitively.

Vocational Interests

Vocational psychology has a proud tradition of research on interests. It can claim the largest and oldest body of work on interests as well as the most sophisticated methods for assessing interests. Despite the reservations of researchers who feel that vocational psychology is becoming marginalized within its historical home of counseling psychology (Tinsley, 2001; Walsh, 2001), basic research on vocational interests seems as strong as ever. One of the most contested problems is the structure of vocational interests. Holland's (1997) RIASEC hexagon has guided basic research and applied practice for several decades. Thus far, it has fared well in the face of alternative models, and the RIASEC model's entrenchment in the industry of interest assessment ensures its long life, if only due to inertia.

One of the most intriguing questions for future vocational research is whether alternative models of interest structure will eventually supplant Holland's hexagon. Tracey's (2002b) spherical model of vocational interests is the most promising alternative to the RIASEC hexagon. It will probably find favor with basic researchers. Alternative structures—such as the RIASEC hexagon and Prediger's (1982) dimensional model—can be understood as special cases of the spherical structure; this makes the model unusually versatile. Research on the reliability and generality of the spherical model will probably grow quickly (e.g., Long, Adams, & Tracey, 2005).

Another direction for vocational research to take is the examination of the role of self-efficacy in the development of vocational interests. It's pretty clear that perceptions of efficacy for activities and interest in the activities correlate with each other (Rottinghaus, Larson, & Borgen, 2003). Why this works is less clear. A small group of studies shows a causal effect of self-efficacy on interest (e.g., Barak, Shiloh, & Haushner, 1992;

Luzzo et al., 1999). This is consistent with the appraisal model of interest developed in part I of this book. Appraising one's ability to understand something as high increases interest in pictures, poetry, and text (chapters 2 and 3). The effects of self-efficacy on interest in vocationally relevant activities can be seen as another example of how appraisals affect interest.

Vocational psychologists are no longer surprised that self-efficacy affects interest; this has been known for some time, although solid causal evidence has been spotty until recently. They should be surprised, however, at recent evidence for effects of interest on self-efficacy (Nauta, Kahn, Angell, & Cantarelli, 2002; Tracey, 2002b). It isn't clear how this works. A likely possibility is that interest motivates the development of knowledge and skills (Fredrickson, 1998; Kashdan, 2004; Sansone & Smith, 2000b), which in turn increase perceptions of self-efficacy. This deserves future research.

Coda

This book has reviewed nearly everything that is known about what interest is and how it works. Yet, beyond simply reviewing what has been said, we have tried to recast the study of interest by contrasting interest's role in emotion and personality, in momentary experience and stable aspects of motivation. Looking at interest in terms of *interest* and *interests* lends clarity to the massive body of work and provides structure for future research. A lot of research is starting to appear—more than this book can hope to review. These are interesting times for the psychology of interest; I'm curious to see what happens.

References

Abe, J. A., & Izard, C. E. (1999). The developmental functions of emotions: An analysis in terms of Differential Emotions Theory. *Cognition and Emotion, 13*, 523–549.

Abele, A. E. (2003). The dynamics of masculine-agentic and feminine-communal traits: Findings from a prospective study. *Journal of Personality and Social Psychology, 85*, 768–776.

Ainley, M. D. (1987). The factor structure of curiosity measures: Breadth and depth of interest curiosity styles. *Australian Journal of Psychology, 39*, 53–59.

Ainley, M. D. (1998). Interest in learning and the disposition of curiosity in secondary students: Investigating process and content. In L. Hoffman, A. Krapp, K. A. Renninger, & J. Baumert (Eds.), *Interest and learning* (pp. 257–266). Kiel, Germany: IPN.

Ainley, M., Hidi, S., & Berndorff, D. (2002). Interest, learning, and the psychological processes that mediate their relationship. *Journal of Educational Psychology, 94*, 545–561.

Aitken, P. P. (1974). Judgments of pleasingness and interestingness as functions of visual complexity. *Journal of Experimental Psychology, 103*, 240–244.

Alexander, P. A., & Jetton, T. L. (1996). The role of importance and interest in the processing of text. *Educational Psychology Review, 8*, 89–121.

Alexander, P. A., Jetton, T. L., & Kulikowich, J. M. (1995). Interrelationship of knowledge, interest, and recall: Assessing a model of domain learning. *Journal of Educational Psychology, 87*, 559–575.

Alexander, P. A., Kulikowich, J. M., & Schulze, S. K. (1994). How subject-matter knowledge affects recall and interest. *American Educational Research Journal, 31*, 313–337.

Allport, G. W. (1937). *Personality: A psychological interpretation.* New York: Holt, Rinehart, & Winston.

Allport, G. W. (1961). *Pattern and growth in personality.* New York: Holt, Rinehart, & Winston.

Allport, G. W. (1962). The general and the unique in psychological science. *Journal of Personality, 30,* 405–422.

Allport, G. W. (1968). The fruits of eclecticism: Bitter or sweet? In G. W. Allport, *The person in psychology: Selected essays* (pp. 3–27). Boston: Beacon.

Anderson, M. Z., Tracey, T. J. G., & Rounds, J. (1997). Examining the invariance of Holland's vocational interest model across gender. *Journal of Vocational Behavior, 50,* 349–364.

Anderson, R. C. (1982). Allocation of attention during reading. In A. Flammer & W. Kintsch (Eds.), *Discourse processing* (pp. 292–305). Amsterdam: North Holland.

Arnold, F. (1910). *Attention and interest: A study in psychology and education.* New York: Macmillan.

Arnold, M. B. (1960). *Emotion and personality, Vol. 1: Psychological aspects.* New York: Columbia University Press.

Aronson, E. (1960). The effect of effort on the attractiveness of rewarded and unrewarded stimuli. *Journal of Abnormal and Social Psychology, 63,* 375–380.

Aronson, E., & Mills, J. (1959). The effect of severity of initiation on liking for a group. *Journal of Abnormal and Social Psychology, 59,* 177–181.

Asher, S. R. (1980). Topic interest and children's reading comprehension. In R. Spiro, B. Bruce, & W. Brewer (Eds.), *Theoretical issues in reading comprehension* (pp. 525–534). Hillsdale, NJ: Lawrence Erlbaum.

Aspinwall, L. G., & Staudinger, U. M. (2003). A psychology of human strengths: Some central issues of an emerging field. In L. G. Aspinwall & U. M. Staudinger (Eds.), *A psychology of human strengths: Fundamental questions and future directions for a positive psychology* (pp. 9–22). Washington, DC: American Psychological Association.

Astin, A. W. (1999). The early years of Holland's research: Some personal reflections. *Journal of Vocational Behavior, 55,* 155–160.

Athanasou, J. A., & Cooksey, R. W. (1993). Self-estimates of vocational interests. *Australian Psychologist, 28,* 118–127.

Athanasou, J. A., & Hosking, K. (1999). *Career interest card sort.* Unpublished manuscript, University of Technology, Sydney, Australia.

Atkinson, J. W. (1964). *An introduction to motivation.* New York: Van Nostrand.

Attneave, F. (1959). *Applications of information theory to psychology.* New York: Holt, Rinehart, & Winston.

Bakan, D. (1958). *Sigmund Freud and the Jewish mystical tradition.* Princeton, NJ: Van Nostrand.

Bakan, D. (1966). Unmitigated agency and Freud's "death instinct." In D. Bakan, *The duality of human existence* (pp. 154–196). Chicago: Rand-McNally.

Bandura, A. (1977). Self-efficacy: Toward a unifying theory of behavioral change. *Psychological Review, 84*, 191–215.

Bandura, A. (1986). *Social foundations of thought and action.* Englewood Cliffs, NJ: Prentice-Hall.

Bandura, A. (1997). *Self-efficacy: The exercise of control.* New York: Freeman.

Banse, R., & Scherer, K. R. (1996). Acoustic profiles in vocal emotion expressions. *Journal of Personality and Social Psychology, 70*, 614–636.

Barak, A. (1981). Vocational interests: A cognitive view. *Journal of Vocational Behavior, 19*, 1–14.

Barak, A., Shiloh, S., & Haushner, O. (1992). Modification of interests through cognitive restructuring: Test of a theoretical model in preschool children. *Journal of Counseling Psychology, 39*, 490–497.

Baumeister, R. F., & Leary, M. R. (1995). The need to belong: Desire for interpersonal attachments as a fundamental human motivation. *Psychological Bulletin, 117*, 497–529.

Baumert, J., & Köller, O. (1998). Interest research in secondary level II: An overview. In L. Hoffman, A. Krapp, K. A. Renninger, & J. Baumert (Eds.), *Interest and learning* (pp. 241–256). Kiel, Germany: IPN.

Benedict, B. M. (2001). *Curiosity: A cultural history of early modern inquiry.* Chicago: University of Chicago Press.

Benet-Martinez, V., & Waller, N. (1997). Further evidence for the cross-cultural generality of the Big Seven Model: Indigenous and imported Spanish personality constructs. *Journal of Personality, 65*, 567–598.

Bergeman, C. S., Chipuer, H. M., Plomin, R., Pedersen, N. L., McClearn, G. E., Nesselroade, J. R., Costa, P. T., Jr., & McCrae, R. R. (1993). Genetic and environmental effects on openness to experience, agreeableness, and conscientiousness: An adoption/twin study. *Journal of Personality, 61*, 159–179.

Bergin, D. A. (1999). Influences on classroom interest. *Educational Psychologist, 34*, 87–98.

Berlyne, D. E. (1949). "Interest" as a psychological concept. *British Journal of Psychology, 39*, 184–195.

Berlyne, D. E. (1954a). A theory of human curiosity. *British Journal of Psychology, 45*, 180–191.

Berlyne, D. E. (1954b). An experimental study of human curiosity. *British Journal of Psychology, 45*, 256–265.

Berlyne, D. E. (1957). Uncertainty and conflict: A point of contact between information-theory and behavior-theory concepts. *Psychological Review, 64*, 329–339.

Berlyne, D. E. (1960). *Conflict, arousal, and curiosity.* New York: McGraw-Hill.

Berlyne, D. E. (1963). Complexity and incongruity variables as determinants of exploratory choice and evaluative ratings. *Canadian Journal of Psychology, 17*, 274–290.

Berlyne, D. E. (1965). *Structure and direction in thinking.* New York: Wiley.

Berlyne, D. E. (1967). Arousal and reinforcement. *Nebraska Symposium on Motivation, 15*, 1–110.

Berlyne, D. E. (1970). Novelty, complexity, and hedonic value. *Perception and Psychophysics, 8,* 279–286.

Berlyne, D. E. (1971a). *Aesthetics and psychobiology.* New York: Appleton-Century-Crofts.

Berlyne, D. E. (1971b). What next? Concluding summary. In H. I. Day, D. E. Berlyne, & D. E. Hunt (Eds.), *Intrinsic motivation: A new direction in education* (pp. 186–196). Toronto: Holt, Rinehart, & Winston.

Berlyne, D. E. (1972). Ends and means of experimental aesthetics. *Canadian Journal of Psychology, 26,* 303–325.

Berlyne, D. E. (1974a). Concluding observations. In D. E. Berlyne (Ed.) *Studies in the new experimental aesthetics* (pp. 305–332). Washington, DC: Hemisphere.

Berlyne, D. E. (1974b). The new experimental aesthetics. In D. E. Berlyne (Ed.), *Studies in the new experimental aesthetics* (pp. 1–25). Washington, DC: Hemisphere.

Berlyne, D. E. (1974c). Novelty, complexity, and interestingness. In D. E. Berlyne (Ed.), *Studies in the new experimental aesthetics* (pp. 175–180). Washington, DC: Hemisphere.

Berlyne, D. E. (Ed.). (1974d). *Studies in the new experimental aesthetics: Steps toward an objective psychology of aesthetic appreciation.* Washington, DC: Hemisphere.

Berlyne, D. E. (1974e). Verbal and exploratory responses to visual patterns varying in uncertainty and in redundancy. In D. E. Berlyne (Ed.), *Studies in the new experimental aesthetics* (pp. 121–158). Washington, DC: Hemisphere.

Berlyne, D. E. (1975). Behaviorism? Cognitive theory? Humanistic psychology? To Hull with them all. *Canadian Psychological Review, 16,* 69–80.

Berlyne, D. E. (1976). Similarity and preference judgments of Indian and Canadian subjects exposed to Western paintings. *International Journal of Psychology, 11,* 43–55.

Berlyne, D. E. (1978). Curiosity and learning. *Motivation and Emotion, 2,* 97–175.

Berlyne, D. E., & Crozier, J. B. (1971). Effects of complexity and prechoice stimulation on exploratory choice. *Perception and Psychophysics, 10,* 242–246.

Berlyne, D. E., Robbins, M. C., & Thompson, R. (1974). A cross-cultural study of exploratory and verbal responses to visual patterns varying in complexity. In D. E. Berlyne (Ed.) *Studies in the new experimental aesthetics* (pp. 259–278). Washington, DC: Hemisphere.

Berlyne, D. E., Salapatek, P. H., Gelman, R. S., & Zener, S. L. (1964). Is light increment really rewarding to the rat? *Journal of Comparative and Physiological Psychology, 58,* 148–151.

Berridge, K. C., & Winkielman, P. (2003). What is an unconscious emotion? (The case for unconscious "liking"). *Cognition and Emotion, 17,* 181–211.

Betz, N. E. (1999). Getting clients to act on their interests: Self-efficacy as a mediator of the implementation of vocational interests. In M. L. Savickas

& A. R. Spokane (Eds.), *Vocational interests* (pp. 327–344). Palo Alto, CA: Davies-Black.

Betz, N. E. (2000). Self-efficacy theory as a basis for career assessment. *Journal of Career Assessment, 8*, 205–222.

Betz, N. E., & Borgen, F. H. (2000). The future of career assessment: Integrating vocational interests with self-efficacy and personal styles. *Journal of Career Assessment, 8*, 329–338.

Betz, N. E., Borgen, F. H., Kaplan, A., & Harmon, L. W. (1998). Gender as a moderator of the validity and interpretive utility of the Skills Confidence Inventory. *Journal of Vocational Behavior, 53*, 281–299.

Betz, N. E., & Gwilliam, L. R. (2002). The utility of measures of self-efficacy for the Holland themes in African American and European American college students. *Journal of Career Assessment, 10*, 283–300.

Betz, N. E., & Hackett, G. (1981). The relationship of career-related self-efficacy expectations to perceived career options in college women and men. *Journal of Counseling Psychology, 28*, 399–410.

Betz, N. E., Harmon, L. W., & Borgen, F. H. (1996). The relationship of self-efficacy for the Holland themes to gender, occupational group membership, and vocational interests. *Journal of Counseling Psychology, 43*, 90–98.

Betz, N. E., & Schifano, R. S. (2000). Evaluation of an intervention to increase Realistic self-efficacy and interests in college women. *Journal of Vocational Behavior, 56*, 35–52.

Biernat, M. R., & Crandall, C. S. (1999). Racial attitudes. In J. P. Robinson, P. R. Shaver, & L. S. Wrightsman (Eds.), *Measures of political attitudes* (pp. 297–411). San Diego, CA: Academic Press.

Block, J. (1995). A contrarian view of the five-factor approach to personality. *Psychological Bulletin, 117*, 187–215.

Block, J. (2001). Millennial contrarianism: The five-factor approach to personality description 5 years later. *Journal of Research in Personality, 35*, 98–107.

Bolles, R. C. (1967). *Theory of motivation.* New York: Harper & Row.

Bonanno, G. A., & Keltner, D. (2004). The coherence of emotion systems: Comparing "on-line" measures of appraisal and facial expressions, and self-report. *Cognition and Emotion, 18*, 431–444.

Borgen, F. H., & Donnay, D. A. C. (1996). Slicing the vocational interest pie one more time: Comment on Tracey and Rounds. *Journal of Vocational Behavior, 48*, 42–52.

Borgen, F. H., & Seling, M. J. (1978). Expressed and inventoried interests revisited: Perspicacity in the person. *Journal of Counseling Psychology, 25*, 536–543.

Boucher, J. D. (1983). Antecedents to emotions across cultures. In S. H. Irvine & J. W. Berry (Eds.), *Human assessment and cultural factors* (pp. 407–420). New York: Plenum.

Boucher, J. D., & Brandt, M. E. (1981). Judgment of emotion: American and Malay antecedents. *Journal of Cross-Cultural Psychology, 12*, 272–283.

Boykin, A. W., Jr. (1977). Verbally expressed preference and problem-solving proficiency. *Journal of Experimental Psychology: Human Perception and Performance, 3,* 165–174.

Boyle, G. J. (1989). Breadth–depth or state–trait curiosity? A factor analysis of state–trait curiosity and anxiety scales. *Personality and Individual Differences, 10,* 175–183.

Bradshaw, G. L., & Anderson, J. R. (1982). Elaborative encoding as an explanation of levels of processing. *Journal of Verbal Learning and Verbal Behavior, 21,* 165–174.

Bragg, B. W. E., & Crozier, J. B. (1974). The development with age of verbal and exploratory responses to sound sequences varying in uncertainty level. In D. E. Berlyne (Ed.), *Studies in the new experimental aesthetics* (pp. 91–108). Washington, DC: Hemisphere.

Brehm, J. W. (1999). The intensity of emotion. *Personality and Social Psychology Review, 3,* 2–22.

Brehm, J. W., & Brummett, B. H. (1998). The emotional control of behavior. In M. Kofta, G. Weary, & G. Sedek (Eds.), *Personal control in action* (pp. 133–154). New York: Plenum.

Brown, L. T., & Farha, W. (1966). Some physical determinants of looking time under three instructional sets. *Perception and Psychophysics, 1,* 2–4.

Brown, S. D., Lent, R. W., & Gore, P. A., Jr. (2000). Self-rated abilities and self-efficacy beliefs: Are they empirically distinct? *Journal of Career Assessment, 8,* 223–235.

Bruner, J. S. (1990). *Acts of meaning.* Cambridge: Harvard University Press.

Campbell, D. P., & Borgen, F. (1999). Holland's theory and the development of interest inventories. *Journal of Vocational Behavior, 55,* 86–101.

Campbell, N. K., & Hackett, G. (1986). The effects of mathematics task performance on math self-efficacy and task interest. *Journal of Vocational Behavior, 28,* 149–162.

Camras, L. A., Meng, Z., Ujiie, T., Dharamsi, S., Miyake, K., Oster, H., Wang, L., Cruz, J., Murdoch, A., & Campos, J. (2002). Observing emotion in infants: Facial expression, body behavior, and rater judgments of responses to an expectancy-violating event. *Emotion, 2,* 179–193.

Carlson, L., & Carlson, R. (1984). Affect and psychological magnification: Derivations from Tomkins' script theory. *Journal of Personality, 52,* 36–45.

Carlson, R. (1981). Studies in script theory: I. Adult analogs of a childhood nuclear scene. *Journal of Personality and Social Psychology, 40,* 501–510.

Carroll, J. B. (2002). The five-factor personality model: How complete and satisfactory is it? In H. I. Braun, D. N. Jackson, & D. E. Wiley (Eds.), *The role of constructs in psychological and educational measurement* (pp. 97–126). Mahwah, NJ: Lawrence Erlbaum.

Chen, A. (2001). A theoretical conceptualization for motivation research in physical education: An integrated perspective. *Quest, 53,* 35–58.

Chen, A., & Darst, P. W. (2001). Situational interest in physical education: A function of learning task design. *Research Quarterly for Exercise and Sport, 72,* 150–164.

Chen, A., & Darst, P. W. (2002). Individual and situational interest: The role of gender and skill. *Contemporary Educational Psychology, 27,* 250–269.

Chen, A., Darst, P. W., & Pangrazi, R. P. (1999). What constitutes situational interest? Validating a construct in physical education. *Measurement in Physical Education and Exercise Science, 3,* 157–180.

Chen, A., Darst, P. W., & Pangrazi, R. P. (2001). An examination of situational interest and its sources. *British Journal of Educational Psychology, 71,* 383–400.

Child, I. L. (1981). Bases of transcultural agreement in response to art. In H. I. Day (Ed.), *Advances in intrinsic motivation and aesthetics* (pp. 415–432). New York: Plenum.

Clore, G. L., & Colcombe, S. (2003). The parallel worlds of affective concepts and feelings. In J. Musch & K. C. Klauer (Eds.), *The psychology of evaluation: Affective processes in cognition and emotion* (pp. 335–369). Mahwah, NJ: Lawrence Erlbaum.

Coie, J. D. (1974). An evaluation of the cross-situational consistency of children's curiosity. *Journal of Personality, 42,* 93–117.

Coke, J. S., Batson, C. D., & McDavis, K. (1978). Empathic mediation of helping: A two-stage model. *Journal of Personality and Social Psychology, 36,* 752–766.

Cole, N. S., Whitney, D. R., & Holland, J. L. (1971). A spatial configuration of occupations. *Journal of Vocational Behavior, 1,* 1–9.

Collins, R. P., Litman, J. A., & Spielberger, C. D. (2003). The measurement of perceptual curiosity. *Personality and Individual Differences, 36,* 1127–1141.

Consedine, N. S., Magai, C., & King, A. R. (2004). Deconstructing positive affect in later life: A differential functionalist analysis of joy and interest. *International Journal of Aging and Human Development, 58,* 49–68.

Cooksey, R. W., & Athanasou, J. A. (1994). Assessing differences in accuracy of self-estimates of vocational interests: An idiographic analysis using profile decomposition. *Australian Journal of Psychology, 46,* 112–117.

Cooper, J. (1998). Unlearning cognitive dissonance: Toward an understanding of the development of dissonance. *Journal of Experimental Social Psychology, 34,* 562–575.

Costa, P. T., Jr., & McCrae, R. R. (1992). *Revised NEO Personality Inventory (NEO-PI-R) and NEO Five-Factor Inventory (NEO-FI) professional manual.* Odessa, FL: Psychological Assessment Resources.

Costa, P. T., Jr., McCrae, R. R., & Holland, J. L. (1984). Personality and vocational interests in an adult sample. *Journal of Applied Psychology, 69,* 390–400.

Crites, J. O. (1999). Operational definitions of interests. In M. L. Savickas & A. R. Spokane (Eds.), *Vocational interests* (pp. 163–170). Palo Alto, CA: Davies-Black.

Cronbach, L. J. (1957). The two disciplines of scientific psychology. *American Psychologist, 12,* 671–684.

Crozier, J. B. (1974). Verbal and exploratory responses to sound sequences varying in uncertainty level. In D. E. Berlyne (Ed.), *Studies in the new experimental aesthetics* (pp. 27–90). Washington, DC: Hemisphere.

Csikszentmihalyi, M. (1975). *Beyond boredom and anxiety: The experience of play in work and games.* San Francisco: Jossey-Bass.

Cupchik, G. C. (1988). The legacy of Daniel E. Berlyne. *Empirical Studies of the Arts, 6,* 171–186.

Cupchik, G. C., & Gebotys, R. J. (1990). Interest and pleasure as dimensions of aesthetic experience. *Empirical Studies of the Arts, 8,* 1–14.

Daffner, K. R., Scinto, L. F. M., Weintraub, S., Guinessey, J., & Mesulam, M. M. (1992). Diminished curiosity in patients with probable Alzheimer's disease as measured by exploratory eye movements. *Neurology, 42,* 320–328.

Darley, J. G., & Hagenah, T. (1955). *Vocational interest measurement: Theory and practice.* Minneapolis: University of Minnesota.

Darwin, C. (1872/1998). *The expression of the emotions in man and animals* (3rd ed.). New York: Oxford University Press.

Day, H. I. (1966). Looking time as a function of stimulus variables and individual differences. *Perceptual and Motor Skills, 22,* 423–428.

Day, H. I. (1967). Evaluations of subjective complexity, pleasingness and interestingness for a series of random polygons varying in complexity. *Perception and Psychophysics, 2,* 281–286.

Day, H. I. (1968). Some determinants of looking time under different instructional sets. *Perception and Psychophysics, 4,* 279–281.

Day, H. I. (1971). The measurement of specific curiosity. In H. I. Day, D. E. Berlyne, & D. E. Hunt (Eds.), *Intrinsic motivation: A new direction in education* (pp. 99–112). Toronto: Holt, Rinehart, & Winston.

Day, H. I. (1981). Preface. In H. I. Day (Ed.), *Advances in intrinsic motivation and aesthetics* (pp. vii–ix). New York: Plenum.

Day, H. I., & Maynes, F. (1972). Curiosity and willingness to become involved. *Psychological Reports, 30,* 807–814.

Day, S. X., & Rounds, J. (1998). Universality of vocational interest structure among racial and ethnic minorities. *American Psychologist, 53,* 728–736.

Day, S. X., Rounds, J., & Swaney, K. (1998). The structure of vocational interests for diverse racial-ethnic groups. *Psychological Science, 9,* 40–44.

Deci, E. (1975). *Intrinsic motivation.* New York: Plenum.

Deci, E. L. (1992). The relation of interest to the motivation of behavior: A self-determination theory perspective. In K. A. Renninger, S. Hidi, & A. Krapp (Eds.), *The role of interest in learning and development* (pp. 43–70). Hillsdale, NJ: Lawrence Erlbaum.

Deci, E. L. (1998). The relation of interest to motivation and human needs—The self-determination theory viewpoint. In L. Hoffman, A. Krapp, K. A. Renninger, & J. Baumert (Eds.), *Interest and learning* (pp. 146–162). Kiel, Germany: IPN.

Deci, E. L., & Ryan, R. M. (1985). *Intrinsic motivation and self-determination in human behavior.* New York: Plenum.

Deci, E. L., & Ryan, R. M. (2000). The "what" and "why" of goal pursuits: Human needs and the self-determination of behavior. *Psychological Inquiry, 11,* 227–268.

De Fruyt, F., & Mervielde, I. (1997). The five-factor model of personality and Holland's RIASEC interest types. *Personality and Individual Differences, 23,* 87–103.

De Raad, B. (1994). An expedition in search of a fifth universal factor: Key issues in the lexical approach. *European Journal of Personality, 8,* 229–250.

De Raad, B. (1998). Five big, Big Five issues: Rationale, content, structure, status, and crosscultural assessment. *European Psychologist, 3,* 113–124.

De Raad, B., & Van Heck, G. L. (1994). The fifth of the big five [Special issue]. *European Journal of Personality, 8*(4).

DeVellis, R. F. (2003). *Scale development: Theory and applications* (2nd ed.). Newbury Park, CA: Sage.

Dewey, J. (1910). *How we think.* Boston: Heath.

Dewey, J. (1913). *Interest and effort in education.* Boston: Riverside.

Di Blas, L., & Forzi, M. (1999). Refining a descriptive structure of personality attributes in the Italian language: The abridged Big Three circumplex structure. *Journal of Personality and Social Psychology, 76,* 451–481.

Diegelman, N. M., & Subich, L. M. (2001). Academic and vocational interests as a function of outcome expectancies in social cognitive career theory. *Journal of Vocational Behavior, 59,* 394–405.

Digman, J. M. (1997). Higher-order factors of the Big Five. *Journal of Personality and Social Psychology, 73,* 1246–1256.

Dollard, J., & Miller, N. E. (1950). *Personality and psychotherapy.* New York: McGraw–Hill.

Dollinger, S. J., Robinson, N. M., & Ross, V. J. (1999). Photographic individuality, breadth of perspective, and creativity. *Journal of Personality, 67,* 623–644.

Dolliver, R. H. (1969). *Strong Vocational Interest Blank* versus expressed vocational interests: A review. *Psychological Bulletin, 72,* 95–107.

Donnay, D. A. C., & Borgen, F. H. (1999). The incremental validity of vocational self-efficacy: An examination of interest, self-efficacy, and occupation. *Journal of Counseling Psychology, 46,* 432–447.

Duffy, E. (1934). Emotion: An example of the need for reorientation in psychology. *Psychological Review, 44,* 184–198.

Dunning, D. (1999). A newer look: Motivated social cognition and the schematic representation of social concepts. *Psychological Inquiry, 10,* 1–11.

Dutton, D. G., & Aron, A. P. (1974). Some evidence for heightened sexual attraction under conditions of high anxiety. *Journal of Personality and Social Psychology, 30,* 510–517.

Duval, T. S., & Duval, V. H. (1983). *Consistency and cognition: A theory of causal attribution.* Hillsdale, NJ: Lawrence Erlbaum.

Duval, T. S., & Lalwani, N. (1999). Objective self-awareness and causal attributions for self-standard discrepancies: Changing self or changing standards of correctness. *Personality and Social Psychology Bulletin, 25,* 1220–1229.

Duval, T. S. & Silvia, P. J. (2001). *Self-awareness and causal attribution: A dual systems theory.* Boston: Kluwer Academic.

Duval, T. S., & Silvia, P. J. (2002). Self-awareness, probability of improvement, and the self-serving bias. *Journal of Personality and Social Psychology, 82,* 49–61.

Einarsdóttir, S., Rounds, J., Ægisdóttir, S., & Gerstein, L. H. (2002). The structure of vocational interests in Iceland: Examining Holland's and Gati's RIASEC models. *European Journal of Psychological Assessment, 18,* 85–95.

Eisenman, R. (1966). Pleasing and interesting visual complexity: Support for Berlyne. *Perceptual and Motor Skills, 23,* 1167–1170.

Ekman, P. (1992). An argument for basic emotions. *Cognition and Emotion, 6,* 169–200.

Ekman, P. (1993). Facial expression and emotion. *American Psychologist, 48,* 384–392.

Ekman, P., & Friesen, W. V. (1978). *Facial Action Coding System: A technique for the measurement of facial movement.* Palo Alto, CA: Consulting Psychologists Press.

Elliot, A. J., & Devine, P. G. (1994). On the motivational nature of cognitive dissonance: Dissonance as psychological discomfort. *Journal of Personality and Social Psychology, 67,* 382–394.

Ellsworth, P. C., & Scherer, K. R. (2003). Appraisal processes in emotion. In R. J. Davidson, K. R. Scherer, & H. H. Goldsmith (Eds.), *Handbook of affective sciences* (pp. 572–595). New York: Oxford University Press.

Ellsworth, P. C., & Smith, C. A. (1988). Shades of joy: Patterns of appraisal differentiating positive emotions. *Cognition and Emotion, 2,* 301–331.

Emmons, R. A. (1999). *The psychology of ultimate concerns: Motivation and spirituality in personality.* New York: Guilford.

Entwistle, N. (1988). Motivational factors in students' approaches to learning. In R. R. Schmeck (Ed.), *Learning strategies and learning styles* (pp. 21–51). New York: Plenum.

Etcoff, N. L., & Magee, J. J. (1992). Categorical perception of facial expression. *Cognition, 44,* 227–240.

Evans, C. (1974). *Cults of unreason.* Frogmore, England: Panther Books.

Evans, D. R. (1971). The Ontario Test of Intrinsic Motivation, question asking, and autistic thinking. *Psychological Reports, 29,* 154.

Evans, D. R., & Day, H. I. (1971). The factorial structure of responses to perceptual complexity. *Psychonomic Science, 27,* 357–359.

Eysenck, H. J. (1967). *The biological basis of personality.* Springfield, IL: Charles C. Thomas.

Eysenck, H. J., & Eysenck, M. W. (1985). *Personality and individual differences: A natural science approach.* New York: Plenum.

Farmer, R., & Sundberg, N. D. (1986). Boredom proneness: The development and correlates of a new scale. *Journal of Personality Assessment, 50,* 4–17.

Feist, G. J. (1998). A meta-analysis of personality on scientific and artistic creativity. *Personality and Social Psychology Review, 2,* 290–309.

Feldman-Barrett, L., & Russell, J. A. (1999). The structure of current affect: Controversies and emerging consensus. *Current Directions in Psychological Science, 8,* 10–14.

Festinger, L. (1957). *A theory of cognitive dissonance.* Stanford, CA: Stanford University Press.

Fisher, C. D., & Noble, C. S. (2004). A within-person examination of correlates of performance and emotions while working. *Human Performance, 17,* 145–168.

Fiske, D. W. (1961). Effects of monotonous and restricted stimulation. In D. W. Fiske & S. R. Maddi (Eds.), *Functions of varied experience* (pp. 106–144). Homewood, IL: Dorsey.

Fiske, D. W., & Maddi, S. R. (1961a). A conceptual framework. In D. W. Fiske & S. R. Maddi (Eds.), *Functions of varied experience* (pp. 11–56). Homewood, IL: Dorsey.

Fiske, D. W., & Maddi, S. R. (Eds.). (1961b). *Functions of varied experience.* Homewood, IL: Dorsey.

Fleeson, W. (2001). Toward a structure- and process-integrated view of personality: Traits as density distributions of states. *Journal of Personality and Social Psychology, 80,* 1011–1027

Försterling, F. (2001). *Attribution: An introduction to theories, research and applications.* Philadelphia: Psychology Press.

Fouad, N. A. (1999). Validity evidence for interest inventories. In M. L. Savickas & A. R. Spokane (Eds.), *Vocational interests* (pp. 193–209). Palo Alto, CA: Davies-Black.

Fouad, N. A. (2002). Cross-cultural differences in vocational interests: Between-group differences on the Strong Interest Inventory. *Journal of Counseling Psychology, 49,* 282–289.

Fowler, H. (1965). *Curiosity and exploratory behavior.* New York: Macmillan.

Francès, R. (1976). Comparative effects of six collative variables on interest and preference in adults of different educational levels. *Journal of Personality and Social Psychology, 33,* 62–79.

Fredrickson, B. L. (1998). What good are positive emotions? *Review of General Psychology, 2,* 300–319.

Fredrickson, B. L. (2001). The role of positive emotions in positive psychology: The broaden-and-build theory of positive emotions. *American Psychologist, 56,* 218–226.

Freud, S. (1920). *Beyond the pleasure principle.* New York: Norton.

Freud, S. (1923). *The ego and the id.* New York: Norton.

Frick, F. C. (1959). Information theory. In S. Koch (Ed.), *Psychology: A study of a science* (Vol. 2, pp. 611–636). New York: McGraw–Hill.

Frick, R. W. (1985). Communicating emotion: The role of prosodic features. *Psychological Bulletin, 97,* 412–429.

Frijda, N. H. (1986). *The emotions.* Cambridge: Cambridge University Press.

Fulker, D. W., Eysenck, S. B. G., & Zuckerman, M. (1980). A genetic and environmental analysis of sensation seeking. *Journal of Research in Personality, 14,* 261–281.

Furedy, J. J., & Furedy, C. P. (1981). "My first interest is interest": Berlyne as an exemplar of the curiosity drive. In H. I. Day (Ed.), *Advances in intrinsic motivation and aesthetics* (pp. 1–17). New York: Plenum.

Furnham, A. F., & Bunyan, M. (1988). Personality and art preferences. *European Journal of Personality, 2,* 67–74.

Gaeddert, D., & Hansen, J. C. (1993). Development of a measure of interest diversity. *Journal of Career Assessment, 1,* 294–308.

Garner, R. (1992). Learning from school texts. *Educational Psychologist, 27,* 53–63.

Garner, R., Alexander, P. A., Gillingham, M. G., Kulikowich, J. M., & Brown, R. (1991). Interest and learning from text. *American Educational Research Journal, 28,* 643–659.

Garner, R., Brown, R., Sanders, S., & Menke, D. J. (1992). "Seductive details" and learning from text. In K. A. Renninger, S. Hidi, & A. Krapp (Eds.), *The role of interest in learning and development* (pp. 239–254). Hillsdale, NJ: Lawrence Erlbaum.

Garner, R., & Gillingham, M. G. (1991). Topic knowledge, cognitive interest, and text recall: A microanalysis. *Journal of Experimental Education, 59,* 310–319.

Garner, R., Gillingham, M. G., & White, C. S. (1989). Effects of "seductive details" on macroprocessing and microprocessing in adults and children. *Cognition and Instruction, 6,* 41–57.

Garner, W. R. (1962). *Uncertainty and structure as psychological concepts.* New York: Wiley.

Gati, I. (1979). A hierarchical model for the structure of vocational interests. *Journal of Vocational Behavior, 15,* 90–106.

Gati, I. (1991). The structure of vocational interests. *Psychological Bulletin, 109,* 309–324.

Gaze, T. (2000). *The oxygen of truth* (Vol. 1). Lawrence, KS: Broken Boulder Press.

Gendolla, G. H. E. (2000). On the impact of mood on behavior: An integrative theory and a review. *Review of General Psychology, 4,* 378–408.

Gerard, H. B., & Mathewson, G. C. (1966). The effects of severity of initiation on liking for a group: A replication. *Journal of Experimental Social Psychology, 2,* 278–287.

Gilbert, D. T., & Ebert, J. E. J. (2002). Decisions and revisions: The affective forecasting of changeable outcomes. *Journal of Personality and Social Psychology, 82,* 503–514.

Gilbert, D. T., & Gill, M. J. (2000). The momentary realist. *Psychological Science, 11,* 394–398.

Gilbert, D. T., Pinel, E. C., Wilson, T. D., Blumberg, S. J., & Wheatley, T. P. (1998). Immune neglect: A source of durability bias in affective forecasting. *Journal of Personality and Social Psychology, 75,* 617–638.

Gilbert, D. T., & Wilson, T. D. (2000). Miswanting: Some problems in the forecasting of future affective states. In J. P. Forgas (Ed.), *Feeling and thinking* (pp. 178–197). New York: Cambridge University Press.

Goetz, E. T., & Sadoski, M. (1995a). The perils of seduction: Distracting details or incomprehensible abstractions? *Reading Research Quarterly, 30,* 500–511.

Goetz, E. T., & Sadoski, M. (1995b). The perils of seduction revisited: A reply to Wade, Alexander, Schraw, & Kulikowich. *Reading Research Quarterly, 30,* 518–519.

Goetz, E. T., Sadoski, M., Fatemi, Z., & Bush, R. (1994). That's news to me: Readers' response to brief newspaper articles. *Journal of Reading Behavior, 26,* 125–138.

Goldberg, L. R. (1994). Resolving a scientific embarrassment: A comment on the articles in this special issue. *European Journal of Personality, 8,* 351–356.

Gordon, A., Wilkinson, R., McGown, A., & Jovanoska, S. (1997). The psychometric properties of the boredom proneness scale: An examination of its validity. *Psychological Studies, 42,* 85–97.

Gottfredson, G. D. (2001). Fostering the scientific practice of vocational psychology. *Journal of Vocational Behavior, 59,* 192–202.

Gottfredson, L. S. (1996). Gottfredson's theory of circumscription and compromise. In D. Brown & L. Brooks (Eds.), *Career choice and development* (3rd ed., pp. 179–232). New York: Guilford.

Gray, J. R. (2001). Emotional modulation of cognitive control: Approach–withdrawal states double-dissociate spatial from verbal two-back task performance. *Journal of Experimental Psychology: General, 130,* 436–452.

Grigg, A. E. (1959). Childhood experience with parental attitudes: A test of Roe's hypothesis. *Journal of Counseling Psychology, 6,* 153–155.

Guilford, J. P., Christensen, P. R., Bond, N. A., Jr., & Sutton, M. A. (1954). A factor analysis study of human interests. *Psychological Monographs: General and Applied, 68*(4), 1–38.

Hackett, G., & Betz, N. E. (1981). A self-efficacy approach to the career development of women. *Journal of Vocational Behavior, 18,* 326–339.

Hall, C. S., & Lindzey, G. (1957). *Theories of personality.* New York: Wiley.

Hansen, J. C. (1996). What goes around, comes around. *Journal of Vocational Behavior, 48,* 73–76.

Hansen, J. C., & Scullard, M. G. (2002). Psychometric evidence for the Leisure Interest Questionnaire and analyses of the structure of leisure interests. *Journal of Counseling Psychology, 49,* 331–341.

Hansen, J. C., & Tan, R. N. (1992). Concurrent validity of the 1985 *Strong Interest Inventory* for college majors selection. *Measurement and Evaluation in Counseling and Development, 19,* 53–57.

Hare, F. G. (1974). Artistic training and responses to visual and auditory patterns varying in uncertainty. In D. E. Berlyne (Ed.), *Studies in the new experimental aesthetics* (pp. 159–168). Washington, DC: Hemisphere.

Hargreaves, D. J. (1986). *The developmental psychology of music.* Cambridge: Cambridge University Press.

Harlow, H. F. (1953). Mice, monkeys, men, and motives. *Psychological Review, 60*, 23–32.

Harmon, L. W. (1996). Lost in space: A response to "The Spherical Representation of Vocational Interests" by Tracey and Rounds. *Journal of Vocational Behavior, 48*, 53–58.

Harp, S. F., & Mayer, R. E. (1997). The role of interest in learning from scientific text and illustrations: On the distinction between emotional interest and cognitive interest. *Journal of Educational Psychology, 89*, 92–102.

Harp, S. F., & Mayer, R. E. (1998). How seductive details do their damage: A theory of cognitive interest in science learning. *Journal of Educational Psychology, 90*, 414–434.

Harris, M. B. (2000). Correlates and characteristics of boredom proneness and boredom. *Journal of Applied Social Psychology, 30*, 576–598.

Hartung, P. J. (1999). Interest assessment using card sorts. In M. L. Savickas & A. R. Spokane (Eds.), *Vocational interests* (pp. 235–252). Palo Alto, CA: Davies-Black.

Haviland-Jones, J. M., & Kahlbaugh, P. (2000). Emotion and identity. In M. Lewis & J. M. Haviland-Jones (Eds.), *Handbook of emotions* (2nd ed., pp. 293–305). New York: Guilford.

Hebb, D. O. (1949). *The organization of behavior.* New York: Wiley.

Hebb, D. O. (1955). Drives and the C.N.S. (conceptual nervous system). *Psychological Review, 62*, 243–254.

Heider, F. (1944). Social perception and phenomenal causality. *Psychological Review, 51*, 358–374.

Heider, F. (1958). *The psychology of interpersonal relations.* New York: Wiley.

Hekkert, P., & van Wieringen, P. C. W. (1996). The impact of level of expertise on the evaluation of original and altered versions of post-impressionistic paintings. *Acta Psychologica, 94*, 117–131.

Herbart, J. F. (1891). *A text-book in psychology: An attempt to found the science of psychology on experience, metaphysics, and mathematics.* New York: Appleton. (Original work published 1816).

Hewstone, M. (1989). *Causal attribution: From cognitive processes to collective beliefs.* Oxford, UK: Blackwell.

Hidi, S. (1990). Interest and its contribution as a mental resource for learning. *Review of Educational Research, 60*, 549–571.

Hidi, S. (1995). A reexamination of the role of attention in learning from text. *Educational Psychology Review, 7*, 323–350.

Hidi, S. (2000). An interest researcher's perspective: The effects of extrinsic and intrinsic factors on motivation. In C. Sansone & J. M. Harackiewicz (Eds.), *Intrinsic and extrinsic motivation* (pp. 309–339). San Diego: Academic Press.

Hidi, S. (2001). Interest, reading, and learning: Theoretical and practical considerations. *Educational Psychology Review, 13*, 191–209.

Hidi, S., & Anderson, V. (1992). Situational interest and its impact on reading and expository writing. In K. A. Renninger, S. Hidi, & A. Krapp (Eds.),

The role of interest in learning and development (pp. 215–238). Hillsdale, NJ: Lawrence Erlbaum.

Hidi, S., & Baird, W. (1986). Interestingness—A neglected variable in discourse processing. *Cognitive Science, 10,* 179–194.

Hidi, S., & Baird, W. (1988). Strategies for increasing text-based interest and students' recall of expository texts. *Reading Research Quarterly, 23,* 465–483.

Hidi, S., Baird, W., & Hildyard, A. (1982). That's important, but is it interesting? Two factors in text processing. In A. Flammer & W. Kintsch (Eds.), *Discourse processing* (pp. 63–75). Amsterdam: North Holland.

Hidi, S., & Berndorff, D. (1998). Situational interest and learning. In L. Hoffman, A. Krapp, K. A. Renninger, & J. Baumert (Eds.), *Interest and learning* (pp. 74–90). Kiel, Germany: IPN.

Hidi, S., & Harackiewicz, J. M. (2000). Motivating the academically unmotivated: A critical issue for the 21st century. *Review of Educational Research, 70,* 151–179.

Hoffman, L., & Häussler, P. (1998). An intervention project promoting girls' and boys' interest in physics. In L. Hoffman, A. Krapp, K. A. Renninger, & J. Baumert (Eds.), *Interest and learning* (pp. 301–316). Kiel, Germany: IPN.

Holland, J. L. (1973). *Making vocational choices.* Englewood Cliffs, NJ: Prentice-Hall.

Holland, J. L. (1985a). *Making vocational choices: A theory of vocational personalities and work environments* (2nd ed.). Odessa, FL: Psychological Assessment Resources.

Holland, J. L. (1985b). *Manual for the Vocational Preference Inventory.* Odessa, FL: Psychological Assessment Resources.

Holland, J. L. (1996). Exploring careers with a typology: What we have learned and some new directions. *American Psychologist, 51,* 397–406.

Holland, J. L. (1997). *Making vocational choices: A theory of vocational personalities and work environments* (3rd ed.). Odessa, FL: Psychological Assessment Resources.

Holland, J. L. (1999). Why interest inventories are also personality inventories. In M. L. Savickas & A. R. Spokane (Eds.), *Vocational interests* (pp. 87–101). Palo Alto, CA: Davies-Black.

Holland, J. L., Fritzsche, B. A., & Powell, A. B. (1994). *The Self-Directed Search technical manual.* Odessa, FL: Psychological Assessment Resources.

Holt, J. (1967). *How children learn.* New York: Pitman.

Hosking, K., & Athanasou, J. A. (1997). Do vocational interest types affect job satisfaction in adult career development? *Australian Journal of Career Development, 6,* 21–25.

Hoyle, R. H., Stephenson, M. T., Palmgreen, P., Lorch, E. P., & Donohew, R. L. (2002). Reliability and validity of a brief measure of sensation seeking. *Personality and Individual Differences, 32,* 401–414.

Hull, C. L. (1943). *Principles of behavior.* New York: Appleton-Century-Crofts.

Hull, C. L. (1952). *A behavior system.* New Haven, CT: Yale University Press.

Hunt, J. M. (1965). Intrinsic motivation and its role in psychological development. *Nebraska Symposium on Motivation, 13,* 189–282.

Hunt, J. M. (1971). Toward a history of intrinsic motivation. In H. I. Day, D. E. Berlyne, & D. E. Hunt (Eds.), *Intrinsic motivation: A new direction in education* (pp. 1–33). Toronto: Holt, Rinehart, & Winston.

Hutt, C. (1970). Specific and diversive exploration. *Advances in Child Development and Behavior, 5,* 119–180.

Iran-Nejad, A. (1987). Cognitive and affective causes of interest and liking. *Journal of Educational Psychology, 79,* 120–130.

Izard, C. E. (1971). *The face of emotion.* New York: Appleton-Century-Crofts.

Izard, C. E. (1977). *Human emotions.* New York: Plenum.

Izard, C. E. (1978). On the development of emotions and emotion-cognition relationships in infancy. In M. Lewis & L. A. Rosenblum (Eds.), *The development of affect* (pp. 389–413). New York: Plenum.

Izard, C. E. (1984). Emotion–cognition relationships and human development. In C. E. Izard, J. Kagan, & R. B. Zajonc (Eds.), *Emotions, cognition, and behavior* (pp. 17–37). Cambridge: Cambridge University Press.

Izard, C. E., & Ackerman, B. P. (2000). Motivational, organizational, and regulatory functions of discrete emotions. In M. Lewis & J. M. Haviland-Jones (Eds.), *Handbook of emotions* (2nd ed., pp. 253–264). New York: Guilford.

Jackson, D. N. (1994). *Jackson Personality Inventory–Revised manual.* Port Huron, MI: Sigma Assessment Systems.

John, O. P. (1990). The "Big Five" factor taxonomy: Dimensions of personality in the natural language and in questionnaires. In L. A. Pervin (Ed.), *Handbook of personality* (pp. 66–100). New York: Guilford.

Johnson, C. D., & Stokes, G. S. (2002). The meaning, development, and career outcomes of breadth of vocational interests. *Journal of Vocational Behavior, 61,* 327–347.

Johnson-Laird, P. N., & Oatley, K. (1992). Basic emotions, rationality, and folk theory. *Cognition and Emotion, 6,* 201–223.

Johnson-Laird, P. N., & Oatley, K. (2000). Cognitive and social construction in emotions. In M. Lewis & J. M. Haviland-Jones (Eds.), *Handbook of emotions* (2nd ed., pp. 458–475). New York: Guilford.

Johnstone, T., & Scherer, K. R. (2000). Vocal communication of emotion. In M. Lewis & J. M. Haviland-Jones (Eds.), *Handbook of emotions* (2nd ed., pp. 220–235). New York: Guilford.

Jones, E. E., & Davis, K, E. (1965). From acts to dispositions: The attribution process in person perception. *Advances in Experimental Social Psychology, 2,* 219–266.

Jose, P. E., & Brewer, W. F. (1984). Development of story liking: Character identification, suspense, and outcome resolution. *Developmental Psychology, 20,* 911–924.

Kaiser, S., & Wehrle, T. (2001). Facial expressions as indicators of appraisal processes. In K. R. Scherer, A. Schorr, & T. Johnstone (Eds.), *Appraisal pro-*

cesses in emotion: Theory, methods, research (pp. 285–300). New York: Oxford University Press.

Kashdan, T. B. (2002). Social anxiety dimensions, neuroticism, and the contours of positive psychological functioning. *Cognitive Therapy and Research, 26,* 789–810.

Kashdan, T. B. (2004). Curiosity. In C. Peterson & M. E. P. Seligman (Eds.), *Character strengths and virtues: A handbook and classification* (pp. 125–141). New York: Oxford University Press.

Kashdan, T. B., Rose, P., & Fincham, F. D. (2004). Curiosity and exploration: Facilitating positive subjective experiences and personal growth opportunities. *Journal of Personality Assessment, 82,* 291–305.

Kass, S. J., Vodanovich, S. J., & Callendar, A. (2001). State–trait boredom: Relationship to absenteeism, tenure, and job satisfaction. *Journal of Business and Psychology, 16,* 317–327.

Kass, S. J., Vodanovich, S. J., Stanny, C. J., & Taylor, T. M. (2001). Watching the clock: Boredom and vigilance performance. *Perceptual and Motor Skills, 92,* 969–976.

Kelley, H. H. (1967). Attribution theory in social psychology. *Nebraska Symposium on Motivation, 15,* 192–238.

Kelley, H. H. (1973). Causal schemata and the attribution process. *American Psychologist, 28,* 107–123.

Keltner, D., & Busswell, B. N. (1996). Evidence for the distinctness of embarrassment, shame, and guilt: A study of recalled antecedents and facial expressions of emotion. *Cognition and Emotion, 10,* 155–171.

Keltner, D., & Ekman, P. (2000). Facial expression of emotion. In M. Lewis & J. M. Haviland-Jones (Eds.), *Handbook of emotions* (2nd ed., pp. 236–249). New York: Guilford.

Keltner, D., & Gross, J. J. (1999). Functional accounts of emotions. *Cognition and Emotion, 13,* 467–480.

Keltner, D., Locke, K. D., & Audrain, P. C. (1993). The influence of attributions on the relevance of negative feelings to personal satisfaction. *Personality and Social Psychology Bulletin, 19,* 21–29.

Kensinger, E. A., & Corkin, S. (2003). Effect of negative emotional content on working memory and long-term memory. *Emotion, 3,* 378–393.

Kinney, D. K., & Kagan, J. (1976). Infant attention to auditory discrepancy. *Child Development, 47,* 155–164.

Kintsch, W. (1980). Learning from text, levels of comprehension, or: Why anyone would read a story anyway. *Poetics, 9,* 87–98.

Kintsch, W., & van Dijk, T. A. (1978). Toward a model of text comprehension and production. *Psychological Review, 85,* 363–394.

Klinger, E. (1971). *Structure and functions of fantasy.* New York: Wiley.

Kluckhohn, C., & Murray, H. A. (1948). Personality formation: The determinants. In C. Kluckhohn, H. A. Murray, & D. M. Schneider (Eds.), *Personality in nature, society and culture* (pp. 35–48). New York: Knopf.

Knowles, E. S., & Byers, B. (1996). Reliability shifts in measurement reactivity: Driven by content engagement or self-engagement? *Journal of Personality and Social Psychology, 70,* 1080–1090.

Köller, O., Baumert, J., & Schnabel, K. (2001). Does interest matter? The relationship between academic interest and achievement in mathematics. *Journal for Research in Mathematics Education, 32,* 448–470.

Konečni, V. J. (1996). Daniel E. Berlyne (1924–1976): Two decades later. *Empirical Studies of the Arts, 14,* 129–142.

Koopmans, J. R., Boomsma, D. I., Heath, A. C., & van Doornen, L. J. P. (1995). A multivariate genetic analysis of sensation seeking. *Behavior Genetics, 25,* 349–356.

Krapp, A. (1999). Interest, motivation and learning: An educational-psychological perspective. *European Journal of Psychology of Education, 14,* 23–40.

Krapp, A. (2002a). An educational-psychological theory of interest and its relation to self-determination theory. In E. L. Deci & R. M. Ryan (Eds.), *Handbook of self-determination research* (pp. 405–427). Rochester, NY: University of Rochester Press.

Krapp, A. (2002b). Structural and dynamic aspects of interest development: Theoretical considerations from an ontogenetic perspective. *Learning and Instruction, 12,* 383–409.

Krapp, A., Hidi, S., & Renninger, K. A. (1992). Interest, learning, and development. In K. A. Renninger, S. Hidi, & A. Krapp (Eds.), *The role of interest in learning and development* (pp. 3–25). Hillsdale, NJ: Lawrence Erlbaum.

Krebs, P. J., Smither, J. W., & Hurley, R. B. (1991). Relationship of vocational personality and research training environment to the research productivity of counseling psychologists. *Professional Psychology, 22,* 362–367.

Kruger, J. (1999). Lake Wobegon be gone! The "below-average-effect" and the egocentric nature of comparative ability judgments. *Journal of Personality and Social Psychology, 77,* 221–232.

Kruger, J., & Dunning, D. (1999). Unskilled and unaware of it: How difficulties in recognizing one's own incompetence lead to inflated self-assessments. *Journal of Personality and Social Psychology, 77,* 1121–1134.

Kruger, J., & Dunning, D. (2002). Unskilled and unaware—but why? A reply to Krueger and Mueller (2002). *Journal of Personality and Social Psychology, 82,* 189–192.

Krull, D. S., & Anderson, C. A. (1997). The process of explanation. *Current Directions in Psychological Science, 6,* 1–5.

Lacey, J. I. (1967). Somatic response patterning and stress: Some revisions of activation theory. In M. H. Appley & R. Trumbull (Eds.), *Psychological stress* (pp. 14–37). New York: Appleton-Century-Crofts.

Lamiell, J. T. (1987). *The psychology of personality: An epistemological inquiry.* New York: Columbia University Press.

Langevin, R. L. (1971). Is curiosity a unitary construct? *Canadian Journal of Psychology, 25,* 360–374.

Langevin, R. L. (1976). Construct validity of sensation seeking and curiosity measures of normal and psychotic subjects. *Canadian Journal of Behavioral Science, 8,* 251–262.

Langsdorf, P., Izard, C. E., Rayias, M., & Hembree, E. A. (1983). Interest expression, visual fixation, and heart rate changes in 2- to 8-month-old infants. *Developmental Psychology, 19,* 375–386.

Larsen, J. T., McGraw, A. P., & Cacioppo, J. T. (2001). Can people feel happy and sad at the same time? *Journal of Personality and Social Psychology, 81,* 684–696.

Larson, L. M., Rottinghaus, P. J., & Borgen, F. H. (2002). Meta-analyses of Big Six interests and Big Five personality factors. *Journal of Vocational Behavior, 61,* 217–239.

Lassiter, G. D., Geers, A. L., Munhall, P. J., Ploutz-Snyder, R. J., & Breitenbecher, D. L. (2002). Illusory causation: Why it occurs. *Psychological Science, 13,* 299–305.

Lazarus, R. S. (1991). *Emotion and adaptation.* New York: Oxford University Press.

Lazarus, R. S. (2001). Relational meaning and discrete emotions. In K. R. Scherer, A. Schorr, & T. Johnstone (Eds.), *Appraisal processes in emotion: Theory, methods, research* (pp. 37–67). New York: Oxford University Press.

LeDoux, J. (1996). *The emotional brain.* New York: Simon & Schuster.

Leeper, R. W. (1948). A motivational theory of emotion to replace "emotion as a disorganized response." *Psychological Review, 55,* 5–21.

Lenox, R. A., & Subich, L. M. (1994). The relationship between self-efficacy beliefs and inventoried vocational interests. *Career Development Quarterly, 42,* 302–313.

Lent, R. W., Brown, S. D., & Hackett, G. (1994). Toward a unifying social cognitive theory of career and academic interest, choice, and performance. *Journal of Vocational Behavior, 45,* 79–122.

Leuba, C. (1955). Toward some integration of learning theories: The concept of optimal stimulation. *Psychological Reports, 1,* 27–33.

Lewis, M. (1997). *Altering fate: Why the past does not predict the future.* New York: Guilford.

Lewis, M. D. (2001). Personal pathways in the development of appraisal: A complex systems/stage theory perspective. In K. R. Scherer, A. Schorr, & T. Johnstone (Eds.), *Appraisal processes in emotion: Theory, methods, research* (pp. 205–220). New York: Oxford University Press.

Libby, W. L., Jr., Lacey, B. C., & Lacey, J. L. (1973). Pupillary and cardiac activity during visual attention. *Psychophysiology, 10,* 270–294.

Lilienfeld, S. O., Lynn, S. J., & Lohr, J. M. (2003). Science and pseudoscience in clinical psychology: Initial thoughts, reflections, and considerations. In S. O. Lilienfeld, S. J. Lynn, & J. M. Lohr (Eds.), *Science and pseudoscience in clinical psychology* (pp. 1–14). New York: Guilford.

Litman, J. A. (2005). Curiosity and the pleasures of learning: Wanting and liking new information. *Cognition and Emotion, 19,* 793–814.

Litman, J. A., Hutchins, T. L., & Russon, R. K. (2005). Epistemic curiosity, feeling-of-knowing, and exploratory behavior. *Cognition and Emotion, 19,* 559–582.

Litman, J. A., & Jimerson, T. L. (2004). The measurement of curiosity as a feeling of deprivation. *Journal of Personality Assessment, 82,* 147–157.

Litman, J. A., & Spielberger, C. D. (2003). Measuring epistemic curiosity and its diversive and specific components. *Journal of Personality Assessment, 80,* 75–86.

Locher, P., & Nagy, Y. (1996). Vision spontaneously establishes the percept of pictorial balance. *Empirical Studies of the Arts, 14,* 17–31.

Loewenstein, G. (1994). The psychology of curiosity: A review and reinterpretation. *Psychological Bulletin, 116,* 75–98.

Long, L., Adams, R. S., & Tracey, T. J. G. (2005). Generalizability of interest structure to China: Application of the Personal Globe Inventory. *Journal of Vocational Behavior, 66,* 66–80.

Looft, W. R., & Baranowski, M. D. (1971). Analysis of five measures of sensation seeking and preference for complexity. *Journal of General Psychology, 85,* 307–313.

Lopez, F. G., Lent, R. W., Brown, S. D., & Gore, P. A., Jr. (1997). Role of social–cognitive expectations in high school students' mathematics-related interest and performance. *Journal of Counseling Psychology, 44,* 44–52.

Luzzo, D. A., Hasper, P., Albert, K. A., Bibby, M. A., & Martinelli, E. A., Jr. (1999). Effects of self-efficacy-enhancing interventions on the math/science self-efficacy and career interests, goals, and actions of career undecided students. *Journal of Counseling Psychology, 46,* 233–243.

MacLeod, S. (1999). *The life of Haifisch.* Lawrence, KS: Broken Boulder Press.

Maddi, S. R. (1971). Comments on Nunnally's and Suchman's papers. In H. I. Day, D. E. Berlyne, & D. E. Hunt (Eds.), *Intrinsic motivation: A new direction in education* (pp. 83–90). Toronto: Holt, Rinehart, & Winston.

Maddux, J. E., & Gosselin, J. T. (2003). Self-efficacy. In M. R. Leary & J. P. Tangney (Eds.), *Handbook of self and identity* (pp. 218–238). New York: Guilford.

Madsen, D. B., Das, A. K., Bogen, I., & Grossman, E. E. (1987). A short sensation-seeking scale. *Psychological Reports, 60,* 1179–1184.

Magai, C., & Haviland-Jones, J. (2002). *The hidden genius of emotion: Lifespan transformations of personality.* New York: Cambridge University Press.

Mandler, G. (1982). The structure of value: Accounting for taste. In M. S. Clark & S. T. Fiske (Eds.), *Affect and cognition* (pp. 3–36). Hillsdale, NJ: Lawrence Erlbaum.

Matsumoto, D. (1992). More evidence for the universality of a contempt expression. *Motivation and Emotion, 16,* 363–368.

Maw, W. H. (1971). Differences in the personalities of children differing in curiosity. In H. I. Day, D. E. Berlyne, & D. E. Hunt (Eds.), *Intrinsic motivation: A new direction in education* (pp. 91–98). Toronto: Holt, Rinehart, & Winston.

Maw, W. H., & Magoon, A. J. (1971). The curiosity dimension of fifth-grade children: A factorial discriminant analysis. *Child Development, 42,* 2023–2031.

Maw, W. H., & Maw, E. W. (1970). Self-concepts of high- and low-curiosity boys. *Child Development, 41,* 123–129.

Maw, W. H., & Maw, E. W. (1975). Contrasting proverbs as a measure of attitudes of college students toward curiosity-related behaviors. *Psychological Reports, 37,* 1085–1086.

Mayer, J. D., & Gaschke, Y. N. (1988). The experience and meta-experience of mood. *Journal of Personality and Social Psychology, 55,* 102–111.

McAdams, D. P. (1992). The five-factor model *in* personality: A critical appraisal. *Journal of Personality, 60,* 329–361.

McAdams, D. P. (1993). *The stories we live by: Personal myths and the making of the self.* New York: Guilford.

McAdams, D. P. (1996). Personality, modernity, and the storied self: A contemporary framework for studying persons. *Psychological Inquiry, 7,* 295–321.

McCall, R. B., & Kennedy, C. B. (1980). Subjective uncertainty, variability of response, and the infant's response to discrepancies. *Child Development, 51,* 285–287.

McCall, R. B., Kennedy, C. B., & Applebaum, M. I. (1977). Magnitude of discrepancy and the distribution of attention in infants. *Child Development, 48,* 772–785.

McCall, R. B., & McGhee, P. E. (1977). The discrepancy hypothesis of attention and affect in human infants. In I. C. Uzgiris & F. Weizmann (Eds.), *The structuring of experience* (pp. 179–210). New York: Plenum.

McCrae, R. R. (1994). Openness to experience: Expanding the boundaries of Factor V. *European Journal of Personality, 8,* 251–272.

McCrae, R. R. (1996). Social consequences of experiential openness. *Psychological Bulletin, 120,* 323–337.

McCrae, R. R., & Costa, P. T., Jr. (1990). *Personality in adulthood.* New York: Guilford.

McCrae, R. R., & Costa, P. T., Jr. (1997). Personality trait structure as a human universal. *American Psychologist, 52,* 509–516.

McCrae, R. R., & Costa, P. T., Jr. (1999). A five-factor theory of personality. In L. A. Pervin & O. P. John (Eds.), *Handbook of personality* (2nd ed., pp. 139–153). New York: Guilford.

McDaniel, M. A., Waddill, P. J., Finstad, K., & Bourg, T. (2000). The effects of text-based interest on attention and recall. *Journal of Educational Psychology, 92,* 492–502.

McDougall, W. (1908/1960). *An introduction to social psychology.* London: Methuen.

McLeod, C. R., & Vodanovich, S. J. (1991). The relationship between self-actualization and boredom proneness. *Journal of Social Behavior and Personality, 6,* 137–146.

Mellers, B. A. (2000). Choice and the relative pleasure of consequences. *Psychological Bulletin, 126,* 910–924.

Mellers, B. A., & McGraw, A. P. (2001). Anticipated emotions as guides to choice. *Current Directions in Psychological Science, 10,* 210–214.

Mellers, B. A., Schwartz, A., & Ritov, I. (1999). Emotion-based choice. *Journal of Experimental Psychology: General, 128,* 332–345.

Meyer, M. (1933). That whale among the fishes—the theory of emotions. *Psychological Review, 40,* 292–300.

Mikulas, W. L., & Vodanovich, S. J. (1993). The essence of boredom. *Psychological Record, 43,* 3–12.

Millis, K. (2001). Making meaning brings pleasure: The influence of titles on aesthetic experience. *Emotion, 1,* 320–329.

Mitchell, M. (1993). Situational interest: Its multifaceted structure in the secondary school mathematics classroom. *Journal of Educational Psychology, 85,* 424–436.

Mohr, P., Glover, J., & Ronning, R. R. (1984). The effect of related and unrelated details on the recall of major ideas in prose. *Journal of Reading Behavior, 16,* 97–109.

Murphy, K. R., & Myors, B. (1998). *Statistical power analysis.* Mahwah, NJ: Lawrence Erlbaum.

Nauta, M. M., Kahn, J. H., Angell, J. W., & Cantarelli, E. A. (2002). Identifying the antecedent in the relation between career interests and self-efficacy: Is it one, the other, or both? *Journal of Counseling Psychology, 49,* 290–301.

Naylor, F. D. (1981). A state–trait curiosity inventory. *Australian Psychologist, 16,* 172–183.

Neiss, R. (1988). Reconceptualizing arousal: Psychobiological states in motor performance. *Psychological Bulletin, 103,* 345–366.

Newberry, A. L., & Duncan, R. D. (2001). Roles of boredom and life goals in juvenile delinquency. *Journal of Applied Social Psychology, 31,* 527–541.

Nezlek, J. B. (2001). Multilevel random coefficient analyses of event- and interval-contingent data in social and personality psychology research. *Personality and Social Psychology Bulletin, 27,* 771–785.

Nickell, J. (1993). *Looking for a miracle: Weeping icons, relics, stigmata, and healing cures.* Buffalo, NY: Prometheus.

Nielsen, D. (2001). *Rugburns* and *Gutter ball.* Santa Barbara, CA: Broken Boulder Press.

Nicholls, J. G., Licht, B. G., & Pearl, R. A. (1982). Some dangers of using personality questionnaires to study personality. *Psychological Bulletin, 92,* 572–580.

Nix, G. A., Ryan, R. M., Manly, J. B., & Deci, E. L. (1999). Revitalization through self-regulation: The effects of autonomous and controlled motivation on happiness and vitality. *Journal of Experimental Social Psychology, 35,* 266–284.

Normore, L. F. (1974). Verbal responses to visual sequences varying in uncertainty level. In D. E. Berlyne (Ed.), *Studies in the new experimental aesthetics* (pp. 109–119). Washington, DC: Hemisphere.

North, A. C., & Hargreaves, D. J. (1995). Subjective complexity, familiarity, and liking for popular music. *Psychomusicology, 14,* 77–93.

Nunnally, J. C. (1971). Determinants of visual exploratory behavior: A human tropism for resolving informational conflicts. In H. I. Day, D. E. Berlyne, & D. E. Hunt (Eds.), *Intrinsic motivation: A new direction in education* (pp. 73–82). Toronto: Holt, Rinehart, & Winston.

Nunnally, J. C. (1972). A human tropism. In S. R. Brown & D. J. Brenner (Eds.), *Science, psychology and communication* (pp. 255–277). New York: Teachers College.

Nunnally, J. C. (1981). Explorations of exploration. In H. I. Day (Ed.), *Advances in intrinsic motivation and aesthetics* (pp. 87–129). New York: Plenum.

Nunnally, J. C., & Lemond, L. C. (1973). Exploratory behavior and human development. *Advances in Child Development and Behavior, 8,* 59–109.

Oatley, K., & Jenkins, J. M. (1992). Human emotions: Function and dysfunction. *Annual Review of Psychology, 43,* 55–85

Ogilvie, D. M. (2004). *Fantasies of flight.* New York: Oxford University Press.

Öhman, A. (2002). Automaticity and the amygdala: Nonconscious responses to emotional faces. *Current Directions in Psychological Science, 11,* 62–66.

Öhman, A., Flykt, A., & Esteves, F. (2001). Emotion drives attention: Detecting the snake in the grass. *Journal of Experimental Psychology: General, 130,* 466–478.

Olds, J. (1962). Hypothalamic substrates of reward. *Physiological Review, 42,* 554–604.

Olds, J. (1973). Brain mechanisms of reinforcement learning. In D. E. Berlyne & K. B. Madsen (Eds.), *Pleasure, reward, preference: Their nature, determinants, and role in behavior* (pp. 35–63). New York: Academic Press.

Olson, K. R., & Camp, C. J. (1984). Factor analysis of curiosity measures in adults. *Psychological Reports, 54,* 491–497.

Olson, K. R., Camp, C. J., & Fuller, D. (1984). Curiosity and need for cognition. *Psychological Reports, 54,* 71–74.

Ortony, A., & Turner, T. J. (1990). What's basic about basic emotions? *Psychological Review, 97,* 315–331.

Osberg, T. M. (1985). Order effects in the administration of personality measures: The case of the Self-Consciousness Scale. *Journal of Personality Assessment, 49,* 536–539.

Ottati, V. C., & Isbell, L. M. (1996). Effects of mood during exposure to target information on subsequently reported judgments: An on-line model of misattribution and correction. *Journal of Personality and Social Psychology, 71,* 39–53.

Paloutzian, R. F., Richardson, J. T., & Rambo, L. R. (1999). Religious conversion and personality change. *Journal of Personality, 67,* 1047–1079.

Panksepp, J. (1998). *Affective neuroscience: The foundations of human and animal emotions.* New York: Oxford University Press.

Parkinson, B. (1995). *Ideas and realities of emotion.* London: Routledge.

Parrott, W. G. (2001). Implications of dysfunctional emotions for understanding how emotions function. *Review of General Psychology, 5,* 180–186.

Paunonen, S. V., & Ashton, M. C. (2001). Big Five factors and facets and the prediction of behavior. *Journal of Personality and Social Psychology, 81,* 524–539.

Paunonen, S. V., & Jackson, D. N. (1996). The Jackson Personality Inventory and the five-factor model of personality. *Journal of Research in Personality, 30,* 42–59.

Pecchinenda, A. (2001). The psychophysiology of appraisals. In K. R. Scherer, A. Schorr, & T. Johnstone (Eds.), *Appraisal processes in emotion: Theory, methods, research* (pp. 301–315). New York: Oxford University Press.

Pecchinenda, A., & Smith, C. A. (1996). The affective significance of skin conductance activity during a difficult problem-solving task. *Cognition and Emotion, 10,* 481–503.

Peters, R. A. (1978). Effects of anxiety, curiosity, and perceived instructor threat on student verbal behavior in the college classroom. *Journal of Educational Psychology, 70,* 388–395.

Phillips, L. H., Bull, R., Adams, E., & Fraser, L. (2002). Positive mood and executive function: Evidence from Stroop and fluency tasks. *Emotion, 2,* 12–22.

Plata, M. (1975). Stability and change in prestige rankings of occupations over 49 years. *Journal of Vocational Behavior, 6,* 95–99.

Plutchik, R. (1962). *The emotions: Facts, theories, and a new model.* New York: Random House.

Polly, L. M., Vodanovich, S. J., Watt, J. D., & Blanchard, M. J. (1993). The effects of attributional processes on boredom proneness. *Journal of Social Behavior and Personality, 8,* 123–132.

Pope, L. K., & Smith, C. A. (1994). On the distinct meanings of smiles and frowns. *Cognition and Emotion, 8,* 65–72.

Prediger, D. J. (1982). Dimensions underlying Holland's hexagon: Missing link between interests and occupations? *Journal of Vocational Behavior, 21,* 259–287.

Prediger, D. J. (1996). Alternative dimensions for the Tracey–Rounds interest sphere. *Journal of Vocational Behavior, 48,* 59–67.

Prediger, D. J., & Vansickle, T. R. (1992). Locating occupations on Holland's hexagon: Beyond RIASEC. *Journal of Vocational Behavior, 40,* 111–128.

Prenzel, M. (1992). The selective persistence of interest. In K. A. Renninger, S. Hidi, & A. Krapp (Eds.), *The role of interest in learning and development* (pp. 71–98). Hillsdale, NJ: Lawrence Erlbaum.

Pribram, K. H., & McGuiness, D. (1975). Arousal, activation and effort in the control of attention. *Psychological Review, 82,* 116–149.

Prince, J. P., & Heiser, L. J. (2000). *Essentials of career interest assessment.* New York: Wiley.

Proudfoot, W., & Shaver, P. (1975). Attribution theory and the psychology of religion. *Journal for the Scientific Study of Religion, 14,* 317–330.

Pryor, J. B., & Kriss, M. (1977). The cognitive dynamics of salience in the attribution process. *Journal of Personality and Social Psychology, 35,* 49–55.

Raine, A., Reynolds, C., Venables, P. H., & Mednick, S. A. (2002). Stimulation seeking and intelligence: A prospective longitudinal study. *Journal of Personality and Social Psychology, 82,* 663–674.

Randahl, G. J. (1991). A typological analysis of the relations between measured vocational interests and abilities. *Journal of Vocational Behavior, 38,* 333–350.

Rathunde, K. (1995). Wisdom and abiding interest: Interviews with three noted historians in later life. *Journal of Adult Development, 2,* 159–172.

Rathunde, K. (1996). Family context and talented adolescents' optimal experience in school-related activities. *Journal of Research on Adolescence, 6,* 603–626.

Rathunde, K. (1998). Undivided and abiding interest: Comparisons across studies of talented adolescents and creative adults. In L. Hoffman, A. Krapp, K. A. Renninger, & J. Baumert (Eds.), *Interest and learning* (pp. 367–376). Kiel, Germany: IPN.

Rathunde, K. (2001). Family context and the development of undivided interest: A longitudinal study of family support and challenge and adolescents' quality of experience. *Applied Developmental Science, 5,* 158–171.

Rathunde, K., & Csikszentmihalyi, M. (1993). Undivided interest and the growth of talent: A longitudinal study of adolescents. *Journal of Youth and Adolescence, 22,* 1–21.

Rawlings, D. (2000). The interaction of openness to experience and schizotypy in predicting preference for abstract and violent paintings. *Empirical Studies of the Arts, 18,* 69–91.

Rawlings, D. (2003). Personality correlates of liking for "unpleasant" paintings and photographs. *Personality and Individual Differences, 23,* 395–410.

Rawson, K. A., & Dunlosky, J. (2002). Are performance predictions for text based on ease of processing? *Journal of Experimental Psychology: Learning, Memory, and Cognition, 28,* 69–80.

Reeve, J. (1989). The interest–enjoyment distinction in intrinsic motivation. *Motivation and Emotion, 13,* 83–103.

Reeve, J. (1993). The face of interest. *Motivation and Emotion, 17,* 353–375.

Reeve, J. (1996). *Motivating others: Nurturing inner motivational resources.* New York: Allyn & Bacon.

Reeve, J., Cole, S. G., & Olson, B. C. (1986). Adding excitement to intrinsic motivation research. *Journal of Social Behavior and Personality, 1,* 349–363.

Reeve, J., & Nix, G. (1997). Expressing intrinsic motivation through acts of exploration and facial displays of interest. *Motivation and Emotion, 21,* 237–250.

Regan, D. T., Straus, E., & Fazio, R. (1974). Liking and the attribution process. *Journal of Experimental Social Psychology, 10,* 385–397.

Reisenzein, R. (2000). Exploring the strength of association between the components of emotion syndromes: The case of surprise. *Cognition and Emotion, 14,* 1–38.

Renninger, K. A. (2000). Individual interest and its implications for understanding intrinsic motivation. In C. Sansone & J. M. Harackiewicz (Eds.), *Intrinsic and extrinsic motivation* (pp. 373–404). San Diego: Academic Press.

Reynolds, R. E. (1992). Selective attention and prose learning: Theoretical and empirical research. *Educational Psychology Review, 4,* 345–391.

Rheingold, H. L., & Eckerman, C. O. (1973). Fear of the stranger: A critical examination. *Advances in Child Behavior and Development, 8,* 185–222.

Ring, K. (1967). Experimental social psychology: Some sober questions about some frivolous values. *Journal of Experimental Social Psychology, 3,* 113-1123.

Rinn, W. E. (1984). The neurophysiology of facial expression: A review of the neurological and psychological mechanisms for producing facial expressions. *Psychological Bulletin, 95,* 52–77.

Roe, A. (1946). Artists and their work. *Journal of Personality, 15,* 1–40.

Roe, A. (1957). Early determinants of vocational choice. *Journal of Counseling Psychology, 4,* 212–217.

Roe, A., & Klos, D. (1969). Occupational classification. *Counseling Psychologist, 1,* 84–92.

Roe, A., & Siegelman, M. (1964). *The origin of interests.* Washington, DC: APGA.

Roseman, I. J. (2001). A model of appraisal in the emotion system: Integrating theory, research, and applications. In K. R. Scherer, A. Schorr, & T. Johnstone (Eds.), *Appraisal processes in emotion: Theory, methods, research* (pp. 68–91). New York: Oxford University Press.

Roseman, I. J., & Evdokas, A. (2004). Appraisals cause experienced emotions: Experimental evidence. *Cognition and Emotion, 18,* 1–28.

Roseman, I. J., & Smith, C. A. (2001). Appraisal theory: Overview, assumptions, varieties, controversies. In K. R. Scherer, A. Schorr, & T. Johnstone (Eds.), *Appraisal processes in emotion: Theory, methods, research* (pp. 3–19). New York: Oxford University Press.

Rosenberg, E., & Ekman, P. (1994). Coherence between expressive and experiential systems in emotion. *Cognition and Emotion, 8,* 201–229.

Ross, L., Rodin, J., & Zimbardo, P. G. (1969). Toward an attribution therapy: The reduction of fear through induced cognitive-emotional misattribution. *Journal of Personality and Social Psychology, 12,* 279–288.

Rottinghaus, P. J., Larson, L. M., & Borgen, F. H. (2003). The relation of self-efficacy and interests: A meta-analysis of 60 samples. *Journal of Vocational Behavior, 62,* 221–236.

Rounds, J. B., & Day, S. X. (1999). Describing, evaluating, and creating vocational interest structures. In M. L. Savickas & A. R. Spokane (Eds.), *Vocational interests* (pp. 103–133). Palo Alto, CA: Davies-Black.

Rounds, J. B., & Tracey, T. J. G. (1993). Prediger's dimensional representation of Holland's RIASEC circumplex. *Journal of Applied Psychology, 78,* 875–890.

Rounds, J. B., & Tracey, T. J. G. (1996). Cross-cultural structural equivalence of RIASEC models and measures. *Journal of Counseling Psychology, 43,* 310–329.

Rounds, J. B., & Zevon, M. B. (1983). Multidimensional scaling research in vocational psychology. *Applied Psychological Measurement, 7,* 491–510.

Routtenberg, A. (1968). The two-arousal hypothesis: Reticular formation and limbic system. *Psychological Review, 75,* 51–80.

Rozin, P., & Cohen, A. B. (2003). High frequency of facial expressions corresponding to confusion, concentration, and worry in an analysis of naturally occurring facial expressions of Americans. *Emotion, 3,* 68–75.

Ruch, W. (1988). Sensation seeking and the enjoyment of structure and content of humor: Stability of findings across four samples. *Personality and Individual Differences, 9,* 861–871.

Ruch, W. (1992). Assessment of appreciation of humor: Studies with the 3 WD Humor Test. In C. D. Spielberger & J. N. Butcher (Eds.), *Advances in personality assessment* (Vol. 9, pp. 27–75). Hillsdale, NJ: Lawrence Erlbaum.

Rudolph, U., & Försterling, F. (1997). The psychological causality implicit in verbs: A review. *Psychological Bulletin, 121,* 192–218.

Rupp, D. E., & Vodanovich, S. J. (1997). The role of boredom proneness in self-reported anger and aggression. *Journal of Social Behavior and Personality, 12,* 925–936.

Russell, J. A. (2003). Core affect and the psychological construction of emotion. *Psychological Review, 110,* 145–172.

Russell, J. A., & Lemay, G. (2000). Emotion concepts. In M. Lewis & J. M. Haviland-Jones (Eds.), *Handbook of emotions* (2nd ed., pp. 491–503). New York: Guilford.

Russell, P. A. (1994). Preferability, pleasingness, and interestingness: Relationships between evaluative judgments in empirical aesthetics. *Empirical Studies of the Arts, 12,* 141–157.

Russell, P. A. (2003). Effort after meaning and the hedonic value of paintings. *British Journal of Psychology, 94,* 99–110.

Russell, P. A., & George, D. A. (1990). Relationships between aesthetic response scales applied to paintings. *Empirical Studies of the Arts, 8,* 15–30.

Russell, P. A., & Gray, C. D. (1991). The heterogeneity of the preferability scale in aesthetic judgments of paintings. *Visual Arts Research, 17,* 76–84.

Russell, P. A., & Milne, S. (1997). Meaningfulness and the hedonic value of paintings: Effects of titles. *Empirical Studies of the Arts, 15,* 61–73.

Ryan, R. M. (1995). Psychological needs and the facilitation of the integrative process. *Journal of Personality, 63,* 397–427.

Ryan, R. M., & Deci, E. L. (2000). When rewards compete with nature: The undermining of intrinsic motivation and self-regulation. In C. Sansone & J. M. Harackiewicz (Eds.), *Intrinsic and extrinsic motivation* (pp. 13–54). San Diego, CA: Academic.

Ryan, R. M., & Frederick, C. (1997). On energy, personality, and health: Subjective vitality as a dynamic reflection of well-being. *Journal of Personality, 65,* 529–565.

Sadoski, M. (2001). Resolving the effects of concreteness on interest, comprehension, and learning important ideas from text. *Educational Psychology Review, 13,* 263–281.

Sadoski, M., Goetz, E. T., & Fritz, J. B. (1993). A causal model of sentence recall: Effects of familiarity, concreteness, comprehensibility, and interestingness. *Journal of Reading Behavior, 25,* 5–16.

Sadoski, M., Goetz, E. T., & Rodriguez, M. (2000). Engaging texts: Effects of concreteness on comprehensibility, interest, and recall in four text types. *Journal of Educational Psychology, 92,* 85–95.

Sadoski, M., & Paivio, A. (2001). *Imagery and text: A dual coding theory of reading and writing.* Mahwah, NJ: Lawrence Erlbaum.

Sadoski, M., & Quast, Z. (1990). Reader recall and long term recall for journalistic text: The roles of imagery, affect, and importance. *Reading Research Quarterly, 25,* 256–272.

Sagan, C. (1995). *The demon-haunted world: Science as a candle in the dark.* New York: Random House.

Sansone, C., & Harackiewicz, J. M. (1996). "I don't feel like it": The function of interest in self-regulation. In L. L. Martin & A. Tesser (Eds.), *Striving and feeling* (pp. 203–228). Mahwah, NJ: Lawrence Erlbaum.

Sansone, C., & Harackiewicz, J. M. (Eds.) (2000). *Intrinsic and extrinsic motivation: The search for optimal motivation and performance.* San Diego, CA: Academic.

Sansone, C., & Smith, J. L. (2000a). The "how" of goal pursuit: Interest and self-regulation. *Psychological Inquiry, 4,* 306–309.

Sansone, C., & Smith, J. L. (2000b). Interest and self-regulation: The relation between having to and wanting to. In C. Sansone & J. M. Harackiewicz (Eds.), *Intrinsic and extrinsic motivation* (pp. 341–372). San Diego, CA: Academic.

Sansone, C., Weir, C., Harpster, L., & Morgan, C. (1992). Once a boring task always a boring task? Interest as a self-regulatory mechanism. *Journal of Personality and Social Psychology, 63,* 379–390.

Sansone, C., Wiebe, D. J., & Morgan, C. (1999). Self-regulating interest: The moderating role of hardiness and conscientiousness. *Journal of Personality, 67,* 701–733.

Savickas, M. L. (1999). The psychology of interests. In M. L. Savickas & A. R. Spokane (Eds.), *Vocational interests* (pp. 19–56). Palo Alto, CA: Davies-Black.

Savickas, M. L., & Spokane, A. R. (Eds.) (1999). *Vocational interests.* Palo Alto, CA: Davies-Black.

Savickas, M. L., Taber, B. J., & Spokane, A. R. (2002). Convergent and discriminant validity of five interest inventories. *Journal of Vocational Behavior, 61,* 139–184.

Schachter, S., & Singer, J. (1962). Cognitive, social and physiological determinants of emotional state. *Psychological Review, 63,* 379–399.

Schank, R. C. (1979). Interestingness: Controlling inferences. *Artificial Intelligence, 12,* 273–297.

Schank, R. C., & Abelson, R. P. (1977). *Scripts, plans, goals, and understanding: An inquiry into human knowledge structures.* Oxford: Lawrence Erlbaum.

Scherer, K. R. (1986). Vocal affect expression: A review and a model for future research. *Psychological Bulletin, 99,* 143–165.

Scherer, K. R. (1997). Profiles of emotion-antecedent appraisal: Testing theoretical predictions across cultures. *Cognition and Emotion, 11,* 113–150.

Scherer, K. R. (1999). On the sequential nature of appraisal processes: Indirect evidence from a recognition task. *Cognition and Emotion, 13,* 763–793.

Scherer, K. R. (2001a). Appraisal considered as a process of multilevel sequential checking. In K. R. Scherer, A. Schorr, & T. Johnstone (Eds.), *Appraisal processes in emotion: Theory, methods, research* (pp. 92–120). New York: Oxford University Press.

Scherer, K. R. (2001b). The nature and study of appraisal: A review of the issues. In K. R. Scherer, A. Schorr, & T. Johnstone (Eds.), *Appraisal processes in emotion: Theory, methods, research* (pp. 369–391). New York: Oxford University Press.

Scherer, K. R., Schorr, A., & Johnstone, T. (2001). (Eds.) *Appraisal processes in emotion: Theory, methods, research.* New York: Oxford University Press.

Schiefele, U. (1991). Interest, learning, and motivation. *Educational Psychologist, 26,* 299–323.

Schiefele, U. (1992). Topic interest and levels of text comprehension. In K. A. Renninger, S. Hidi, & A. Krapp (Eds.), *The role of interest in learning and development* (pp. 151–182). Hillsdale, NJ: Lawrence Erlbaum.

Schiefele, U. (1996). Topic interest, text representation, and quality of experience. *Contemporary Educational Psychology, 21,* 3–18.

Schiefele, U. (1998). Individual interest and learning—What we know and what we don't know. In L. Hoffman, A. Krapp, K. A. Renninger, & J. Baumert (Eds.), *Interest and learning* (pp. 91–104). Kiel, Germany: IPN.

Schiefele, U. (1999). Interest and learning from text. *Scientific Studies of Reading, 3,* 257–279.

Schiefele, U. (2001). The role of interest in motivation and learning. In J. M. Collis & S. Messick (Eds.), *Intelligence and personality: Bridging the gap in theory and measurement* (pp. 163–194). Mahwah, NJ: Lawrence Erlbaum.

Schiefele, U., & Krapp, A. (1996). Topic interest and free recall of expository text. *Learning and Individual Differences, 8,* 141–160.

Schiefele, U., Krapp, A., & Winteler, A. (1992). Interest as a predictor of academic achievement: A meta-analysis of research. In K. A. Renninger, S. Hidi, & A. Krapp (Eds.), *The role of interest in learning and development* (pp. 183–212). Hillsdale, NJ: Lawrence Erlbaum.

Schiefele, U., & Wild, K.-P. (Eds.) (2000). *Interesse und Lernmotivation* [Interest and learning motivation]. Münster, Germany: Waxmann.

Schlottmann, A. (2001). Perception versus knowledge of cause and effect in children: Seeing is believing. *Current Directions in Psychological Science, 10,* 111–115

Schorr, A. (2001a). Appraisal: The evolution of an idea. In K. R. Scherer, A.

Schorr, & T. Johnstone (Eds.), *Appraisal processes in emotion: Theory, methods, research* (pp. 20–34). New York: Oxford University Press.

Schorr, A. (2001b). Subjective measurement in appraisal research: Present state and future perspectives. In K. R. Scherer, A. Schorr, & T. Johnstone (Eds.), *Appraisal processes in emotion: Theory, methods, research* (pp. 331–349). New York: Oxford University Press.

Schraw, G. (1997). Situational interest in literary text. *Contemporary Educational Psychology, 22,* 436–456.

Schraw, G. (1998). Processing and recall differences among seductive details. *Journal of Educational Psychology, 90,* 3–12.

Schraw, G., Bruning, R., & Svoboda, C. (1995). Sources of situational interest. *Journal of Reading Behavior, 27,* 1–17.

Schraw, G., & Lehman, S. (2001). Situational interest: A review of the literature and directions for future research. *Educational Psychology Review, 13,* 23–52.

Schultz, D. P. (1965). *Sensory restriction.* New York: Academic Press.

Schwartz, N. (1999). Self-reports: How the questions shape the answers. *American Psychologist, 54,* 93–105.

Schwartz, N., & Clore, G. L. (1983). Mood, misattribution, and judgments of well-being: Informative and directive functions of affective states. *Journal of Personality and Social Psychology, 45,* 513–523.

Scott, T. H., Bexton, W. H., Heron, W., & Doane, B. K. (1959). Cognitive effects of perceptual isolation. *Canadian Journal of Psychology, 13,* 200–209.

Seager, W. (2002). Emotional introspection. *Consciousness and Cognition, 11,* 666–687.

Sedikides, C., & Strube, M. J. (1997). Self-evaluation: To thine own self be good, to thine own self be sure, to thine own self be true, and to thine own self be better. *Advances in Experimental Social Psychology, 29,* 206–269.

Seib, H. M., & Vodanovich, S. J. (1998). Cognitive correlates of boredom proneness: The role of private self-consciousness and absorption. *Journal of Psychology, 132,* 642–652.

Seligman, M. E. P., & Csikszentmihalyi, M. (2000). Positive psychology: An introduction. *American Psychologist, 55,* 5–14.

Shah, J. Y., & Kruglanski, A. W. (2000). The structure and substance of intrinsic motivation. In C. Sansone & J. M. Harackiewicz (Eds.), *Intrinsic and extrinsic motivation* (pp. 105–127). San Diego, CA: Academic Press.

Shannon, C. E., & Weaver, W. (1949). *Mathematical theory of communication.* Urbana, IL: University of Illinois.

Sheffield, F. D., Roby, T. B., & Campbell, B. A. (1954). Drive reduction versus consummatory behavior as determinants of reinforcement. *Journal of Comparative and Physiological Psychology, 47,* 349–354.

Shirey, L. L. (1992). Importance, interest, and selective attention. In K. A. Renninger, S. Hidi, & A. Krapp (Eds.), *The role of interest in learning and development* (pp. 281–296). Hillsdale, NJ: Lawrence Erlbaum.

Shirey, L. L., & Reynolds, R. E. (1988). Effect of interest on attention and learning. *Journal of Educational Psychology, 80*, 159–166.

Silvia, P. J. (1999). Explaining personality or explaining variance? A comment on Creed and Funder (1998). *European Journal of Personality, 13*, 533–538.

Silvia, P. J. (2001a). Expressed and measured vocational interests: Definitions and distinctions. *Journal of Vocational Behavior, 59*, 382–393.

Silvia, P. J. (2001b). Interest and interests: The psychology of constructive capriciousness. *Review of General Psychology, 5*, 270–290.

Silvia, P. J. (2003). Self-efficacy and interest: Experimental studies of optimal incompetence. *Journal of Vocational Behavior, 62*, 237–249.

Silvia, P. J. (2004). *Emotions, attributions, and the development of interests.* Unpublished manuscript.

Silvia, P. J. (2005a). Cognitive appraisals and interest in visual art: Exploring an appraisal theory of aesthetic emotions. *Empirical Studies of the Arts, 23*, 119–133.

Silvia, P. J. (2005b). Emotional responses to art: From collation and arousal to cognition and emotion. *Review of General Psychology, 9*.

Silvia, P. J. (2005c). What is interesting? Exploring the appraisal structure of interest. *Emotion, 5*, 89–102.

Silvia, P. J., & Brehm, J. W. (2001). Exploring alternative deterrents to emotional intensity: Anticipated happiness, distraction, and sadness. *Cognition and Emotion, 15*, 575–592.

Silvia, P. J., & Duval, T. S. (2001a). Objective self-awareness theory: Recent progress and enduring problems. *Personality and Social Psychology Review, 5*, 230–241.

Silvia, P. J., & Duval, T. S. (2001b). Predicting the interpersonal targets of self-serving attributions. *Journal of Experimental Social Psychology, 37*, 333–340.

Silvia, P. J., & Duval, T. S. (2004). Self-awareness, self-motives, and self-motivation. In R. A. Wright, J. Greenberg, & S. S. Brehm (Eds.), *Motivational analyses of social behavior: Building on Jack Brehm's contributions to psychology* (pp. 57–75). Mahwah, NJ: Lawrence Erlbaum.

Silvia, P. J., & Gendolla, G. H. E. (2001). On introspection and self-perception: Does self-focused attention enable accurate self-knowledge? *Review of General Psychology, 5*, 241–269.

Silvia, P. J., & Warburton, J. B. (2006). Positive and negative affect: Bridging states and traits. In D. L. Segal & J. C. Thomas (Eds.) *Comprehensive handbook of personality and psychopathology, Vol. 1: Personality and everyday functioning* (pp. 268–284). New York: Wiley.

Smith, C. A., & Ellsworth, P. C. (1985). Patterns of cognitive appraisal in emotion. *Journal of Personality and Social Psychology, 48*, 813–838.

Smith, C. A., & Kirby, L. D. (2001). Toward delivering on the promise of appraisal theory. In K. R. Scherer, A. Schorr, & T. Johnstone (Eds.), *Appraisal processes in emotion: Theory, methods, research* (pp. 121–138). New York: Oxford University Press.

Somer, E., & Goldberg, L. R. (1999). The structure of Turkish trait-descriptive adjectives. *Journal of Personality and Social Psychology, 76,* 431–450.

Sommers, J., & Vodanovich, S. J. (2000). Boredom proneness: Its relationship to psychological- and physical-health symptoms. *Journal of Clinical Psychology, 56,* 149–155.

Son, L. K., & Metcalfe, J. (2000). Metacognitive and control strategies in study-time allocation. *Journal of Experimental Psychology: Learning, Memory, and Cognition, 26,* 204–221.

Spacks, P. M. (1995). *Boredom: The literary history of a state of mind.* Chicago: University of Chicago.

Spence, K. W. (1956). *Behavior theory and conditioning.* New Haven, CT: Yale University Press.

Spielberger, C. D., Jacobs, G., Crane, R., Russél, S., Westberry, L., Barker, E., Johnson, E., Knight, J., & Marks, E. (1979). *Preliminary manual for the State-Trait Personality Inventory.* Unpublished manual, University of South Florida.

Spielberger, C. D., & Starr, L. M. (1994). Curiosity and exploratory behavior. In H. F. O'Neil, Jr., & M. Drillings (Eds.), *Motivation: Theory and research* (pp. 221–243). Hillsdale, NJ: Lawrence Erlbaum.

Spokane, A. R. (1985). A review of research on person–environment congruence in Holland's theory of careers. *Journal of Vocational Behavior, 26,* 306–343.

Spokane, A. R., & Decker, A. R. (1999). Expressed and measured interests. In M. L. Savickas & A. R. Spokane (Eds.), *Vocational interests* (pp. 211–233). Palo Alto, CA: Davies-Black.

Stapel, D. A., Koomen, W., & Ruys, K. I. (2002). The effects of diffuse and distinct affect. *Journal of Personality and Social Psychology, 83,* 60–74.

Strong, E. K., Jr. (1943). *The vocational interests of men and women.* Stanford, CA: Stanford University Press.

Strong, E. K., Jr. (1955). *Vocational interests 18 years after college.* Minneapolis: University of Minnesota.

Super, D. E. (1940). *Avocational interest patterns: A study in the psychology of avocations.* Stanford, CA: Stanford University Press.

Super, D. E. (1949). *Appraising vocational fitness by means of psychological tests.* New York: Harper & Row.

Swanson, J. L. (1999). Stability and change in vocational interests. In M. L. Savickas & A. R. Spokane (Eds.), *Vocational interests* (pp. 135–158). Palo Alto, CA: Davies–Black.

Switzer, D. K., Grigg, A. E., Miller, J. S., & Young, R. K. (1962). Early experiences and occupational choice: A test of Roe's hypothesis. *Journal of Counseling Psychology, 9,* 45–48.

Tan, E. S. (2000). Emotion, art, and the humanities. In M. Lewis & J. M. Haviland-Jones (Eds.), *Handbook of emotions* (2nd ed., pp. 116–134). New York: Guilford.

Thayer, R. E. (2001). *Calm energy: How people regulate mood with food and exercise.* New York: Oxford University Press.

Thorndike, E. L. (1935a). *Adult interests.* New York: Macmillan.

Thorndike, E. L. (1935b). *The psychology of wants, interests and attitudes.* New York: Appleton-Century.

Tinsley, H. E. A. (2000). The congruence myth: An analysis of the efficacy of the person–environment fit model. *Journal of Vocational Behavior, 56,* 147–183.

Tinsley, H. E. A. (2001). Marginalization of vocational psychology. *Journal of Vocational Behavior, 59,* 243–251.

Tobias, S. (1994). Interest, prior knowledge, and learning. *Review of Educational Research, 64,* 37–54.

Todt, E., & Schreiber, S. (1998). Development of interests. In L. Hoffman, A. Krapp, K. A. Renninger, & J. Baumert (Eds.), *Interest and learning* (pp. 25–40). Kiel, Germany: IPN.

Tokar, D. M., & Swanson, J. L. (1995). Evaluation of the correspondence between Holland's vocational personality typology and the five-factor model. *Journal of Vocational Behavior, 46,* 89–108.

Tomkins, S. S. (1962). *Affect, imagery, consciousness, Vol. 1: The positive affects.* New York: Springer.

Tomkins, S. S. (1963). *Affect, imagery, consciousness, Vol. 2: The negative affects.* New York: Springer.

Tomkins, S. S. (Speaker). (1976). *A theory of psychological magnification* [cassette recording]. Philadelphia, PA: Silvan S. Tomkins Institute.

Tomkins, S. S. (1979). Script theory: Differential magnification of affects. *Nebraska Symposium on Motivation, 26,* 201–236.

Tomkins, S. S. (1987). Script theory. In J. Aronoff, A. I. Rabin, & R. A. Zucker (Eds.), *The emergence of personality* (pp. 147–216). New York: Springer.

Tomkins, S. S. (1991). *Affect, imagery, consciousness, Vol. 3: The negative affects: Anger and fear.* New York: Springer.

Tracey, T. J. G. (1997). The structure of interests and self-efficacy expectations: An expanded examination of the spherical model of interests. *Journal of Counseling Psychology, 44,* 32–43.

Tracey, T. J. G. (2001). The development of structure of interests in children: Setting the stage. *Journal of Vocational Behavior, 59,* 89–104.

Tracey, T. J. G. (2002a). Development of interests and competency beliefs: A 1-year longitudinal study of fifth- to eighth-grade students using the ICA–R and structural equation modeling. *Journal of Counseling Psychology, 49,* 148–163.

Tracey, T. J. G. (2002b). Personal globe inventory: Measurement of the spherical model of interests and competence beliefs. *Journal of Vocational Behavior, 60,* 113–172.

Tracey, T. J. G., & Rounds, J. B. (1992). Evaluating the RIASEC circumplex using high-point codes. *Journal of Vocational Behavior, 41,* 295–311.

244   REFERENCES

Tracey, T. J. G., & Rounds, J. B. (1993). Evaluating Holland's and Gati's vocational interest models: A structural meta-analysis. *Psychological Bulletin, 113,* 229–246.

Tracey, T. J. G., & Rounds, J. (1994). An examination of the structure of Roe's eight interest fields. *Journal of Vocational Behavior, 44,* 279–296.

Tracey, T. J. G., & Rounds, J. (1995). The arbitrary nature of Holland's RIASEC types: A concentric-circles structure. *Journal of Counseling Psychology, 42,* 431–439.

Tracey, T. J. G., & Rounds, J. (1996a). Contributions of the spherical representation of vocational interests. *Journal of Vocational Behavior, 48,* 85–95.

Tracey, T. J. G., & Rounds, J. (1996b). The spherical representation of vocational interests. *Journal of Vocational Behavior, 48,* 3–41.

Tracey, T. J. G., & Ward, C. C. (1998). The structure of children's interests and competence perceptions. *Journal of Counseling Psychology, 45,* 290–303.

Tracey, T. J. G., Watanabe, N., & Schneider, P. L. (1997). Structural invariance of vocational interests across Japanese and American cultures. *Journal of Counseling Psychology, 44,* 346–354.

Underwood, B. J. (1975). Individual differences as a crucible for theory construction. *American Psychologist, 30,* 128–134.

Van den Bergh, O., & Vrana, S. R. (1998). Repetition and boredom in a perceptual fluency/attributional model of affective judgements. *Cognition and Emotion, 12,* 533–553.

van Dijk, T. A., & Kintsch, W. (1983). *Strategies of discourse comprehension.* Orlando, FL: Academic Press.

van Reekum, C. M., & Scherer, K. R. (1997). Levels of processing in emotion-antecedent appraisal. In G. Matthews (Ed.), *Cognitive science perspectives on personality and emotion* (pp. 259–330). Amsterdam: Elsevier.

Vidler, D. C., & Rawan, H. R. (1974). Construct validation of a scale of academic curiosity. *Psychological Reports, 35,* 263–266.

Vidler, D. C., & Rawan, H. R. (1975). Further validation of a scale of academic curiosity. *Psychological Reports, 37,* 115–118.

Vodanovich, S. J., & Kass, S. J. (1990a). Age and gender differences in boredom proneness. *Journal of Social Behavior and Personality, 5,* 285–295.

Vodanovich, S. J., & Kass, S. J. (1990b). A factor analytic study of the boredom proneness scale. *Journal of Personality Assessment, 55,* 115–123.

Vodanovich, S. J., & Rupp, D. E. (1999). Are procrastinators prone to boredom? *Social Behavior and Personality, 27,* 11–16.

Vodanovich, S. J., Verner, K. M., & Gilbride, T. V. (1991). Boredom proneness: Its relationship to positive and negative affect. *Psychological Reports, 69,* 1139–1146.

Wade, S. E. (1992). How interest affects learning from text. In K. A. Renninger, S. Hidi, & A. Krapp (Eds.), *The role of interest in learning and development* (pp. 255–277). Hillsdale, NJ: Lawrence Erlbaum.

Wade, S. E. (2001). Research on importance and interest: Implications for cur-

riculum development and future research. *Educational Psychology Review,*
13, 243–261.

Wade, S. E., & Adams, R. B. (1990). Effects of importance and interest on recall of biographical text. *Journal of Reading Behavior, 22,* 331–353.

Wade, S. E., Alexander, P., Schraw, G., & Kulikowich, J. (1995). The perils of criticism: Response to Goetz and Sadoski. *Reading Research Quarterly, 30,* 512–515.

Wade, S. E., Buxton, W. M., & Kelly, M. (1999). Using think-alouds to examine reader–text interest. *Reading Research Quarterly, 34,* 194–216.

Wade, S. E., Schraw, G., Buxton, W. M., & Hayes, M. T. (1993). Seduction of the strategic reader: Effects of interest on strategies and recall. *Reading Research Quarterly, 28,* 93–114.

Walker, E. L. (1980). *Psychological complexity and preference: A hedgehog theory of behavior.* New York: Brooks–Cole.

Walker, E. L. (1981). The quest for the inverted U. In H. I. Day (Ed.), *Advances in intrinsic motivation and aesthetics* (pp. 39–70). New York: Plenum.

Wallace, J. C., Vodanovich, S. J., & Restino, B. M. (2003). Predicting cognitive failures from boredom proneness and daytime sleepiness scores: An investigation within military and undergraduate samples. *Personality and Individual Differences, 34,* 635–644.

Wallerstein, H. (1954). An electromyographic study of attentive listening. *Canadian Journal of Psychology, 8,* 228–238.

Walsh, W. B. (1999). What we know and need to know: A few comments. In M. L. Savickas & A. R. Spokane (Eds.), *Vocational interests* (pp. 371–382). Palo Alto, CA: Davies-Black.

Walsh, W. B. (2001). The changing nature of the science of vocational psychology. *Journal of Vocational Behavior, 59,* 262–274.

Watson, D. (2000). *Mood and temperament.* New York: Guilford.

Watson, D., & Tellegen, A. (1985). Toward a consensual structure of mood. *Psychological Bulletin, 98,* 219–235.

Watson, D., Wiese, D., Vaidya, J., & Tellegen, A. (1999). The two general systems of affect: Structural findings, evolutionary considerations, and psychobiological evidence. *Journal of Personality and Social Psychology, 76,* 820–838.

Watt, J. D., & Vodanovich, S. J. (1992a). An examination of race and gender differences in boredom proneness. *Journal of Social Behavior and Personality, 7,* 169–175.

Watt, J. D., & Vodanovich, S. J. (1992b). Relationship between boredom proneness and impulsivity. *Psychological Reports, 70,* 688–690.

Weick, K. E. (1964). Reduction of cognitive dissonance through task enhancement and effort expenditure. *Journal of Abnormal and Social Psychology, 68,* 533–539.

Weiner, B. (1985). An attributional model of achievement motivation and emotion. *Psychological Review, 92,* 548–573.

Weiner, B. (1986). *An attributional theory of motivation and emotion.* New York: Springer.

Weiner, B. (1991). On perceiving the other as responsible. *Nebraska Symposium on Motivation, 38,* 165–198.

Weiner, B. (1995) Inferences of responsibility and social motivation. *Advances in Experimental Social Psychology, 27,* 1–47.

Weiner, B. (2000). Intrapersonal and interpersonal theories of motivation from an attributional perspective. *Educational Psychology Review, 12,* 1–14.

White, R. W. (1963). *Ego and reality in psychoanalytic theory: A proposal regarding independent ego energies* (Psychological Issues Series, Monograph 11). New York: International Universities.

White, R. W. (1972). *The enterprise of living: Growth and organization in personality.* New York: Holt, Rinehart, & Winston.

Wicklund, R. A. (1990). *Zero-variable theories and the psychology of the explainer.* New York: Springer.

Wicklund, R. A. (1998). Self-esteem. In H. S. Friedman (Ed.), *Encyclopedia of mental health* (Vol. 3, pp. 433–439). San Diego, CA: Academic Press.

Wicklund, R. A., & Brehm, J. W. (1976). *Perspectives on cognitive dissonance.* Hillsdale, NJ: Lawrence Erlbaum.

Wilde, O. (1998). *Oscar Wilde's wit and wisdom: A book of quotations.* Mineola, NY: Dover.

Wilson, P. S. (1971). *Interest and discipline in education.* London: Routledge & Kegan Paul.

Wilson, T. D. (2002). *Strangers to ourselves: Discovering the adaptive unconscious.* Cambridge: Harvard University Press.

Wilson, T. D., Centerbar, D. B., Kermer, D. A., & Gilbert, D. T. (2005). The pleasures of uncertainty: Prolonging positive moods in ways people do not anticipate. *Journal of Personality and Social Psychology, 88,* 5–21.

Wohlwill, J. F. (1987). Curiosity, imagination, and play: Communality and interrelationships. In D. Görlitz & J. F. Wohlwill (Eds.), *Curiosity, imagination, and play* (pp. 2–21). Hillsdale, NJ: Lawrence Erlbaum.

Wolfradt, U., & Pretz, J. E. (2001). Individual differences in creativity: Personality, story writing, and hobbies. *European Journal of Personality, 15,* 297–310.

Wright, R. A., & Kirby, L. D. (2001). Effort determination of cardiovascular response: An integrative analysis with applications in social psychology. *Advances in Experimental Social Psychology, 33,* 255–307.

Zajonc, R. B. (2001). Mere exposure: A gateway to the subliminal. *Current Directions in Psychological Science, 10,* 224–228.

Zanna, M. P., & Cooper, J. (1974). Dissonance and the pill: An attribution approach to studying the arousal properties of dissonance. *Journal of Personality and Social Psychology, 29,* 703–709.

Zubek, J. P., Pushkar, D., Sansom, W., & Gowing, J. (1961). Perceptual changes after prolonged sensory isolation (darkness and silence). *Canadian Journal of Psychology, 15,* 83–100.

Zuckerman, M. (1969). Theoretical formulations: I. In J. P. Zubek (Ed.), *Sensory deprivation* (pp. 407–432). New York: Appleton-Century-Crofts.

Zuckerman, M. (1991). *Psychobiology of personality.* Cambridge: Cambridge University Press.

Zuckerman, M. (1994). *Behavioral expressions and biosocial bases of sensation seeking.* New York: Cambridge University Press.

Zuckerman, M. (1999). *Vulnerability to psychopathology: A biosocial model.* Washington, DC: American Psychological Association.

Author Index

Subject Index

aesthetics, 27–28, 202
  Berlyne's theory of, 50
  and effects of titles on interest, 59
  and expertise in art, 58
  and interest in poetry, 61
  and interest in visual art, 61–62
affective forecasting, 139, 191
appraisal structure of interest, 8, 58, 63
  as applied to other areas, 201–202
  and coping-potential appraisals, 8,
    57–58, 78, 81, 204, 209
  direct evidence for, 59, 61–62
  and facial expressions, 203–204
  indirect evidence for, 58–59
  and individual differences, 206
  and novelty–complexity appraisals,
    57, 78, 81, 204
  and reappraisal, 58
  and self-efficacy, 209
  and text, 78, 81–84, 204–205
appraisal theories of emotion, 8, 14,
    24, 31–32, 44, 62
  and appraisal processes, 56, 204
  and appraisal structure, 55–56
  and core relational themes, 24, 56,
    58
  and interest. *See* appraisal structure
    of interest

and the psychology of interest, 201
  and reappraisal, 56–57
  subjective emphasis of, 8, 54
arousal jag, 39, 47, 50
arousal potential, 37–38, 41, 43
attributions
  accuracy of, 134–137
  and action, 140–141
  and automaticity, 137, 143
  definition of, 132–133
  for emotions, 10, 133, 138
  and expectations, 137–140, 141
  and misattribution, 136–137
  and salience, 134

behaviorism, 3, 13–14
Berlyne, Daniel E., 8
  and cognitive psychology, 54
  and emotions, 42–43
  evaluation of, 42–44
  first arousal theory, 37–40
  and the information-gaps theory, 50–
    51
  second arousal theory, 40–42
Big Five model, 104
  and openness to experience, 105
  and the RIASEC interest types, 156
boredom, 19, 37, 47, 102

sensation seeking, 4, 7, 9, 88, 94, 103–
104, 110
definition of, 99
heritability of, 100
and humor, 101–102
and interest, 100–101
psychobiology of, 99–100
sensory deprivation, 23, 37
situational interest, 4, 10, 150, 183,
199
and actualized interest, 185
alternative model of, 189
causes of, 184
criticisms of, 187–188
definition of, 184
and psychological state of interest,
186

text-based interest, 5, 8, 64–65
and appraisals, 64, 78–79, 81–84,
202, 204–205
and attention, 67–68, 73, 83
and coherence, 79
and concreteness, 80, 82
and ease of comprehension, 8, 79, 81–
82
and learning, 64, 66–73, 204
and levels of processing, 69–71, 73,
83
and prior knowledge, 80
and reading, 65
and seductive details. See seductive
details
sources of, 66, 77–81
and strategy use, 71–72, 83, 204
and surprisingness, 80–82
and vividness, 79–81
Tomkins, Silvan S.
and criticism of his theory of
interest, 45
and the innate activator theory of
interest, 44–46
and script theory, 117–119

trait curiosity, 4, 9, 59, 88, 110, 206
and appraisals, 206
in children, 92–94
future research directions for, 206–
207
and intelligence, 93
Kashdan's model of, 91–92
Maw's model of, 92–94
Naylor's model of, 91
older measures of, 108
peer reports of, 92–93
similarity of models of, 206–207
Spielberger's model of, 89–91
teacher reports of, 92–93

uncertainty, 24, 35, 50

vocational interests, 4, 10
basic and applied aspects of, 154,
164, 167, 179
and children, 174, 178
and criticisms of spherical model,
164–165
definitions of, 153
and ethnicity, 158, 163
expressed versus measured, 166
and gender, 158, 163
hexagonal versus circular structure
of, 160–161
and interest inventories. See interest
inventories
measurement of, 153–154, 165–166
occupational prestige and, 161, 163
origins of. See development of
vocational interests
and personality, 88
person–environment congruence
and, 158
Prediger's model of, 155, 158–160, 208
and RIASEC. See RIASEC
spherical model of, 155, 160–165,
179, 208
structure of, 155–165